LABORATORY Manual

CHEMISTRY

CBSE Class XI

Author
Shikha Soni

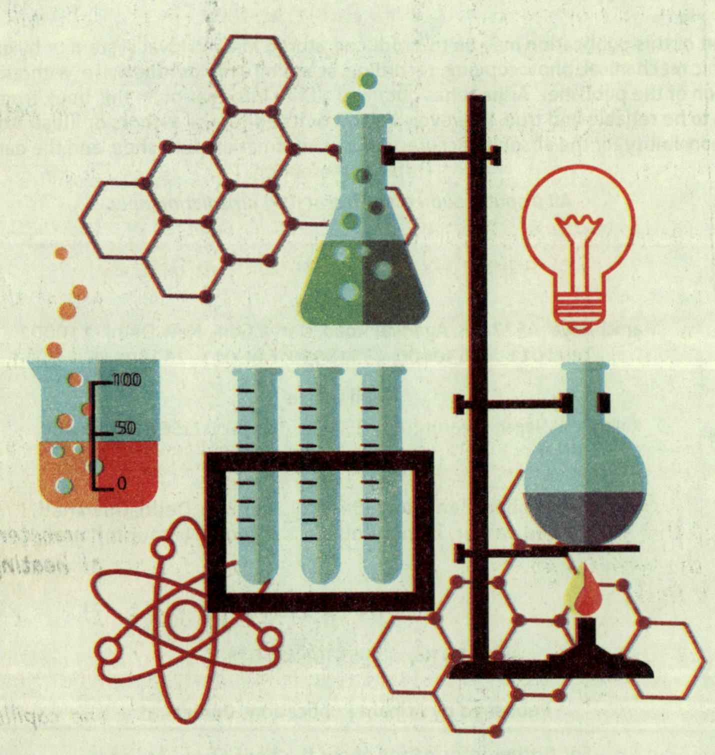

Name..

Class........................ **Section**........................**Roll No**.......................

School..

Arihant Prakashan (School Division Series)

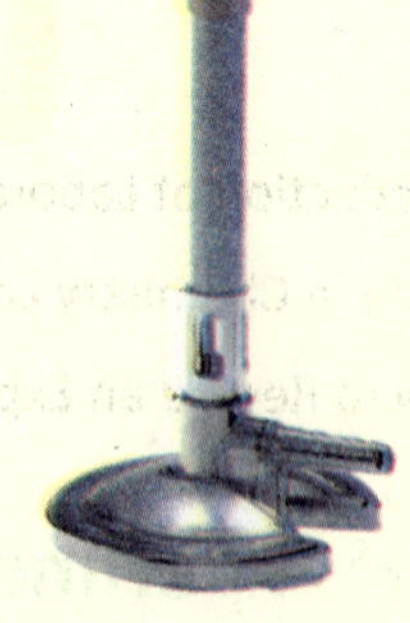

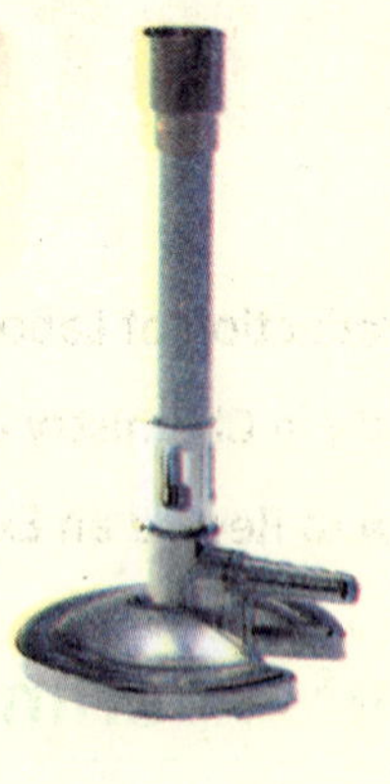

Arihant Prakashan (School Division Series)

卐 Administrative & Production Offices

Regd. Office
'Ramchhaya' 4577/15, Agarwal Road, Darya Ganj, New Delhi -110002
Tele: 011- 47630600, 43518550; Fax: 011- 23280316

Head Office
Kalindi, TP Nagar, Meerut (UP) - 250002, Tel: 0121-7156203, 7156204

卐 Sales & Support Offices
Agra, Ahmedabad, Bengaluru, Bareilly, Chennai, Delhi, Guwahati, Hyderabad, Jaipur, Jhansi, Kolkata, Lucknow, Nagpur & Pune

卐 Price : ₹ 350.00

卐 **PO No.** : TXT-59-T070820-5-26

Published by Arihant Publications (India) Ltd.

For further information about the books from Arihant, log on to **www.arihantbooks.com** or email to **info@arihantbooks.com**

Follow us on   

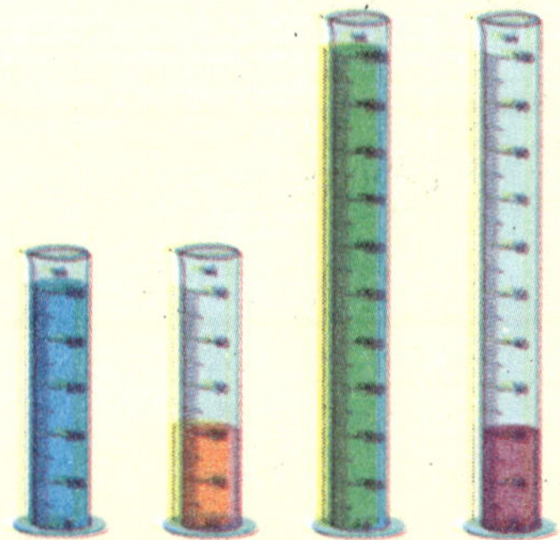

Contents

List of Experiments

INVESTIGATORY PROJECTS

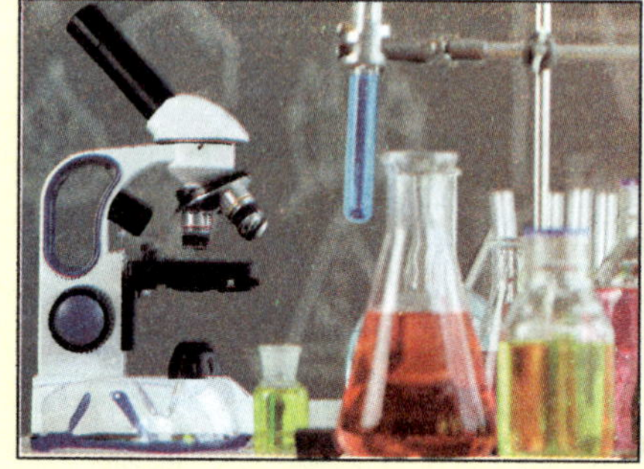

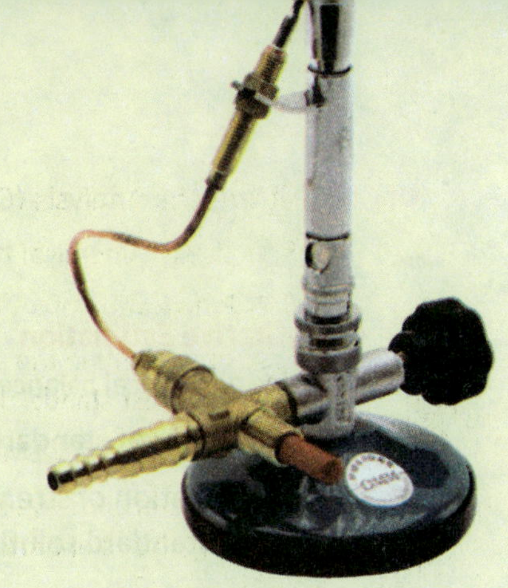

Syllabus

PRACTICAL

Micro-chemical methods are available for several of the practical experiments. Wherever possible such techniques should be used:

A. Basic Laboratory Techniques

1. Cutting glass tube and glass rod
2. Bending a glass tube
3. Drawing out a glass jet
4. Boring a cork

B. Characterisation and Purification of Chemical Substances

1. Determination of melting point of an organic compound.
2. Determination of boiling point of an organic compound.
3. Crystallization of impure sample of any one of the following: Alum, Copper Sulphate, Benzoic Acid.

C. Experiments based on pH

a) Any one of the following experiments:

- Determination of pH of some solutions obtained from fruit juices, solution of known and varied concentrations of acids, bases and salts using pH paper or universal indicator.
- Comparing the pH of solutions of strong and weak acids of same concentration.
- Study the pH change in the titration of a strong base using universal indicator.

b) Study the pH change by common-ion in case of weak acids and weak bases.

D. Chemical Equilibrium

One of the following experiments:

a) Study the shift in equilibrium between ferric ions and thiocyanate ions by increasing/decreasing the concentration of either of the ions.

b) Study the shift in equilibrium between $[Co(H_2O)_6]^{2+}$ and chloride ions by changing the concentration of either of the ions.

E. Quantitative Estimation

i) Using a chemical balance.

ii) Preparation of standard solution of oxalic acid.

iii) Determination of strength of a given solution of sodium hydroxide by titrating it against standard solution of oxalic acid.

iv) Preparation of standard solution of sodium carbonate.

v) Determination of strength of a given solution of hydrochloric acid by titrating it against standard sodium carbonate solution.

F. Qualitative Analysis

a) Determination of one anion and one cation in a given salt

Cations Pb^{2+}, Cu^{2+}, As^{3+}, Al^{3+}, Fe^{3+}, Mn^{2+}, Ni^{2+}, Zn^{2+}, Co^{2+}, Ca^{2+}, Sr^{2+}, Ba^{2+}, Mg^{2+}, NH_4^+

Anions CO_3^{2-} , S^{2-} , SO_3^{2-} , SO_4^{2-} , NO_2^- , NO_3 , Cl^- , Br^- , I^- , PO_4^{3-} , CH_3COO^-

(Insoluble salts excluded)

b) Detection of -nitrogen, sulphur, chlorine in organic compounds.

PROJECTS

Scientific investigations involving laboratory testing and collecting information from other sources.

A few suggested Projects

- Checking the bacterial contamination in drinking water by testing sulphide ion.
- Study of the methods of purification of water.
- Testing the hardness, presence of Iron, Fluoride, Chloride, etc., depending upon the regional variation in drinking water and study of causes of presence of these ions above permissible limit (if any).
- Investigation of the foaming capacity of different washing soaps and the effect of addition of sodium carbonate on it.
- Study the acidity of different samples of tea leaves.
- Determination of the rate of evaporation of different liquids.
- Study the effect of acids and bases on the tensile strength of fibers.
- Study of acidity of fruit and vegetable juices.

Note: Any other investigatory project, which involves about 10 periods of work, can be chosen with the approval of the teacher.

INDEX

S.No.	Name of the Experiments	Page No.	Date	Remarks

INDEX

S.No.	Name of the Experiments	Page No.	Date	Remarks

LABORATORY Manual

CHEMISTRY

CERTIFICATE

This is to certify that Activities & Projects recorded in this Practical Notebook have been performed by ______________________
(Student's name)

of __________ of ______________________________
(class/section) (school name)

during academic session ____________________

....	....	....
Examiner Signature	Principal Signature (with school stamp)	Teacher Signature

Introduction to Laboratory Equipments

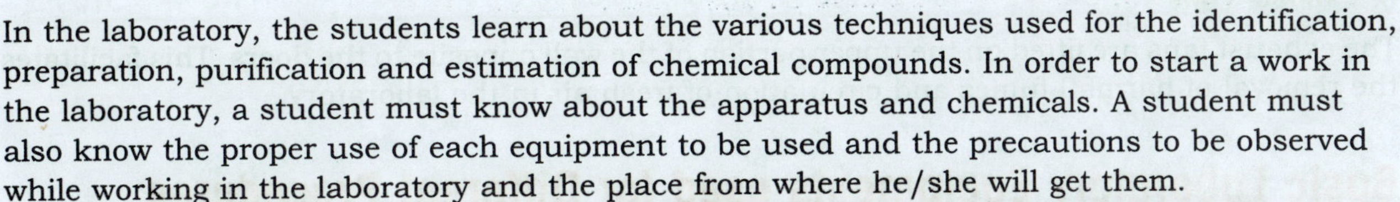

In the laboratory, the students learn about the various techniques used for the identification, preparation, purification and estimation of chemical compounds. In order to start a work in the laboratory, a student must know about the apparatus and chemicals. A student must also know the proper use of each equipment to be used and the precautions to be observed while working in the laboratory and the place from where he/she will get them.

A **chemistry laboratory** is provided with the following elements with which the student must become familiar.

1. Demonstration Table

This table is meant for the teacher to give instructions and to demonstrates any part of the experiment to be carried out by the students. The teacher explains the correct procedure which is to be followed and precautions to be taken while performing the experiments. The students stand around the demonstration table and note the instructions given to them by their teacher.

2. Student's Working Table

A number of concrete or wooden table are provided for the working of students. Each seat is complete in itself and is provided with

(i) **Gas Taps** These are fitted on the working table for supply of LPG to the burners for heating purposes. These must be used carefully and kept tightly closed when not in use.

(ii) **Water Taps and Sinks** For supply of water, a water tap is fixed on each seat and waste liquids are thrown in the sink. Never throw any insoluble solid materials like filter papers, broken glass apparatus etc., into the sink as these can block the drain.

(iii) **Reagent Shelves** Reagents or chemicals to be used very frequently are kept on these shelves. e.g. HCl, H_2SO_4, HNO_3, NaOH, NH_4OH etc.

(iv) **Dustbin** It is meant for disposing waste materials like used filter papers, broken apparatus, etc.

3. Side Shelves

Mostly, there are big shelves fitted on the walls of the laboratory. Chemicals and reagents, which are less frequently used are kept in these shelves. e.g. Nessler's reagent, potassium ferricyanide, starch solution, silver nitrate, dimethylglyoxime, etc.

4. Fume Closet or Cupboard

There is atleast one fume closet in the corner of the laboratory. It is a small chamber having a sliding glass wall and a chimney fitted with an exhaust fan at the top. All experiments giving out poisonous gases or vapours are performed in this closet.

5. Balance Room

It is a small room attached to the laboratory. In this, a number of chemical balances are kept for weighing the substances.

6. Exhaust Fans

The exhaust fans are fitted on the upper portion of the wall opposite to the doors. This facilitates the removal of harmful fumes and circulation of fresh air in the laboratory.

Basic Laboratory Equipments used for Different Procedures

Procedures like heating, filtration, decantation, weighing liquids and solids, measuring volumes are used very frequently while doing the experiments in laboratory. To perform these procedures, a student must be aware of the glass apparatus and equipments and should understand the techniques to handle them properly.

The basic laboratory apparatus and their utility in experimentations are listed below

Name of the Apparatus	Use	Figures
Test tubes These are the hollow glass tube closed at one end and has a circular rim at the other. These are available in different diameter and lengths and different volumes.	These are used to carry out the chemical reactions and to boil the solutions. Only one-third of the test tube should be filled while carrying out a reaction.	
Test tube stand It is made up of plastic polypropylene. The holes in the top plate can hold the test tubes and its vertical pins for drying the tubes.	It is used to keep test tubes vertically and provides protection to the contents of the tube.	
Test tube holder It contains an iron strip fitted in cylindrical wooden base.	It is used to hold the test tube containing liquids or solids during heating.	
Test tube brush It is made up of thick hard iron wire with soft plastic bristles.	It is used for cleaning the test tube.	

Name of the Apparatus	Use	Figures
Boiling tube It is similar to the test tube but with large diameter.	It is used when large volume of solution is required to be heated.	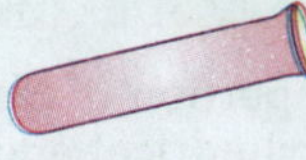
Beakers These are the cylindrical vessels with a large diameter and are usually made up of pyrex or corning glass. These are available in various sizes, ranging from 5 mL to 2000 mL.	These are used for keeping liquid solution during experimental work and to pour solution from one beaker to another.	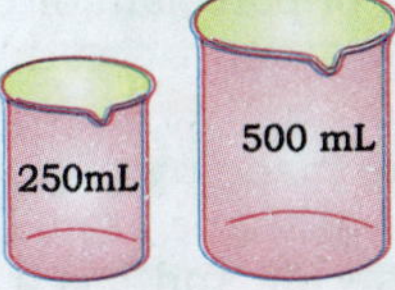
Conical flask It is a hollow glass vessel which is of conical shape and is available in various sizes ranging from 5 mL to 2000 mL, also referred as Erlen meyer Flask.	It is usually used for carrying out volumetric titrations and hence, also called titration flask.	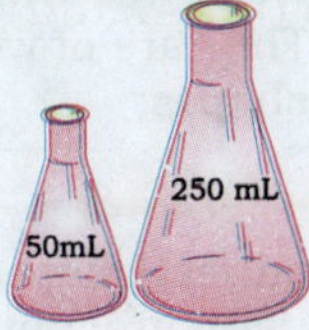
Round bottom flask It is round glass bottle flask and cannot be placed on the table directly due to its round bottom.	It is used where heating is necessary and in the preparation of organic compounds and gases.	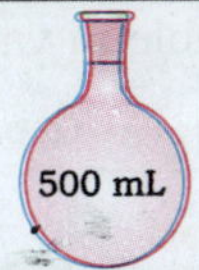
Flat bottom flask It is a glass bottle having a flat bottom with a long narrow neck. It can be kept on the table without falling.	It is used for carrying out chemical reactions and distillation processes.	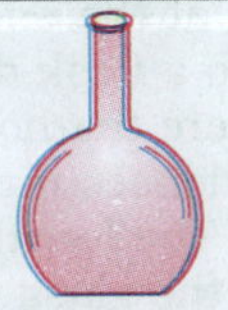
Measuring flask It is usually made up of borosil/pyrex/corning glass and is of different sizes and volumes like 50 mL, 100 mL, 250 mL or 500 mL. They have long and narrow neck with a flat bottom. At the upper part of the long neck, a mark is engraved upto which the liquid is to be filled.	They are used for making definite volumes of standard solutions.	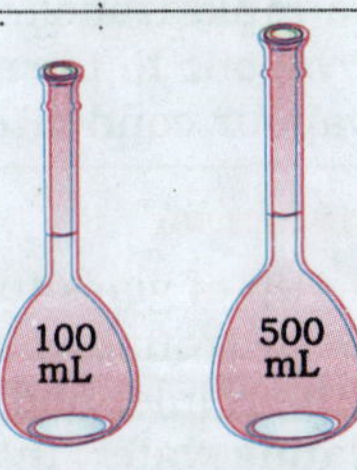
Distilling flask It is a round bottom flask containing a tube at the cylindrical neck.	It is used in the distillation process.	
Funnel It is a cone shaped hollow glass apparatus with a narrow long stem and are available in various sizes.	It is used for filtration and sublimation.	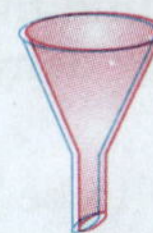

Name of the Apparatus	Use	Figures
Buchner funnel The upper portion of Buchner funnel is cylindrical and lower base has conical shape with a stem pipe like structure. It is made up of porcelain or ceramic.	It is used for filtration.	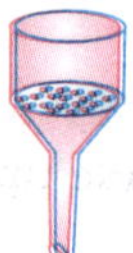
Separating funnels These are made up of glass having oval shape at mid. The mouth is wide and has a glass cap stopper. The other end is having a tube fitted with a stopcork. They are of various sizes and shapes.	It is used to separate two immiscible liquids.	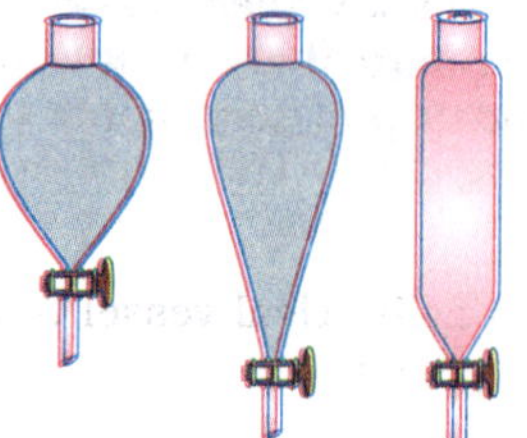
Measuring cylinder It is a cylindrical shaped apparatus with graduated marks. It is made up of glass or plastic and is available in various volumes.	It is used for measuring different volumes of liquids.	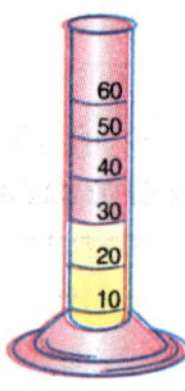
Air condenser It is a long tube having a slightly wide mouth at the end. It is connected to a flask during a reaction where the hot vapour rises up and condenses in colder regions of the tube. The length and diameter of the glass tube vary. There is a rapid transfer of heat from hot vapour to the surrounding air and vapour condenses.	It is used for refluxing and distillation of solutions or liquids with high boiling points.	
Water condenser It is made up of glass tubes with an inner tube surrounded by an outer jacket with an inlet and an outlet for circulating water. Inlet is connected to the tap. Heat is transferred from hot vapour to the surrounding water.	It is used for refluxing and distillation of solutions of low boiling point.	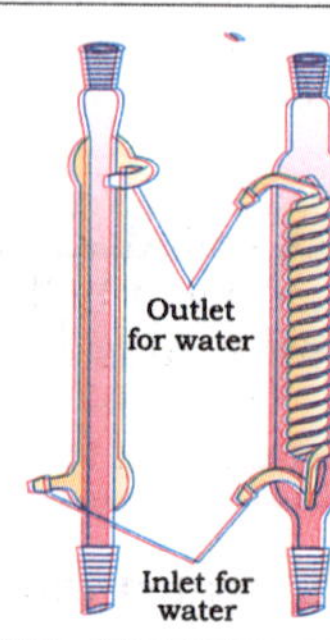
Desiccator It is made up of glass and has two compartments. The lower portion contains a ground tile which is used for placing dehydrating agent such as $CaCl_2$. The substance to be dried is kept at the upper portion of the desiccator.	It is used to remove moisture from a substance.	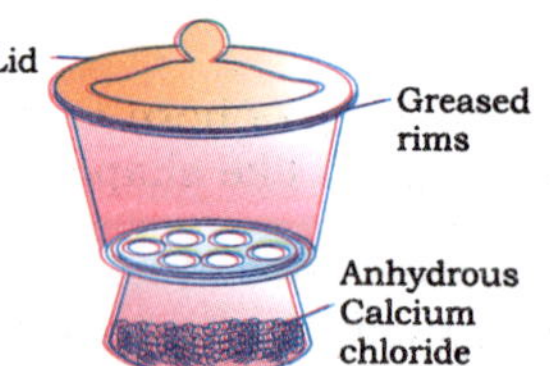

Name of the Apparatus	Use	Figures
China dish It is a hollow hemispherical shaped apparatus made up of porcelain.	It is used for evaporating mixtures and also keeping solids exposed to air.	
Mortar-pestle It is a thick walled vessel with a hemispherical shape with a base. It is made up of porcelain.	It is used for grinding the salts and other substances with the help of pestle.	
Gas jar It is a cylindrical vessel having one side opened.	It is used to collect a gas during their preparation.	
Burette It is a hollow long cylindrical tube with graduated marks. There is a stopcork and nozzle at the end of the tube. The stopper can move in such a way so that dropwise addition of liquid is also possible.	It is used in volumetric titrations to transfer accurate volume of solutions.	
Pipette It is a thin hollow cylindrical tube with a bulb in the middle portion. It is available in various capacities such as 1 mL, 5 mL, 15 mL or 20 mL.	It is used to measure and transfer a particular volume of liquid accurately during titrations.	
Fusion tube It is a very small test tube of about 1-2 mL capacity made up of easily breakable glass.	It is used for preparing Lassaigne's extract required to test extra elements present in an organic compound.	
Glass rod It is a thick cylindrical stick of glass which is not hollow and available in various thickness.	It is mainly used for stirring and mixing substances.	
Platinum wire A platinum coated wire fitted with a glass rod.	It is used for performing flame test.	
Spatula It is made up of horn or plastic with a spoon like shape.	It is used to take chemicals from a container.	
Triangular file It is made up of hard cast iron and are available in various shapes and sizes.	It is used to mark scratch while cutting a glass rod or tube.	

Name of the Apparatus	Use	Figures
Cork borers These are made up of brass or copper.	These are used to make holes of various sizes in corks.	
Watch glass It is a curve shaped transparent glass apparatus so that the substance do not fall off.	It is used for crystallisation and mixture analysis.	
Wire gauze A flat square piece of iron wire mesh in which asbestos paper is trapped at the centre of the gauze.	It is kept on the tripod stand so that the glass container do not come in direct contact of flame.	
Water bath It is a vessel made up of brass having oval shape.	It is used for heating water. Inflammable substance cannot be warmed on a direct flame, thus, heated in a vessel kept on the water bath. Electric water baths are also available in laboratories.	
Sand bath It is a metal plate in which sand is kept and it is heated from below.	Any apparatus that requires uniform heating is kept on a sand bath.	
Crucible tongs It is made up of steel or iron.	It is used to hold hot beaker, China dish, etc.	
Tripod stand It is made up of cast iron and possesses a triangular shape fitted with three rods acting as legs.	It is used to place wire gauze on it during heating.	
Wash bottle It is made up of plastic, polythene containing a thin tube.	It is used for washing and rinsing glass apparatus.	

CLEANING OF GLASSWARE APPARATUS

Glassware apparatus should be cleaned before starting of an experiment. If they were not clean and contaminated with dirt and other chemicals, experimental errors are caused after the experiment and the student would not get the appropriate results.

Depending upon the type of impurities or contamination, the apparatus can be cleaned with tap water to remove dust, concentrated acids like HCl, HNO_3 or chromic acid [5 g of potassium dichromate dissolved in 100 mL of conc. sulphuric acid] to remove grease. Sodium carbonate (or washing soda) can also be used to clean the apparatus. Employ a suitable brush to clean the inner surface of burettes, test tubes, flask, etc. Place the washed apparatus in an inverted position so that the water is drained off.

Heating Devices

Heating work in laboratories can be done with the help of a gas burner, spirit lamp or a kerosene lamp.

Bunsen Burner

In chemistry laboratories where gas supply is available, Bunsen burners are used. This burner was devised by Robert Bunsen in 1855.

Various parts of Bunsen burner are described as

- **The Base** The burner rests on a cast iron base. It keeps the burner in a stable upright position. The base has a side tube connected to a gas tap called gas tube.
- **The Burner Tube** It is a long metallic tube which has two holes diametrically opposite to each other near the lower end which form the air vent. The tube can be screwed at the base. The gas coming from the nozzle gets mixed with the air coming through the air vent and burns at its upper end.
- **The Air Regulator** It is a short metallic cylindrical sleeve with two holes diametrically opposite to each other. When it is fitted to the burner tube, it surrounds the air vent of the burner tube. In order to control the flow of air through the air vent, size of its hole is adjusted by rotating the sleeve.

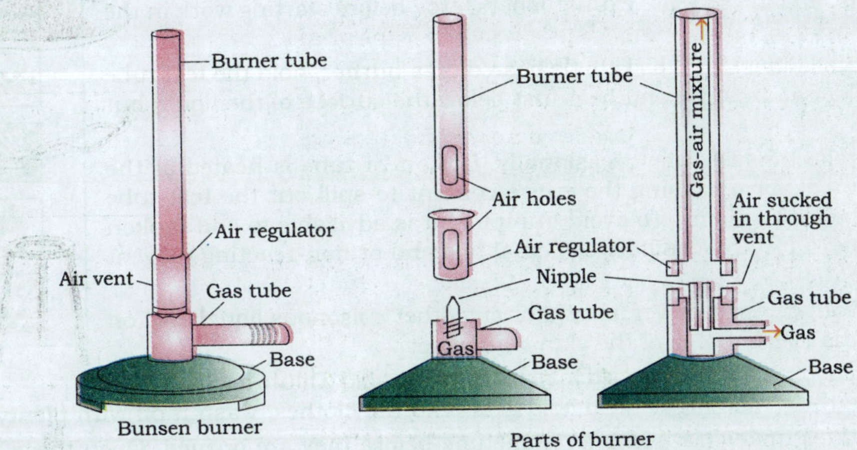

Bunsen burner

Parts of burner

Working of Burner

When the burner is connected to the gas supply, the gas escapes through the nozzle and there is a fall of pressure due to which air is sucked through the air holes. The mixture of air and gas burns at the upper end of the burner producing a flame.

The flame can be luminous or non-luminous depending upon the quantity of air mixed. The hottest zone is oxidising flame called non-luminous zone and is used for heating purposes.

SAFETY IN CHEMISTRY LABORATORY

Do's and Dont's in the Chemistry Laboratory

To work efficiently in a laboratory without any injury or accident, students are advised to follow the practices listed below.

Do's

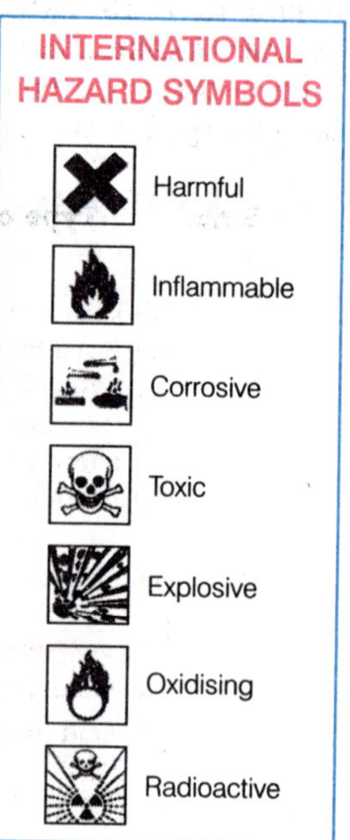

- Always perform the experiments under supervision of a teacher.
- Wear lab coat and shoes while working in the laboratory in order to protect your clothes and foot from corrosive chemicals.
- Wear safety glasses at all times in the laboratory. Eye protection is required while working inside the laboratory. Accidents never occur ahead of time so eye protection is a prerequisite. If chemical splashes accidentaly in the eye, wash the eye with a large amount of water.
- Make sure of the location and operation of emergency equipments like eyewash fountains, first aid box, fire extinguishers, etc., before starting work in the laboratory.
- If a solution contained in a test tube is to be heated on a burner, hold the test tube with test tube holder at an angle and heat just below the surface of the liquid but not at bottom.
- While heating, shake the test tube occasionally. If the test tube is heated at the bottom, a bubble may form causing the entire content to spill out the test tube violently. This is called bumping. To avoid bumping, it is advisable to add broken China dish/marble/a piece of capillary sealed at one end or non-reacting reagent like pumice stone.
- Handle the acids with care, whenever an acid or any other poisonous liquid spill on your body, wash the affected area of the skin with water.
- Dilute ammonium hydroxide may be used to neutralise the acid. Dilute acetic acid is used to neutralise the remaining base. If acid gets onto the clothes, wash it off with plenty of water.
- Cool ammonia bottles under tap water for sometime before they are opened. Open these bottles in fume cupboards.
- Before using a reagent bottle, read the label very carefully to be sure that you are using the correct reagent.
- Clean every piece of apparatus as soon as the work is finished and keep these at proper place.
- Look for the symbols on the labels of chemical bottles.

Dont's

- Do not touch the chemicals with hands as it may be poisonous or it may contaminated with poisonous chemicals.
- Never mix the chemicals unless it is required in the experiment as it may result in serious accidents.
- Do not heat the test tube containing solution with its mouth pointing towards yourself or your neighbour as the spurting of content may harm you or your neighbour.
- Do not smell the gases directly. They may be highly toxic. Keep the test tube atleast 8-10 inches away from your nose and wave the vapours gently towards your nose.
- Hot apparatus should not be placed on working table directly because it may spoil the working table. Place it on a glazed tile or a wire gauze.

- Do not heat the apparatus which is made up of thick glass. e.g. Graduated cylinder, bottles, measuring flasks, etc., as they may break on heating. Always heat glass apparatus with wire gauze, don't heat them directly.
- Do not hold reagent bottles by the neck and must use both hands to carry bottles from one place to another.
- Never return unused chemicals to the stock bottles. If you commit a mistake in putting the material back into the correct bottle, experiments of other students will be spoiled.
- Do not waste water or gas. Close the taps whenever they are not in use. Do not leave the lighted burner under the wire gauze when nothing is being heated, extinguish it.
- Don't taste anything in the laboratory (poisonous substances are not always so labelled in the laboratory) and never use laboratory as an eating place.
- Never use glass apparatus of the laboratory for eating and drinking purposes. Never work in laboratory alone. Seek the permission of your teacher for working for extra hours, in case it is needed.

Probable Accidents and their First Aid Treatment

Accidents in the laboratory are often the result of carelessness or ignorance of the students. Most of the accidents take place due to improper handling of chemicals and apparatus. In any case, if it happens, take necessary steps immediately by using first aid box. The probable accidents, injuries and their first aid emergency treatments are listed below :

S.No.	Type of accident	First aid emergency treatment
1.	**Burns**	
	(i) Burns causing blisters	Apply burnol at once.
	(ii) Burn by dry heat (i.e. flame, hot object, etc.) **Caution** Heat burns should never be washed.	Apply mustard oil or burnol.
	(iii) Bromine burns	Wash liberally with 2% NH_3 solution and then rub glycerine. Wipe off glycerine after sometime and later apply burnol.
	(iv) Acid burns	Firstly wash freely with water, then with 1% acetic acid and, then again with water. Dry the skin and apply burnol to it.
2.	**Eye accidents**	
	(i) Alkali in eye	Wash thoroughly with water and then with 1% boric acid solution.
	(ii) Acid in eye	Wash thoroughly with water, afterwards with 1% sodium bicarbonate solution and then with water again.
3.	**Cuts**	
	(i) Minor cuts	Allow to bleed for a few seconds. Remove the glass piece if any. Apply methylated spirit and cover it with a piece of cotton or you can apply $FeCl_3$ solution to stop bleeding.
	(ii) Major cuts	Apply pressure above the cut to stop bleeding. Call the doctor immediately.
4.	**Poisons**	
	(i) Poisons not swallowed	Spit out immediately. Wash mouth with plenty of water.
	(ii) Inhalation of gases like Cl_2, SO_2, Br_2, etc., causing suffocation	Loosen the clothes at the neck. At once go in the open air. Inhale dilute vapours of ammonia or gargle with sodium bicarbonate solution.
	(iii) Acid swallowed	Drink lot of water. Drink lime water. No emetic [a substance causing vomiting] should be taken.
	(iv) Caustic alkalies swallowed	Drink plenty of water. Drink a glass of lemon or orange juice. No emetic should be taken.
5.	**Fire**	
	(i) Beaker containing inflammable liquid catches fire.	Immediately cover the beaker with duster or damp cloth.
	(ii) Clothes catch fire.	Do not run in hastle. Wrap with a blanket, then lie down on the floor and roll.

Go to the doctor after getting first aid.

HOW TO RECORD AN EXPERIMENT?

A neat and systematic recording of the experiment in the laboratory notebook is very important for keeping an upto date record of the work which has been done in the laboratory.

Infact, a proper record of the experimental results and conclusions is an indispensable part of scientific work. The laboratory notebook must be well maintained and protected from mechanical and chemical damage. It should be made checked regularly by the teacher.

The experiment should be recorded in the laboratory notebook under the following heads as

Date......	Experiment No.	Page No. ......

Aim or Objective of the Experiment *State clearly and precisely the objective of the experiment to be performed.*

Materials Required *Mention the name of the apparatus and chemicals to be used in the experiment clearly.*

Theory or Principle *Mention the concept on which the experiment is based in a very brief manner. Also, write the formula used, clearly explaining the symbols involved.*

Procedure *Mention various steps in the experiment followed with precautions.*

Chemical Reactions *The chemical reactions that takes place in the experiment should be written on the left hand side of the notebook.*

Diagrams *Wherever required, draw the diagrams on the left hand side of the notebook.*

Observations *Record the observations or data in a tabular form as far as possible, neatly and without any overwriting.*

Calculations *[wherever desirable] For writing the calculations, substitute the observed value in the formula and do the computations systematically and neatly.*

Result *State the conclusions drawn from the experimental observations. If the result depends upon the conditions of temperature and pressure, mention these conditions also along with the result.*

Precautions *Mention the precautions observed during the course of setting an apparatus and the steps followed while performing the experiment.*

Discussion *Under this heading mention any special inferences or special difficulties faced during the experimentation.*

These may include points for making the experiment more accurate and for better understanding of the basic principle involved.

Unit 1

Basic Laboratory Techniques

In the chemical laboratory, a student is required to carry out from simplest operations (like cutting and bending of glass tube and glass rod, boring a cork) to complex process (analysing the compounds qualitatively and quantitatively).

In the following pages, you will learn about some of the techniques of handling glass tubes and glass rods without injuring yourself. Also, you will learn the techniques of using laboratory apparatus and equipments.

The laboratory apparatus for carrying out reactions, in general, is made up of glass. It is because glass is resistant to the action of most of the chemicals. Generally, two types of glass are used for making apparatus for laboratory work. These are soda-lime glass and borosilicate glass which are discussed below.

(i) **Soda-lime glass** It is made by heating soda, limestone and silica softens at about 300-400°C in the burner flame. Thus, glass tubings made of soda lime glass easily softens on heating and hence, can be bent. It should be heated and cooled gradually to avoid breaking as coefficient of expansion of soda glass is very high. Annealing by mild reheating and uniform cooling prevents breakage.

(ii) **Borosilicate glass** It does not soften below 700-800°C and requires oxygen-natural gas flame for working. The apparatus made of this glass can withstand sudden changes in temperature due to low coefficient of expansion. The apparatus used for heating purposes is made from this glass because it does not distort.

1.1 CUTTING OF GLASS TUBE AND GLASS ROD

Theory/Principle

Cutting of glass tube is required for making U-shaped tubes and delivery tubes.

Materials Required

- Soda-glass tube or rod : 15 cm long
- Wire gauze : 1
- Bunsen burner : 1
- Triangular file : 1

Procedure

To cut a glass tube, proceed in the following manner

Making a Scratch on a Tube

1. Place the glass tube or rod on the table and make a mark on the tube at required length.

2. Press the glass tube with your left hand and keep the lower end of a triangular file with its sharp edge perpendicular to the tube on the mark. Make a single deep scratch on the glass tube or rod at a desired length with triangular file by moving it only in downward direction, i.e. towards yourself [Fig. 1.1].

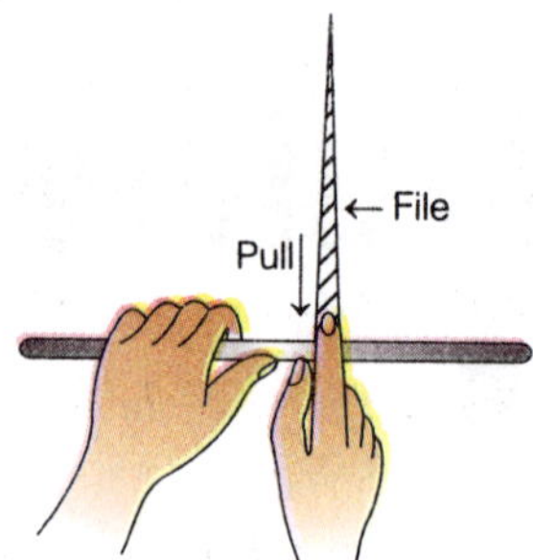

Fig. 1.1 *Marking a scratch on a glass rod or a glass tube with a triangular file*

Breaking of Tube

3. Hold the tube/rod with both the hands at equal distances from the scratch and break it by applying a gentle pressure with your thumbs in a direction away from you as shown in the figure [1.2 (i), (ii)].

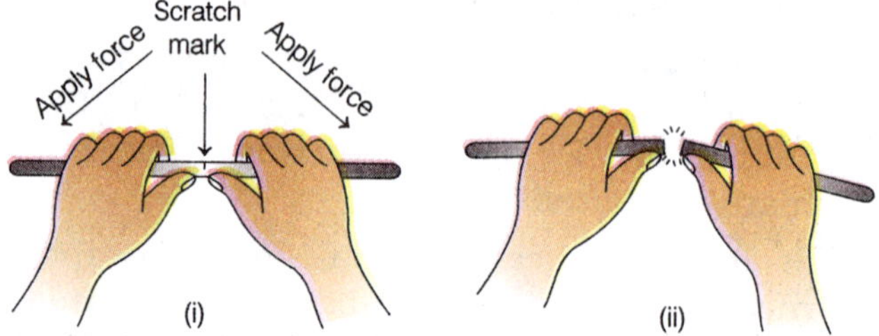

Fig.1.2 *(i) Placing the thumbs together opposite to the scratch mark*
(ii) Breaking the glass rod or glass tube by applying moderate force

4. If the glass tube does not break, make a deeper scratch at the point marked earlier and make a fresh attempt.

Fire Polishing

5. If the edges of the tube/rod are not smooth, then to make them round and smooth, first trim the jagged edges by rubbing with a wire gauze. Heat the freshly cut edge of the tube gently in the flame. This is called **fire polishing**.
6. For fire polishing, first continuously warm the cut end in the Bunsen flame till it becomes red hot and then rotate it back and forth until the edge is rounded. Too much heating may distort the rounded edge [Fig. 1.3].

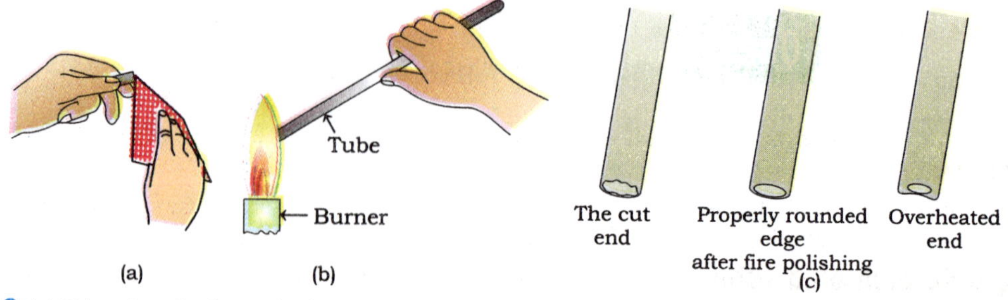

Fig. 1.3 *(a) Trimming the jagged edges (b) Rounding the edges, (c) Properly and improperly rounded edges.*

PRECAUTIONS

- *The selected glass tube or rod should be free from cracks.*
- *With one stroke of the triangular file, make a single deep scratch at the desired length.*
- *The file should be moved on the tube only in downward direction.*
- *Break the tube or rod by holding it with the help of a piece of cloth so that hands are not harmed.*
- *To avoid injury, the filing and breaking of the glass tube or rod should be carried away from the face as far as possible.*
- *Make sure that a gentle pressure should be applied on the scratched mark to break a glass tube or rod as large pressure may break it into small pieces .*
- *Do not heat the tube over strong flame and not even for a long time as long heating will distort the rounded ends.*

Viva-Voce

Q.1 Why is glass preferred for manufacturing laboratory apparatus?

Ans. Glass is chemically resistant and can be easily shaped when heated which makes it ideal for laboratory use.

Q.2 What raw materials are used in the preparation of soda-lime glass?

Ans. Soda, limestone, and silica.

Q.3 Why does soda-lime glass tend to break upon sudden heating or cooling?

Ans. Because it has a high coefficient of expansion, which makes it vulnerable to thermal stress.

Q.4 Which tool is used to mark or scratch the glass tube for cutting?

Ans. A triangular file.

Q.5 What is meant by annealing in the context of glasswork?

Ans. Annealing is the process of gently reheating and gradually cooling glass to prevent breakage due to internal stress.

Q.6 What is fire polishing and why is it done?

Ans. Fire polishing is the process of gently heating the cut edge of glass to make it smooth and safe to handle.

Q.7 Why is a single deep scratch preferred over multiple shallow ones while cutting glass?

Ans. A single deep scratch creates a clean break line, whereas multiple scratches may lead to irregular or unsafe breaks.

Questions From NCERT Lab Manual

Q.1 Why is it required to round off the freshly cut edges of the glass tube or the glass rod?

Ans. It is required to round off the freshly cut edges of the glass tube or rod because the freshly cut edges are sharp. They might injured your fingers.

Q.2 Why does glass not possess a sharp melting point?

Ans. Glass does not have a sharp melting point because it is an amorphous solid, so it does not have a regular arrangement of constituent particles.

1.2 BENDING OF A GLASS TUBE

Theory/Principle

In chemical laboratories, bended glass tubes are required for delivery of gases and for carrying out distillation. On heating a glass tube at a particular place, it becomes soft and can be bent at a desired angle.

Materials Required

- Glass tube : 20-25 cm long
- Bunsen burner : 1
- Glazed tile : 1
- Triangular file : 1

Procedure

To bend a glass tube proceed in the following manner

Cutting of Glass Tube

1. Cut a tube of desired length by using a triangular file as described in experiment in Fig. 1.1.

Heating of Glass Tube

2. Heat the portions of the glass tube from where it is to be bent by placing it in luminous flame (i.e. hottest zone) of the Bunsen burner [Fig. 1.4].

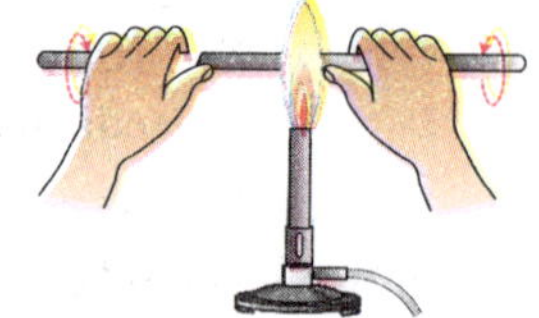

Fig. 1.4 *Heating the tube*

3. While heating the tube in the flame, keep it rotating slowly until the portion, which is to be bent, becomes red hot and soft and starts bending under its own weight [Fig. 1.5].

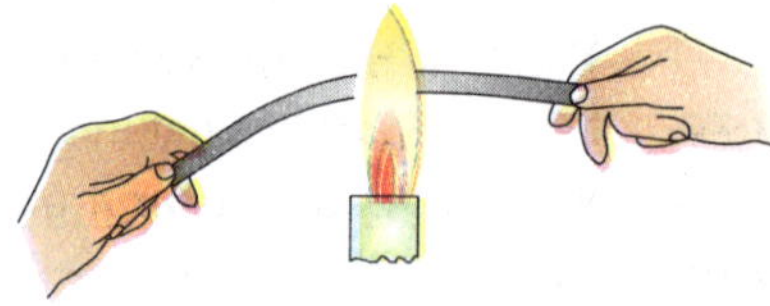

Fig. 1.5 *The tube softens and starts bending under its own weight*

Bending of Glass Tube

4. Now, remove the tube from the flame and bend it slowly at a desired angle in a coplanar manner by gently pressing it against a glazed tile. Allow it to cool on the glazed tile [Fig 1.6].

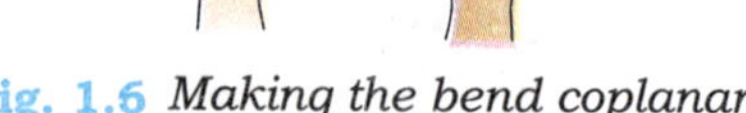

Fig. 1.6 *Making the bend coplanar*

5. Bend the other tubes at different angles [Fig 1.7] in the same manner as described above [Fig 1.6].

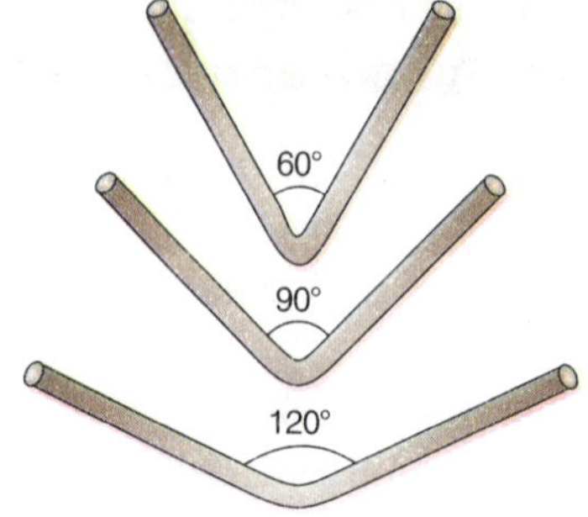

Fig. 1.7 *Making the bend coplanar*

PRECAUTIONS

- *Avoid heating the glass tube only on one side, rather rotate it continuously while heating.*
- *Carry out the process slowly to avoid flattening of the glass tube while bending.*
- *Start bending only when it is soft.*
- *Select a glass tube of appropriate length (nearly 25-30 cm long) to keep your hands safe from heat.*
- *Never try to change the angle of a bent tube by reheating.*
- *Always use the blue flame of the burner for bending the tube.*

Viva-Voce

Q.1 What is meant by the 'hottest zone' of a Bunsen burner flame?
Ans. The tip of the inner blue cone where the temperature is maximum.

Q.2 Why is the tube not bent immediately after heating?
Ans. Because it needs to be soft enough to bend without cracking.

Q.3 Why is the bent tube cooled on a glazed tile and not under running water?
Ans. Sudden cooling can cause the glass to crack due to thermal shock.

Q.4 What safety precaution should you take while heating glass?
Ans. Wear safety goggles and handle the tube with tongs or from a safe distance.

Q.5 What is meant by 'coplanar' bending?
Ans. The bent part lies flat in the same plane as the unbent part.

Q.6 What is the risk of overheating the glass tube?
Ans. It may become too soft and collapse or stick to itself.

Q.7 Can you bend glass with an alcohol lamp? Why or why not?
Ans. No, because it does not produce enough heat compared to a Bunsen burner.

Questions From NCERT Lab Manual

Q.1 Why should the tube be rotated while heating?
Ans. To ensure uniform heating from all the sides, the tube is rotated while heating.

Q.2 Why is the red hot tube bent slowly?
Ans. Red hot tube is very soft, hence slow process of bending prevents the flattening of glass tube.

1.3 DRAWING OUT A GLASS JET

Theory/Principle

A tube made up of soda-lime glass is used for drawing out a jet. On heating soda-lime glass tube at the centre, it easily softens and can be stretched into a fine jet by pulling the two ends of the tube apart. For drawing out a jet, a glass tube of smaller diameter is chosen. If the glass tube has a smaller diameter, then the jet can be drawn easily as small stretching is required. But if the diameter is large, then the tube has to be stretched too far which can be inconvenient.

Materials Required

- Glass tube : 20-25 cm long
- Bunsen burner : 1
- Triangular file : 1
- Sand paper : As per need

Procedure

To drawn out a glass jet, proceed in the following manner.

Cutting and Heating of Tube

1. Take a glass tube of appropriate length and diameter for drawing a jet.
2. Cut the glass tube of desired length with the help of a triangular file.
3. Heat the tube in the hottest portion of the Bunsen burner flame by holding it at both the ends.
4. Continuously heat and rotate the tube slowly until the portion, which is kept in the flame, becomes red hot and soft.

Fig. 1.8 *Heating the tube to draw a jet*

Stretching of Tube

5. Remove the tube from the flame and pull the ends apart slowly and smoothly, until it becomes narrow in the middle and stretches into a fine jet as shown in [Fig. 1.9].

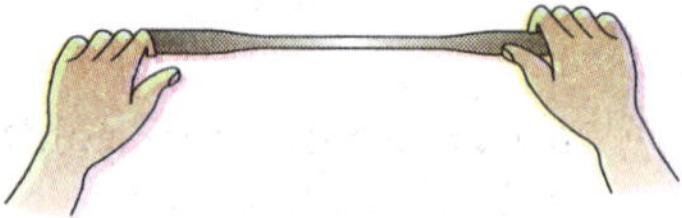

Fig. 1.9 *Before cutting*

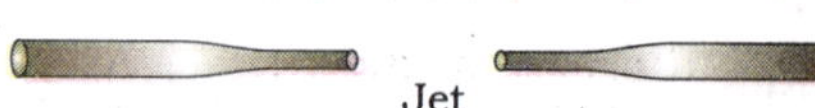

Fig. 1.10 *After cutting*

6. Cut the tube in the middle at the narrow portion with a triangular file and make the two jets uniform [Fig. 1.10].
7. Finally, smooth the ends of the jet by rubbing it with sand paper and by fire polishing.

PRECAUTIONS

- *Select the glass tube of right diameter while heating the glass tube, rotate it continuously.*
- *While drawing a jet, pull apart the two ends of the red-hot tube slowly so that it becomes thin uniformly.*

Viva-Voce

Q.1 What is meant by drawing out a jet from a glass tube?
Ans. It refers to heating and stretching a glass tube to form a thin, narrow nozzle-like end.

Q.2 Why is sandpaper used after cutting the jet?
Ans. The sandpaper is used to smoothen the sharp edges and make the jet safe for use.

Q.3 What is the purpose of fire polishing after cutting the jet?
Ans. Fire polishing melts and seals the rough edges thus giving a clean and finished look.

Q.4 How does the temperature affect the ease of jet drawing?
Ans. Higher temperatures soften the glass more quickly and allow smoother stretching.

Q.5 What should you do if the drawn jet has a sharp or jagged edge?
Ans. Rub it with sandpaper and fire polish it for safety and precision.

Q.6 Can any type of glass tube be used for drawing a jet?
Ans. No, only laboratory grade borosilicate glass is suitable due to its heat resistance.

Q.7 What precautions must be taken during the stretching of the glass tube?
Ans. Pull slowly and evenly to maintain uniformity and avoid sudden stress.

Q.8 How can you identify that the glass is ready to be stretched?
Ans. It becomes red hot and soft, slightly sagging under its own weight.

Questions From NCERT Lab Manual

Q.1 Which type of glass is preferred for drawing out a jet?

Ans. Soda-lime glass (soft glass) is preferred for drawing out a jet.

Q.2 Why is the glass tube of small diameter chosen for drawing out a jet?

Ans. If a tube of larger diameter is chosen then, the tube has to be stretched too far which is not convenient. Hence, a tube of smaller diameter is always chosen for drawing out a jet.

1.4 BORING A CORK

Theory/Principle

Boring a cork is required for fitting a cork in a wash bottle. Also, for insertion of a glass tube through the cork into the flask for setting up an apparatus for the delivery and preparation of gas or for carrying out distillation.

Materials Required

- Rubber corks : As per need
- Cork borer set : 1
- Water or Glycerine solution : As per need [Shelf reagent]

Procedure

To bore a cork, proceed in the following manner :

Selection of Cork

1. Such cork should be selected which is free from cracks. The size of the cork should be such that it should fit properly into the mouth of the flask.

Softening of Cork

2. Wet the selected cork with water so that it becomes flexible. Press the cork with a cork presser, [Fig 1.11 (i)] a mechanical device, if available in the laboratory. If not, then simply press it under your shoe after wrapping the cork in a piece of paper [Fig 1.11 (ii)].

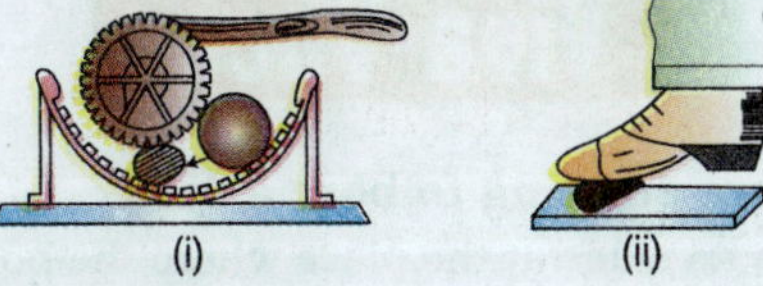

Fig. 1.11 (i) Pressing the cork with the cork presser
(ii) Pressing the cork with shoe

Selection of Borer

3. To select the perfect borer look for that borer whose diameter is slightly smaller in size than the diameter of the tube to be inserted in the hole of the cork [Fig. 1.12].]

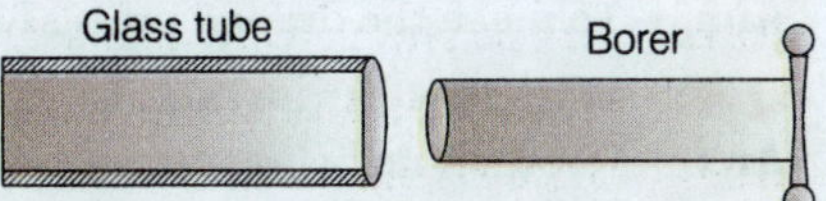

Fig. 1.12 *Choosing the borer*

Marking on Cork

4. Make a mark on both sides of the cork at the place where a hole is to be made or drilled [Fig. 1.13].

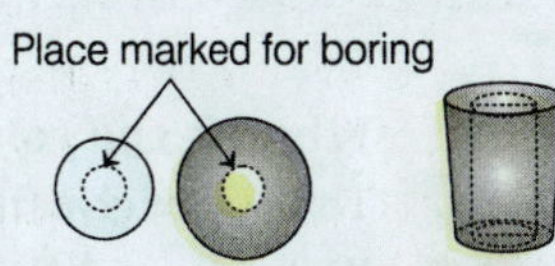

Fig. 1.13 *Marked cork*

Boring the Hole in the Cork

5. Place the rubber cork on the table with its smaller end in the upward direction as shown in [Fig. 1.13]. Hold the cork tightly in position with the left hand and put a suitable borer, lubricated by dipping in water or glycerine, at the place where the hole is to be drilled. [Fig. 1.13]. By lubricating the borer with glycerine or water a smooth hole is drilled.
6. Now, hold and push the borer vertically in the downward direction, and drill the hole by rotating the borer and simultaneously apply the pressure gently.

Reverse Boring

7. When half of the cork has been bored, take the borer out and reverse the cork. Start the process of boring taking care that the borer remains vertically throughout.

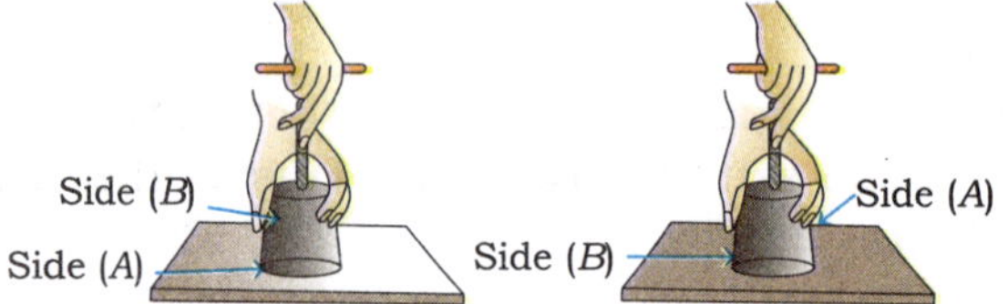

Fig. 1.14 *(a) Boring process* *(b) Reverse boring process*

8. Remove the borer after the cork has been bored from one face to the other. Remove the pieces of cork inside by inserting the needle.
9. For making two holes in the same cork, keep appropriate distance between the two holes and use borers of proper size. If the distance is very small, then the thin cork layer may break.

PRECAUTIONS

- *Make a mark on both sides of the cork and select borer of proper size.*
- *Drill half the hole from one side and another half from other side of the cork to obtain a smooth hole.*
- *Bore should be straight and the tube of the borer must be moistened before pushing it in the cork.*
- *The cork should not be pressed too hard.*

Viva-Voce

Q.1 What is the first step before starting to bore a cork?
Ans. Mark the rubber cork on both its sides at the place where the hole is to be drilled.

Q.2 How do you choose the correct cork borer size?
Ans. Select a borer whose diameter is slightly smaller than that of the tube to be inserted.

Q.3. What is the purpose of lubricating the borer with water or glycerine?
Ans. To make the drilling process smoother and avoid tearing the cork.

Q.4. Why is it important to rotate the borer while drilling?
Ans. Rotation helps in cutting the cork uniformly and easily.

Questions From NCERT Lab Manual

Q.1 What is the role of glycerine in the process of boring?
Ans. The role of glycerine in this process is to lubricate the borer which gives a smooth hole on boring.

Q.2 Why should the diameter of the borer be less than the diameter of the tube to be inserted in the hole?
Ans. To fit the tube tightly in the hole, diameter of the borer should be less than the diameter of the tube to be inserted in the hole.

Unit 2

Characterisation and Purification of Chemical Substances

Qualitative analysis of pure substance is required for the identification of a compound. Therefore, first the substance is to be purified and then its purity is checked. The purity of a compound may be checked by determining its melting and boiling points as pure compound (whether it is solid or liquid) possess sharp melting and boiling points.

There are many techniques, namely, crystallisation, distillation, sublimation, chromatography, etc., available for the purification process of a compound. But in this unit, you will only learn about the crystallisation as a technique used for the purification of a compound.

Crystallisation is one of the most important and effective technique used for the purification of an impure compound particularly when the original crude material obtained after a reaction is in a very impure condition. Thus, crystallisation is done to purify impure sample of a solid, prepare crystals of double salts from single salts and recrystallise the crystals to further improve the quality.

Experiment 2.1

AIM

To determine the melting point of an organic compound.

Theory/Principle

The temperature at which the solid starts to melt is called its **melting point**. The melting point is said to be **sharp**, when the solid substance melts completely within a range of 1°C. If impurities are present in the substance, even in traces, it lowers the melting point of the substance and it melts over a wide range.

Therefore, determination of melting point is very convenient method to check the purity of a solid substance and also helps in its identification.

Materials Required

▪ Thermometer	: 1	Beaker	:	1
▪ Porous plates	: As per need	Wire gauze	:	As per need
▪ Capillary tubes	: As per need	Iron stand with clamps	:	1
▪ Bunsen burner	: 1			

- Heating medium (paraffin oil or conc. H_2SO_4 or water) : As per need
- Thiele's tube/Kjeldahl's flask/beaker : 1
- The given organic compound (Naphthalene/*p*-dichlorobenzene/*p*-toluidine) : As per need

Procedure

Sealing the Capillary Tube

1. Take a glass capillary tube of approximately 8 cm in length. Seal its one open end by heating it in a bunsen flame for few minutes. Rotate the capillary tube while sealing to ensure complete closure of the opening. [Fig. 2.1 (i)]

⚠ ALERT

- *p-dichlorobenzene and naphthalene are harmful substance .*
- *Conc. H_2SO_4 is corrosive and irritant.*
- *Do not inhale vapours of these chemicals and avoid their direct contact with eyes and skin.*

Powdering and Filling the Compound in Capillary Tube

2. Take the desired quantity of the given crystalline substance on a dry and clean porous plate and powder it into fine particles. For filling the substance in the capillary tube, make a heap of the powdered substance.
3. Push the open end of the capillary tube into the powdered heap such that some of the powdered substance enters into the capillary tube. Fill upto nearly 1 cm in length. [Fig. 2.1 (ii)]
4. Hold the sealed end between the index finger and the thumb and tap the upper end gently with the other hand so that solid particles are tightly packed and capillary is prevented from breaking. [Fig. 2.1(iii)]
5. Fill the capillary tube upto 2-3 cm by repeating steps 2 and 3.

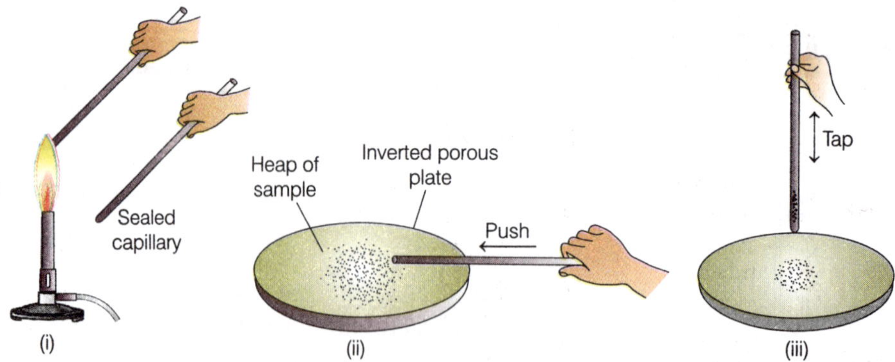

Fig. 2.1 *(i) Sealing one end of the capillary tube*
(ii) Filling a capillary tube
(iii) Packing the compound in a capillary tube by tapping the tube

Fixing the Capillary Tube with Thermometer

6. Moisten the capillary tube with liquid paraffin and stick the capillary tube to the thermometer. The capillary tube will stick to the thermometer by cohesive forces. Make sure that the lower ends of the capillary tube and thermometer bulb are at the same level [Fig. 2.2].

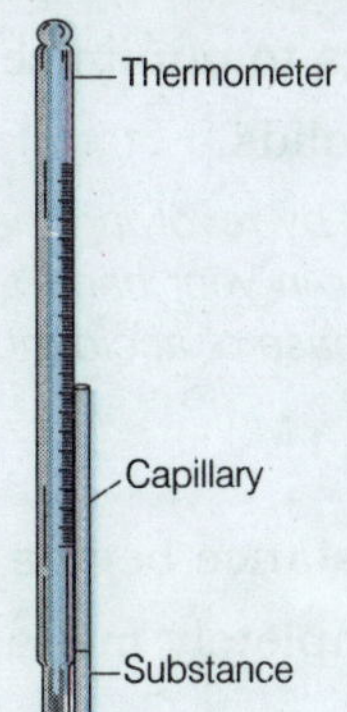

Fig. 2.2 *Arrangement of sample and thermometer at the same level*

Heating the Compound in Thiele's Tube and Finding the Melting Point

7. Fit the thermometer into a rubber cork, which has a groove on its side for the escape of air and vapours to prevent bursting of the tube or flask. [Fig. 2.3 (i)]
8. Take a Thiele's tube and fill it with 50-60 mL of liquid paraffin such that it crosses the bent portion of the Thiele's tube. Alternatively, Kjeldahl's flask or beaker may also be used in place of Thiele's tube. [Fig. 2.3 (i), (ii) and (iii)]
9. Dip the thermometer along with the capillary tube in liquid paraffin and adjust the rubber cork in such a way that the thermometer bulb and filled portion of the capillary is completely dipped in the liquid paraffin and the open end of the capillary tube remains in the air as shown in [Fig. 2.3(i)]. The surface tension of the liquid paraffin is sufficient to keep the capillary tube in position. The thermometer and capillary tube should not touch the sides of the Thiele's tube.
10. Now, heat the side arm of Thiele's tube with a low flame of Bunsen burner from the side opposite to that of the capillary tube and note the rise in temperature from time to time. Stir the liquid occasionally thereby the temperature remains uniform throughout. [Fig. 2.3 (i)]

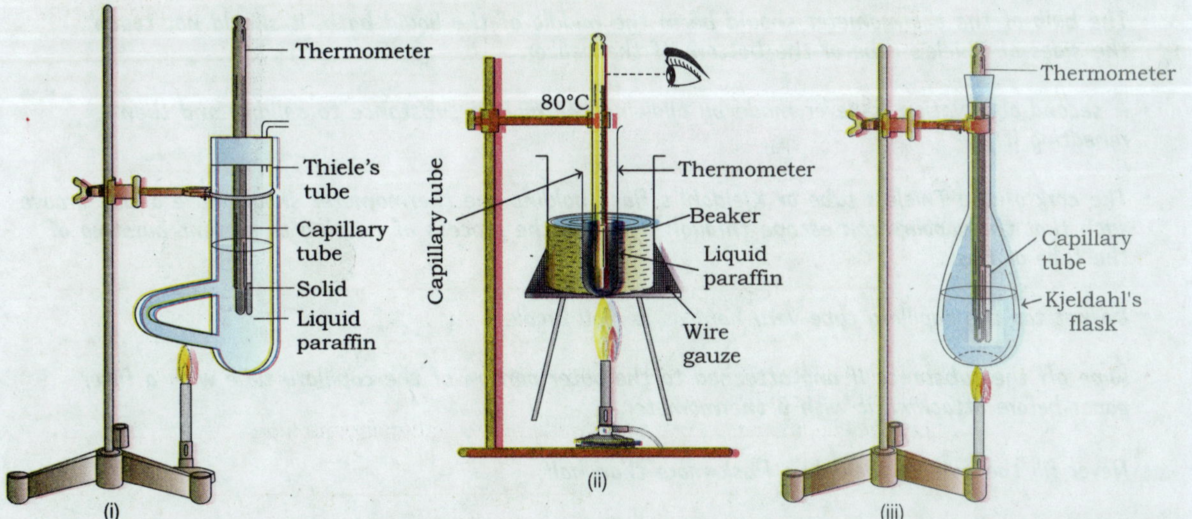

Fig. 2.3 *Determination of melting point using (i) Thiele's tube (ii) Beaker and (iii) Kjeldahl's flask*

11. When the solid shows sign of melting, note the temperature at which solid starts melting.
12. Again note the temperature when the solid substance is completely melted. The range of melting may be 1-2°C. In case, the melting range is more, the solid is not pure.
13. Cool the liquid bath and repeat the experiment with a new filled capillary.
14. Take the average of the two readings to minimise experimental errors.
15. Repeat the experiment with other solids.

Note *If you have taken Kjeldahl's flask, heat it by revolving the flame around the bottom of the flask to ensure uniform heating. For this, hold the burner in your hand and also keep a sand bath below the flask while heating. It will prevent spilling of acid in case of accident.*

Observation

Temperature at which the unknown substance begins to melt, t_1 = ... °C

Temperature at which the substance completely melts, t_2 = ...°C

Average melting point $= \dfrac{t_1\,°C + t_2\,°C}{2}$ = ...°C

Result

Melting point of the given substance is ......°C.

PRECAUTIONS

- *Keep the lower end of the capillary tube and the thermometer at the same level.*
- *The solid must be finely and uniformly powdered otherwise the solid will not enter the capillary tube easily and hence, it will not melt uniformly.*
- *Packing of the powder should be uniform without any big air gaps in between the solid particles.*
- *Gradually heat the liquid bath and stir it to ensure uniform heating.*
- *Do not attach capillary tube with thermometer by a rubber band.*
- *Keep the thermometer straight and note the reading by fixing eye at the level of mercury.*
- *The bulb of the thermometer should be in the middle of the liquid bath, it should not touch the sides of Thiele's tube or the bottom of the beaker.*
- *A second observation is never made by allowing the molten substance to solidify and then reheating it.*
- *The cork of the Thiele's tube or Kjeldahl's flask holding the thermometer should have a side groove such that the vapours can escape through it during the process of heating to prevent bursting of the tube or flask.*
- *Do not tap the capillary tube very hard as it may break.*
- *Wipe off the substance if any attached to the outer portion of the capillary tube with a filter paper before attaching it with a thermometer.*
- *Never fill the bulb of Kjeldahl's flask more than half.*
- *Capillary tube should not be very thick.*

Selection of Heating Medium

Choose the heating medium for the experiment on the basis of the melting point of the sample.Use water as heating medium for the sample having melting point less than 100°C. Paraffin oil is a stable high boiling liquid and can be safely heated upto 220°C. Therefore, for determination of melting point of a sample possessing melting point higher than this, conc. H_2SO_4 may be used which can be heated upto 280°C. Thus, the boiling point of heating medium must be higher than the melting point of the sample H_2SO_4 has been suggested for use but is not recommended. Silicone oils are most satisfactory liquids and can be used in place of sulphuric acid. A list of melting points of some known organic compounds is given below for the sake of convenience of students in the laboratory.

Melting Points of Some Organic Compounds

Compound	Melting point (°C)	Compound	Melting point (°C)
Phenol	42	Acetamide	82
α-naphthol	95	Benzamide	128
β-naphthol	123	Urea	132
Oxalic acid	101	Fructose	103
Benzoic acid	121	Glucose	146
Cinnamic acid	133	Sucrose	160
p-toluidine	43	Naphthalene	80
α-naphthylamine	50	Benzophenone	46
Chloral hydrate	57	Trichloroacetic acid	57

Viva-Voce

Q.1 What is the principle involved in determination of melting point?
Ans. On heating, the kinetic energy of molecules increases and overcomes intermolecular forces, causing the solid to melt.

Q.2 What is the melting point of a substance?
Ans. It is the temperature at which a solid begins to change into liquid at one atmosphere pressure.

Q.3 What is the purpose of sealing one end of the capillary tube?
Ans. Sealing prevents the solid from falling out during heating.

Q.4 How is the substance filled in the capillary tube?
Ans. By dipping its open end into the powder and tapping gently so that the powder settles and packs uniformly.

Q.5 Why is it important to pack the substance tightly in the capillary tube?
Ans. Loose packing can cause uneven melting and give an inaccurate result.

Q.6 What helps the capillary stick to the thermometer?
Ans. Cohesive forces and a slight moistening with liquid paraffin help it stick.

Q.7 At what level should the thermometer bulb and capillary end be placed?
Ans. The lower end of the capillary and the thermometer bulb should be at the same level.

Q.8 What is the role of the side groove in the cork?
Ans. It allows vapours to escape and prevents bursting of the tube or flask.

Q.9 **What volume of liquid paraffin is filled in the Thiele's tube?**

Ans. 50 to 60 mL, so that it crosses the bent portion of the tube.

Q.10 **What should be ensured while heating in a Kjeldahl flask?**

Ans. The burner should be rotated around the bottom and a sand bath used.

Q.11 **What is the safe upper heating limit of paraffin oil?**

Ans. Paraffin can be safely heated up to 220°C.

Q.12 **Why should the capillary and thermometer not touch the tube sides?**

Ans. To avoid direct contact with glass that may cause uneven heating or breakage.

Q.13 **What is observed to note the melting point?**

Ans. The temperature at which the solid starts to melt is recorded as its melting point.

Questions From NCERT Lab Manual

Q.1 **Why do pure solids possess sharp melting point?**

Ans. A pure solid has same force of attraction between the constituent particles at different places and thus, melts at a constant temperature.

Q.2 **What is the effect of impurities on the melting point of a solid?**

Ans. Impurities decreases the melting point of the solid.

Q.3 **Can any other liquid be used in place of liquid paraffin to determine the melting point?**

Ans. Yes, concentrated H_2SO_4 or water or silicone oils can also be used.

Q.4 **Can we heat the capillary directly for the determination of melting point?**

Ans. No, because direct heating would result in uneven and fast heating which melts the solid rapidly before melting point is reached.

Q.5 **Why is liquid paraffin filled in the Thiele's tube/Kjeldahl's flask?**

Ans. Liquid paraffin serves as the heating medium and being transparent it also acts as a magnifying glass and hence, the compound at the bottom of capillary is easily visible.

Q.6 **Why is Thiele's tube heated at the side arm?**

Ans. Thiele's tube is heated at the side arm to maintain the even and uniform heating through convection currents.

Q.7 **Why is the melting point of benzamide more than acetamide?**

Ans. Both the compounds contain same functional group but the molecular mass of benzamide is more than that of acetamide. As a result, benzamide has stronger intermolecular forces and hence, it has higher melting point than acetamide.

Experiment 2.2

AIM

To determine the boiling point of a liquid organic compound.

Theory/Principle

The boiling point of a liquid is the temperature at which vapour pressure of the liquid becomes equal to the atmospheric pressure, which is being experienced by the surface of the liquid. Different liquids have different boiling point due to the difference in the intermolecular forces operating between these molecules.

The boiling point of a liquid increases if any non-volatile impurity is present in the given liquid. Just like the melting point, the boiling point is an important physical property of a liquid which is used to check the purity of a liquid.

Materials Required

- A small thin walled ignition tube : 1
- Thiele's tube or Kjeldahl's flask : 1
- Capillary tube : 1
- Thermometer (110° C or 360°C) : 1
- Iron stand with clamp : 1
- Liquid paraffin or conc. sulphuric acid : As per need
- Given organic liquid compound : 1 mL

Procedure

> ⚠ **ALERT**
> *Conc. H_2SO_4 is a highly corrosive liquid.*

Fixing the Apparatus

1. Fill the Thiele's tube with the liquid paraffin such that it crosses the bent portion of the Thiele's tube.
2. Take a ignition tube and fill it about two-third with the given liquid whose boiling point is to be determined.
3. Attach this ignition tube to the thermometer with a rubber band as shown in [Fig 2.4].

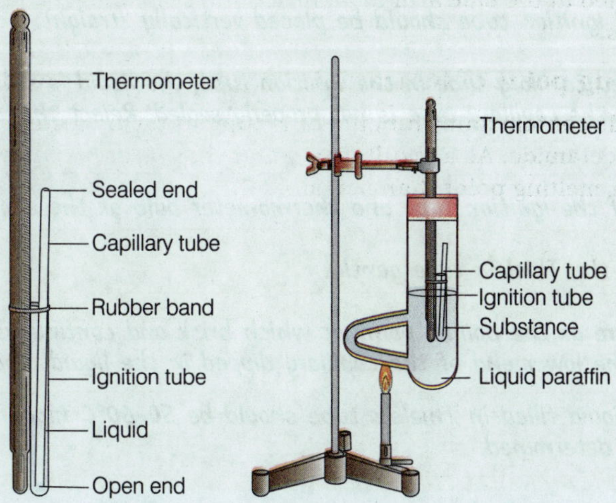

Fig 2.4 *Determination of boiling point*

4. Make sure that the rubber band should be fixed near the mouth of the tube so that it remains outside the liquid paraffin bath. Also, note that the lower end of the ignition tube and the thermometer bulb should be at the same level.
5. Take a capillary tube of approximately 8 cm length and seal its one end by heating in the flame.
6. Place the capillary tube with its open end dipped in the liquid present in the ignition tube.
7. Clamp the thermometer along with the ignition tube having capillary tube with an iron stand.
8. Through the rubber cork, lower the thermometer along with the ignition tube into a liquid paraffin bath in the Thiele's tube. Adjust the thermometer in such a way so that its bulb is well inside the liquid paraffin bath and the open end of the ignition tube along with the rubber band is sufficiently outside the bath.

Heating the Compound to Find out the Boiling Point

9. Heat the side arm of Thiele's tube with a low flame.
10. Keep an eye on the liquid in the ignition tube and on the thread of mercury in the thermometer too.
11. Observe the escape of bubbles at the lower end of the capillary dipped in the liquid organic compound.
12. Note the temperature when continuous stream of bubbles start coming out, briskly. This is the boiling point of the liquid.

Note *For the determination of boiling point of liquids having high boiling points, paraffin cannot be used as heating medium.*

Observation

Temperature at which continuous stream of bubbles formation takes place, t_1 = ... °C

Result

Boiling point of the given liquid is .... °C.

PRECAUTIONS

- *The thermometer and ignition tube should be placed vertically straight.*
- *If on placing the sealed capillary tube in the ignition tube, the liquid is seen rising in capillary tube, it indicates that the capillary tube is not properly sealed. Reject this capillary and use a new sealed one.*
- *Keep the lower end of the ignition tube and thermometer bulb at the same level.*
- *Heat the side arm of the Thiele's tube gently.*
- *Record the temperature as the boiling point at which brisk and continuous evolution of the bubbles starts from the lower end of the capillary dipped in the liquid organic compound.*
- *Boiling point of the liquid filled in Thiele's tube should be 50-60°C higher than the liquid whose boiling point is to be determined.*

Note *List of boiling points of some known organic liquids is given below for the sake of convenience of students in the laboratory.*

Boiling Points of Some Organic Compounds

Compound	Boiling point (°C)	Compound	Boiling point (°C)
Acetophenone	202	Ethyl benzoate	212
Aniline	184	Glycerol	290
Benzaldehyde	179	Methyl salicylate	223
Bromobenzene	157	Nitrobenzene	211
Benzyl alcohol	205	*o*-toluidine	200
Benzoyl chloride	197	*o*-cresol	190
Chlorobenzene	132	Phenol	182
Ethylene glycol	197	Phenyl acetate	196

Viva-Voce

Q.1 Define the point at which a liquid changes to vapour under atmospheric pressure.

Ans. Boiling point is the temperature at which the vapour pressure of a liquid becomes equal to the atmospheric pressure on its surface.

Q.2 What is meant by normal boiling point?

Ans. It is the boiling point of a liquid at an atmospheric pressure of 1.013 bar.

Q.3 Why do different liquids have different boiling points?

Ans. Because the intermolecular forces between molecules are different for different liquids.

Q.4 Name the apparatus used to keep the thermometer upright during the experiment.

Ans. An iron stand with a clamp is used.

Q.5 What type of thermometer is suitable for this experiment?

Ans. A thermometer of 110°C or 360°C depending on the boiling point range.

Q.6 What should be the position of the ignition tube and thermometer bulb?

Ans. Their lower ends should be at the same level.

Q.7 What is the function of the capillary tube in this experiment?

Ans. The capillary allows observation of bubbles which help determine the boiling point.

Q.8 What is observed at the boiling point of the liquid?

Ans. Brisk and continuous evolution of bubbles from the lower end of the capillary tube.

Q.9 What is the ideal temperature difference between a heating medium and test liquid?

Ans. It should be 50–60°C higher than the boiling point of the test liquid.

Q.10 Name the material used to fix the ignition tube with the thermometer?

Ans. A rubber band is used to tie the ignition tube to the thermometer.

Questions From NCERT Lab Manual

Q.1 Suggest a suitable liquid, which can be filled in the Thiele's tube for the determination of the boiling point of carbon tetrachloride?

Ans. Water can be filled because the boiling point of carbon tetrachloride (CCl_4), is less than 100°C.

Q.2 Why is food cooked more quickly in a pressure cooker?

Ans. In a pressure cooker, water is made to boil at a higher temperature under high pressure and hence, cooking takes place rapidly at a higher temperature.

Q.3 **In place of liquid paraffin, can any other liquid be used for the purpose of determination of the boiling point?**

Ans. Conc. H_2SO_4, silicone oils can also be used for the determination of the boiling point in place of liquid paraffin.

Q.4 **How would the boiling point of water vary with the addition of equimolar quantities of urea, potassium chloride and potassium sulphate?**

Ans. Addition of all of the given solutes will increase the boiling point of water because all are non-volatile in nature and the addition of non-volatile solute into water (or any pure solvent) raises the boiling point of water (or any pure solvent).

Q.5 **Why do different isomers of alcohol represented by the formula $C_4H_{10}O$ differ in their boiling points?**

Ans. All the isomers of alcohol representing a general molecular formula $C_4H_{10}O$ differs in structure with respect to branching. Thus, all possess different intermolecular forces of attraction. Hence, due to the relative strength of intermolecular forces of attraction and branching, different isomers of alcohol having same molecular formula, $C_4H_{10}O$ differ in their boiling points.

Q.6 **Suppose boiling point of a liquid in Delhi is 100°C. At hill station, will it be the same or different? Give reason.**

Ans. The boiling point of the liquid will be less than 100°C at the hill station because boiling point decreases with decrease in atmospheric pressure. At hill stations, the atmospheric pressure is less than that in plains. Hence, the boiling point of a liquid in Delhi is different from that in hill station.

Experiment 2.3

AIM

To purify a given sample of a compound (potash alum) copper sulphate/Benzoic acid by the process of crystallisation.

(i) Alum (ii) Copper sulphate (iii) Benzoic acid

Theory/Principle

Crystallisation is the process of obtaining crystals of a pure substance from a solution of impure or mixture of substances. The purity of crystals is often judged from the colour of crystals. e.g. Pure crystals of alum, copper sulphate and benzoic acid are white, blue and greenish white, respectively. Impurities impart colour to the crystals, therefore, impure crystals have a colour different from pure crystals. Now, let us have an overview regarding the given samples.

Alum

Potash alum, commonly known as Phitkari, is a double salt of potassium sulphate and aluminium sulphate, i.e., $K_2SO_4 \cdot Al_2(SO_4)_3 \cdot 24H_2O$. It is highly soluble in water. Its crystals are octahedral in shape. The crystals of potash alum are prepared from its commercial sample containing soluble as well as insoluble impurities.

Copper Sulphate

Its common name is blue vitriol and is chemically known as hydrated copper sulphate. It is a blue coloured compound having chemical formula, $CuSO_4 \cdot 5H_2O$. It is also water soluble. Its crystals are triclinic in shape. These crystals are prepared when given sample is shaken with water.

Benzoic Acid

It is a crystalline solid organic compound whose structure is represented as

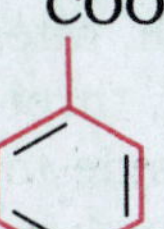

It is moderately soluble in hot water and almost insoluble in cold water. It is highly soluble in benzene and hence, it is crystallised by making its saturated solution in benzene.

Materials Required

▪ Beaker (250 mL)	:	1	▪ Tripod stand	:	1
▪ Glass rod	:	1	▪ Beam balance	:	1
▪ China dish	:	1	▪ Sand bath	:	1
▪ Glass funnel	:	1	▪ Powdered sample (potash alum, copper sulphate or benzoic acid)	:	As per need
▪ Bunsen burner	:	1	▪ Alcohol, distilled water, benzene, dil. H_2SO_4 and filter paper.	:	As per need

Procedure

The crystallisation of impure samples of alum or copper sulphate or benzoic acid involves the following steps

Preparation of Saturated Solution of the Impure Sample

1. Weigh about 10 g of the given sample of alum or copper sulphate or benzoic acid using a beam balance.
2. Take a beaker of 250 mL and fill it with 30-50 mL of distilled water.
3. Dissolve the sample in small quantities at a time in distilled water with constant stirring with a glass rod.

ALERT

- *Copper sulphate is toxic and harmful.*
- *The vapours of benzene should be kept away from flame.*

Note *Steps 2 and 3 are only applicable in the preparation of alum and copper sulphate but not in benzoic acid. In case of benzoic acid, use benzene or hot water to dissolve it. Sometimes, animal charcoal is added in benzoic acid to decolourise coloured impurities if present in the sample.*

4. Keep dissolving until the saturation point is achieved, i.e. when no more sample can be dissolved in water at room temperature. Stop adding the solid when it does not dissolve further. Warm the contents of the beaker by heating the beaker at 60-70°C on a wire gauze [Fig. 2.5].

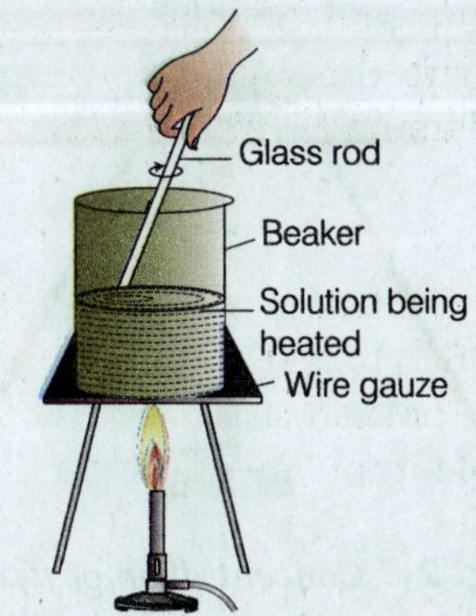

Fig. 2.5 *Heating of solution*

5. Add 5 mL of dil. H_2SO_4 to avoid hydrolysis of salt [discard this step 5 in case of benzoic acid].

Filtration of Hot Solution

6. For filtration of the prepared solution, first take a circular filter paper then fold it one-half, after that fold it one-fourth. Open the filter paper, three folds on one side and one fold on the other side to get a cone.
7. Now, take a funnel and fit the filter paper into it so that the filter paper cone fit in the proper position in the funnel.
8. Then, wet the filter paper cone with a spray of water from a wash bottle. Gently press the upper part of the filter paper cone against the wall of the funnel with thumb. So that, no air gap is left between paper cone and the funnel.
9. Place the funnel on a funnel stand and place a clean China dish below the funnel for collecting a filtrate. To avoid splashing of filtrate, adjust the funnel such that its stem touches the wall of dish. [Fig. 2.6]

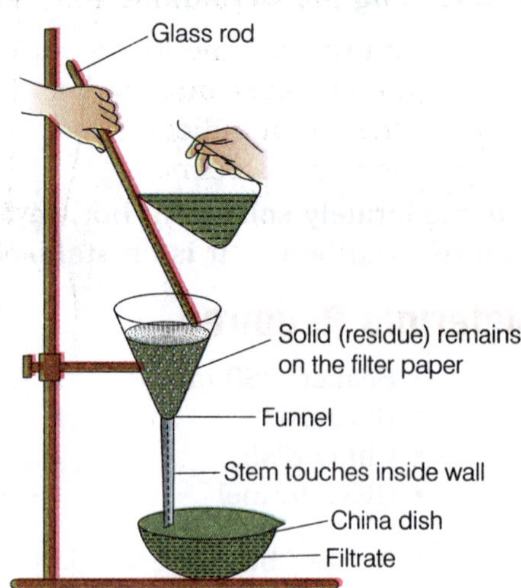

Fig. 2.6 *Filtration of insoluble impurities*

10. Hold a glass rod in a slanting position in your hand with a precaution that the lower end of the rod should reaches into the filter paper cone but does not touch it. Pour the solution along the glass rod as shown in [Fig. 2.6]. The filtrate passes through the filter paper and is collected into the China dish placed below [Fig. 2.6].
11. The insoluble impurities are left as residue on the filter paper which will be discarded.

Concentration of the Filtrate

12. Heat the filtrate collected in China dish over a sand bath (in case of benzoic acid, water bath is used). Do not boil the solution, just heat slowly with continuous stirring with a glass rod [Fig. 2.7] till nearly 3/4th of the solvent is evaporated. The stirring is done to ensure uniform heating and to prevent the formation of solid crust. On the other hand, concentration of filtrate is done to reduce the volume or to concentrate the filtrate to get the crystallisation point.

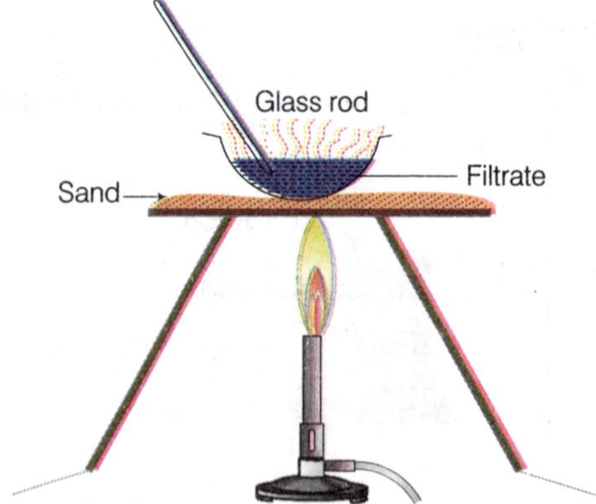

Fig. 2.7 *Concentration of filtrate*

Checking the Crystallisation Point

13. When the volume of the solution reduces to one half, dip one end of a glass rod into the solution, take it out and cool it by blowing air from the mouth [Fig. 2.8]. If a solid film deposits on the rod, it indicates that crystallisation point has reached. Stop heating the solution by removing the burner.

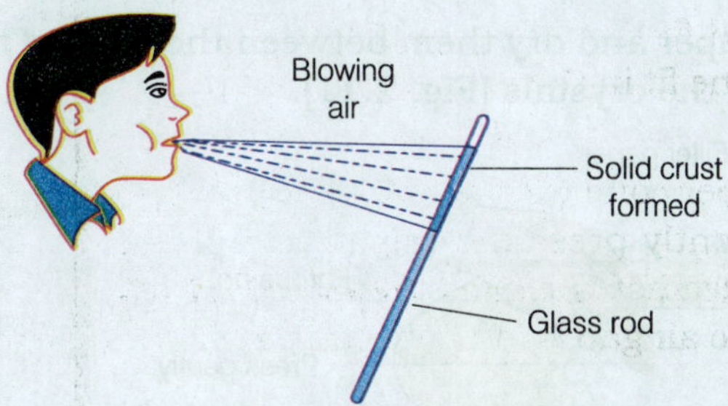

Fig. 2.8 *Checking of the crystallisation point*

Cooling the Hot Concentrated Solution

14. Carefully remove the China dish (porcelain dish) from the sand bath, cover it with a watch glass and keep the contents of the dish undisturbed for cooling.

15. You may also add few already prepared tiny pure crystals to the respective solution while it is cooling. The crystals are added to the solution to facilitate the initial crystallisation. This is called **seeding**.

    The added tiny crystals act as the 'nucleus' for the growth of new crystals as growth depends upon the conditions in which crystallisation is carried out. For obtaining good crystals, rapid cooling should be avoided because it results into small or disfigured crystals.

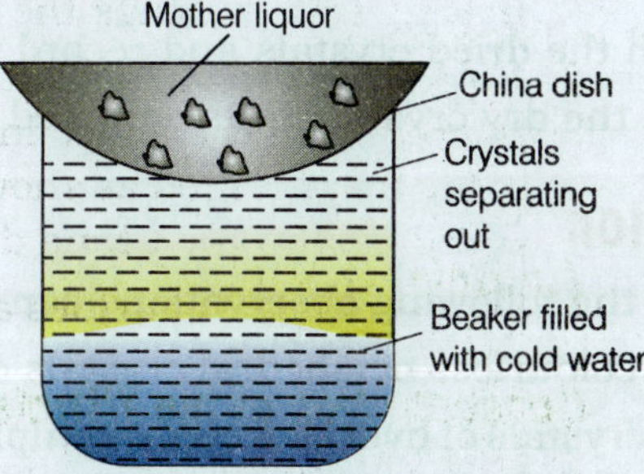

Fig. 2.9 *Cooling the filtrate in China dish kept on a beaker filled with cold water*

Sometimes, cooling is done by placing the China dish containing concentrated solution on a beaker filled to the brim with a cold water [Fig. 2.9].

Separation and Drying of Crystals

16. Once the crystals are formed, decant off the mother liquor (liquid left after crystallisation) by tilting the China dish (decantation). [Fig 2.10]

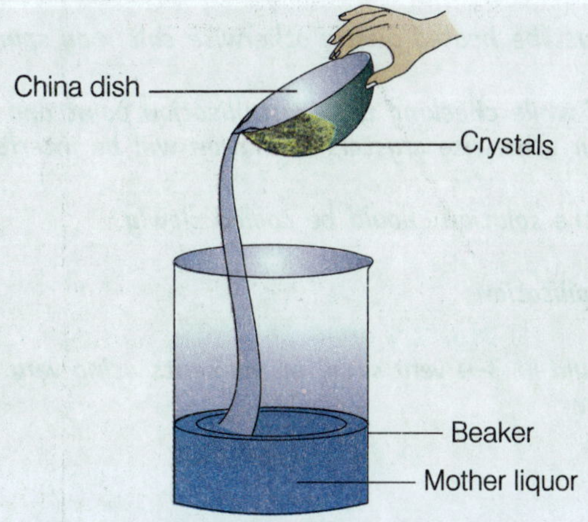

Fig 2.10 *Decanting the mother liquor*

17. Wash the crystals of copper sulphate or potash alum, thus obtained first with very small quantity of alcohol containing small amount of cold water to remove the adhering mother liquor and then with alcohol to remove moisture.

    Wash the crystals of benzoic acid with cold water. Benzoic acid is soluble in alcohol. Do not use alcohol to wash its crystals.

18. Transfer the crystals on a filter paper and dry them between the folds of the filter paper by pressing gently without crushing the crystals [Fig. 2.11].

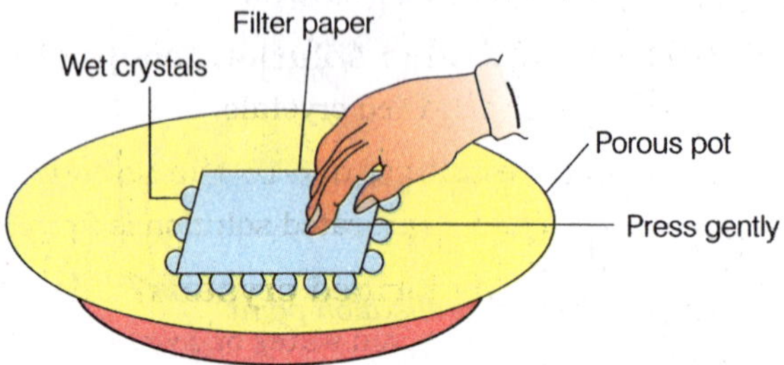

Fig. 2.11 *Drying of the crystals between filter papers*

19. Weigh the dried crystals and record the yield.
20. Store the dry crystals thus obtained at a safe and dry place.

Observation

Any one of the following observations can be seen depending on the sample taken

1. Long colourless octahedral crystals of pure potash alum are obtained.
2. Blue crystals of hydrated copper sulphate ($CuSO_4 \cdot 5H_2O$) with triclinic shape are obtained.
3. Opaque white crystals of pure benzoic acid are obtained.

Result

Yield of the crystals = ... g

PRECAUTIONS

- *Do not heat the beaker or any glass apparatus directly. Always use wire gauze or sand bath to avoid the breaking of apparatus due to direct heating.*
- *While concentrating the solution, it must be heated gently otherwise salt may spurt.*
- *Keep the glass rod away from yourself while checking the crystallisation point and also there should be no moisture while blowing air otherwise crystals formation will be interfered.*
- *After crystallisation point is reached, the solution should be cooled slowly.*
- *Seeding may be done to improve crystallisation.*
- *Wash the crystals with the washing liquid in 3-4 very small installments using very small amount of the liquid rather than in one installment.*

Viva-Voce

Q.1 How is an appropriate solvent selected while performing crystallisation?

Ans. The solvent should dissolve the impure compound readily when hot but only slightly when cold.

Q.2 Which step helps remove insoluble impurities during crystallisation?

Ans. Filtering the hot saturated solution removes insoluble impurities.

Q.3 What is the drawback of cooling a concentrated solution too quickly?

Ans. Rapid cooling results in the formation of small or distorted crystals.

Q.4 When should you stop adding the impure substance to the solvent?

Ans. When the added substance no longer dissolves and a saturated solution is formed.

Q.5 What steps are followed to clean the freshly formed crystals?

Ans. Crystals are washed in small quantities of alcohol and cold water or just cold water, depending on the compound.

Q.6 Why is the dish covered with a watch glass during cooling?

Ans. To prevent contamination from dust and to maintain clean conditions.

Q.7 What precaution is related to solvent evaporation during the experiment?

Ans. One should not evaporate the entire solvent, as it may hinder crystallisation.

Q.8 Which type of container is used for concentrating the hot solution?

Ans. A porcelain dish is used for evaporating the solvent.

Q.9 How is benzoic acid made to dissolve to form its saturated solution?

Ans. By using hot water as benzoic acid dissolves better when heated.

Q.10 What must be repeated to obtain a greater amount of purified crystals?

Ans. Steps of concentration, cooling, filtration, washing, and drying are repeated until a good yield of pure crystals is obtained.

Questions From NCERT Lab Manual

Q.1 What is meant by the term, 'water of crystallisation'?

Ans. Water of crystallisation is the definite number of water molecules present in one formula weight of the crystalline substance. It is necessary for the maintenance of a particular crystalline structure but capable of being removed by sufficient heat.

Q.2 Which thermodynamic functions favour the process of crystallisation?

Ans. Entropy and enthalpy favours the process of crystallisation.

Q.3 Explain the term saturated solution.

Ans. The solution in which no more solute can be dissolved at a particular temperature is known as saturated solution.

Q.4 Why is the preparation of a saturated solution essential for making crystals?

Ans. It is essential to get large clear crystals in maximum yield.

Q.5 What do you understand by the term mother liquor?

Ans. Mother liquor is the liquid left behind after the separation of crystals from a saturated solution.

Q.6 **Which one of the following formula is correct representation of potash alum (Phitkari)?**

(a) $K^{+}(H_2O)_6 Al^{3+}(H_2O)_6(SO_4^{2-})_2$ (b) $K_2SO_4 \cdot Al_2(SO_4)_3 \cdot 24H_2O$

Ans. (b) $K_2SO_4 \cdot Al_2(SO_4)_3 \cdot 24H_2O$

Q.7 **What are isomorphous compounds?**

Ans. In crystallography, isomorphous compounds are those compounds which possess crystals of similar shape.

Q.8 **Name the processes involved in crystallisation.**

Ans. The following processes are involved in crystallisation.

(i) Preparation of the saturated solution of the impure sample.
(ii) Filtration of the saturated solution.
(iii) Concentration of the filtrate.
(iv) Checking the crystallisation point.
(v) Cooling of the hot concentrated solution.
(vi) Separation and drying of the pure crystals.

Unit 3

Experiments Based on pH

Theory/Principle

In this unit, we will learn about shift in ionic equilibrium between unionised water molecules and H^+ and OH^- ions. Pure water ionises to small extent although it has low conductivity which is proved by conductivity experiments.

Thus, ionic equilibrium in pure water can be represented as

$$2H_2O(l) \rightleftharpoons H_3O^+(aq) + OH^-(aq)$$

This is called **self ionisation** of water. The equilibrium constant can be written as

$$K = \frac{[H_3O^+][OH]}{[H_2O]^2}$$

Also, $$K_w = [H_3O^+][OH^-] \qquad [\because [H_2O] \text{ is large}]$$

where, $K_w = K[H_2O]^2$ = ionisation constant of water

$$K_w = 1.0 \times 10^{-14} \text{ [At 25°C]}$$

At a given temperature in any aqueous solution, $[H_3O^+][OH^-]$ remains constant whether acidic, alkaline or neutral in nature. If dissolution of a substance shifts the equilibrium in such a way that at equilibrium

$[H_3O^+] > [OH^-]$, then acidic solution

$[H_3O^+] < [OH^-]$, then alkaline solution

In 1909, P.L. Sorensen suggested a new term for expressing the acidic and basic nature of a solution or concentration of hydrogen ions (or hydronium ions) known as pH or pH scale. The term pH is derived from Danish word 'Potenz' which means power.

There are several substances which are helpful in the determination of pH. Some of them are discussed below.

Acid-Base Indicators

A substance that changes its colour when the medium changes from acidic to basic or *vice-versa,* is called an acid-base indicator. There are several organic dyes which show different colours at different pH.

For e.g., litmus solution, methyl red and methyl orange. These indicators generally show a colour change within a narrow range of one or two pH units.

The table given below shows some common indicators, their pH ranges and the expected results when added to an acid or base :

Indicator	pH Range	Colour in Acidic Medium	Colour in Basic Medium	Indicator	pH Range	Colour in Acidic Medium	Colour in Basic Medium
Thymol blue	1.2 – 2.8	Red	Yellow	Phenol red	6.4 – 8.4	Yellow	Red
2, 4-dinitrophenol	2.4 – 4.0	Colourless	Yellow	Phenolphthalein	8.0 – 10.0	Colourless	Pink
Methyl yellow	2.9 – 4.0	Red	Yellow	Thymolphthalein	9.4 – 10.5	Colourless	Blue
Bromophenol blue	3.0 – 4.6	Yellow	Blue-violet	Alizarin yellow	10.0 – 12.0	Yellow	Lilac
Methyl orange	3.1 – 4.4	Red	Orange	Salicyl yellow	10.0 – 12.0	Yellow	Orange-brown
Methyl red	4.4 – 6.3	Red	Yellow	Trinitrobenzoic acid	12.0 – 13.4	Colourless	Orange-brown
p-nitrophenol	5.0 – 7.0	Colourless	Yellow				

Universal Indicators

By mixing a solution of number of dyes, it is possible to prepare an indicator which passes through a series of colour changes over a much wider pH range. This is called **universal indicator** and gives approximate pH value of a solution. Hence, a solution of a mixture of dyes can be used to measure the pH values from 0 to 14.

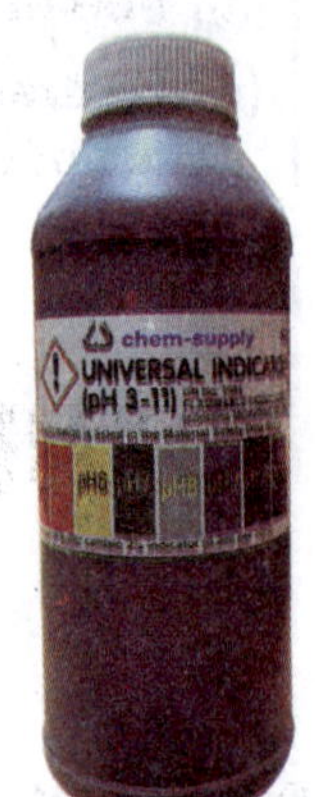

Fig. 3.1 Universal indicator

Some universal indicators can measure the pH change of even 0.5. In fact, dyes themselves are weak acids or bases. Colour change occurs as a result of change in the structure of dye due to acceptance or release of protons.

Different forms of a dye have different colours and hence, colour change is observed when pH of the solution changes. A common universal indicator is available in the market under the name of **Yamada's indicator.** A standard chart for the colour change of the universal indicator with pH is supplied with the indicator paper or solution and the comparison of observed colour change with the chart provides a good estimate of the pH of the solution.

The colours that indicate the pH of a solution, after adding a universal indicator are

Colours of universal indicators at different pH values

pH	Colour
2.0	Red
5.0	Orange-red
5.5	Orange
6.0	Orange-yellow
7.0-7.5	Greenish-yellow
8.0	Green
9.5	Blue
10.0	Violet

pH Papers

These papers are prepared by dipping the strips of paper in the solution of different indicators and then drying them.These are used to find out the approximate pH value of the solution. It is dipped in the given sample solution, the colour obtained is compared with the colour chart and thus, approximate pH of the solution can be predicted.

Natural pH Indicators

These are derived from plants. The most common natural pH indicator is **anthocyanin.** These are water soluble pigments found in most plants that may appear red, violet or blue (in colour) depending on the pH. Some common natural indicators are as follows

(i) **Red cabbage** It has a vast pH range.

pH	Colour
1	Red
7	Purple
12	Green
14	Yellow

(ii) **Rose petals** It is red or pink in acidic solution which turns blue or green in basic solution depending on pH of solution.

(iii) **Poison primrose** It is red-orange in acidic solution which turns to blue in a basic solution.

(iv) **Hydrangeas** The colour of hydrangeas depends on the pH of the soil in which they grow. If pH of the soil is acidic, flowers are blue and in alkaline pH, flowers are pink.

Experiment 3.1

AIM

Determination of pH of some solutions obtained from fruit juices by using pH paper or universal indicator.

Theory/Principle

pH of a solution is mathematically defined as the negative logarithm of hydronium ion concentration, i.e.

$$pH = -\log [H_3O^+] \quad \text{or} \quad pH = \log \frac{1}{[H_3O^+]}$$

(i) If pH of the solution is < 7, then the solution is acidic.

(ii) If pH of the solution is > 7, then the solution is basic.

(iii) If pH of the solution is = 7, then the solution is neutral.

pH of most of the fruit juices are less than 7 which suggests that fruit juices are acidic in nature. Fruits contain various acids like citric acid, oxalic acid, maleic acid, etc.

pH of a solution can be determined by using pH paper or a universal indicator.

Materials Required

- Test tubes : 4
- Glass droppers : 4
- Beakers (100 mL) : 4
- Dropper : 4
- pH papers or universal indicator solution : As per need
- pH chart : 1
- Fruit juices : Lemon, orange, apple and pineapple

Procedure

Using pH Paper

1. Take fresh juices of lemon, orange, apple and pineapple in four separate beakers of 100 mL capacity each.
2. Take a strip of pH paper and put a drops of juice to be tested from each beaker with the help of a separate dropper for each on the pH paper.
3. Note down the colour of the pH paper and match it with the pH indicator chart provided with the pH paper booklet in each case. Note down the pH corresponding to the observed colour. (use Table 3.1)
4. Arrange the pH value of the four juices in the increasing order.

Using Universal Indicator

1. Take nearly 2 mL of each fresh juices (20 drops) with the help of a separate dropper for each juice in four different test tubes marked as *A*, *B*, *C* and *D* respectively.
2. Add 2-3 drops of the universal indicator in each test tube and mix the content of each test tube by shaking thoroughly.
3. Match the colour appearing in each test tube with the standard pH chart.
4. Record your observations in a tabular form. (use Table 3.1)
5. Arrange the pH value of the four juices in the increasing order.

Observations

Table 3.1 pH value of different fruit juices

S. No.	Sample	With pH paper		With universal indicator		Inference
		Colour produced	pH	Colour produced	pH	
1.	Lemon juice					
2.	Orange juice					
3.	Apple juice					
4.	Pineapple juice					

Result

Increasing order of pH value of different juices is ....

PRECAUTIONS

- *Equal number of drops of universal indicator should be added to equal volumes of solutions in each of the test tubes.*
- *Match the colour of the solution with pH chart carefully.*
- *Use only fresh juice for the experiment.*
- *Store pH papers at a safe place to avoid contact with acidic and basic reagents kept in the laboratory.*
- *Use separate dropper for each different samples.*

Viva-Voce

Q.1 Which indicator helps in determining pH values across the entire scale from 0 to 14?

Ans. Universal indicator helps in measuring pH across the full scale from 0 to 14.

Q.2 Why should a separate dropper be used for each fruit juice?

Ans. To prevent mixing or contamination between juices and ensure reliable pH readings.

Q.3 What happens to the pH value when a juice is diluted with water?

Ans. The pH increases as the hydrogen ion concentration decreases.

Q.4 What precaution must be taken while adding universal indicators to each test tube?

Ans. Equal drops of the indicator should be added to equal volumes for consistency.

Q.5 Why must fresh juice be used in this experiment?

Ans. Fresh juice gives more accurate pH readings, as stored juice may undergo fermentation.

Q.6 What is a key inference drawn from comparing the pH of different juices?

Ans. It helps identify the relative acidity of various fruit juices.

Q.7 How would mixing two different juices affect the pH?

Ans. The resulting pH may be intermediate, depending on the acids present in each juice.

Q.8 In what way can the pH of a soft drink be determined using the same principle?

Ans. By adding a universal indicator or pH paper to a sample and matching its colour to a chart.

Q.9 Why is it necessary to handle pH papers carefully in the laboratory?

Ans. Because contact with acidic or basic reagents may damage them and give false readings.

Questions From NCERT Lab Manual

Q.1 Out of the four juices, which one is least basic? Explain.

Ans. Lemon juice is least basic or most acidic because its pH ranges from 2.2-2.4.

Q.2 If we dilute each of the juices, what effect is likely to be observed on the pH values?

Ans. pH of the diluted solutions of juices will be more than those of the pure juices.

Q.3 On mixing any two juices, would the pH alter or remains the same? Verify your answer experimentally.

Ans. pH of the mixture of two juices will get altered and lies between the pH values of the two juices. This can be verified experimentally as, take the pH of two juices separately in two different test tubes and then mix them in equal proportions in another test tube. Observe the colour change by adding the drops on pH paper and compare with the standard pH chart and note down the corresponding pH.

Q.4 How can you ascertain the pH of a soft drink?

Ans. Take 20 mL of soft drink in a test tube. Add 2-3 drops of universal indicator into it. Note down the colour change and compare the colour with the standard pH chart and note down the corresponding pH.

Experiment 3.2

AIM

To determine the pH of solutions of known and varied concentrations of acids, bases and salts, by using pH paper or universal indicator.

Theory/Principle

Hydrogen ion concentration per unit volume decreases on dilution. Hence, change in pH is expected on dilution of the solution. Dilution will increase the pH of an acid whereas it will decrease the pH of a base. It means that dilution tends to shift the pH towards neutrality, i.e. pH equals to 7.

In contrast to acids and bases, salts formed by different strength of acids and bases have different pH values when dissolved in water. Salts when diluted with water produces either acidic or basic solutions. The approximate pH of some of the salts obtained when dissolved in water are given below.

Approximate pH of some salts (when dissolved in water)

S.No.	Salt	pH
1.	Salt of strong acid (HCl) and strong base (NaOH), i.e. NaCl	= 7
2.	Salt of strong acid (HCl) and weak base (NH_4OH), i.e. NH_4Cl	< 7
3.	Salt of weak acid (CH_3COOH) and strong base (NaOH), i.e. CH_3COONa	> 7
4.	Salt of weak acid (CH_3COOH) and weak base (NH_4OH), i.e. CH_3COONH_4	Depends which is stronger

The phenomenon of interaction of ions of the salt with water, producing acidic or basic solution is termed as **salt hydrolysis**.

Materials Required

- Test tubes : As per need
- Boiling tubes : As per need
- Glass droppers : 4
- Glazed tile : As per need
- 0.1 M HCl solution (acid) : 10 mL
- 0.1 M NaOH solution (base) : 10 mL
- 0.1 M NH_4Cl solution (salt) : 10 mL
- pH paper and universal indicator : As per need

Procedure

1. Take four boiling tubes and mark them as 1, 2, 3 and 4. [Fig. 4.1]
2. Take 2 mL of 0.1 M HCl in boiling tube 1.
3. Take 2 mL of 0.1 M HCl in boiling tube 2 and add 18 mL of water into it. Mix them thoroughly.
4. Take 5 mL of dilute HCl solution from boiling tube 2 in boiling tube 3 and add 15 mL of water into it. Mix them well.

5. Again, take 5 mL of dilute HCl solution from boiling tube 3 in boiling tube 4 and add 15 mL of water into it. Mix them thoroughly.

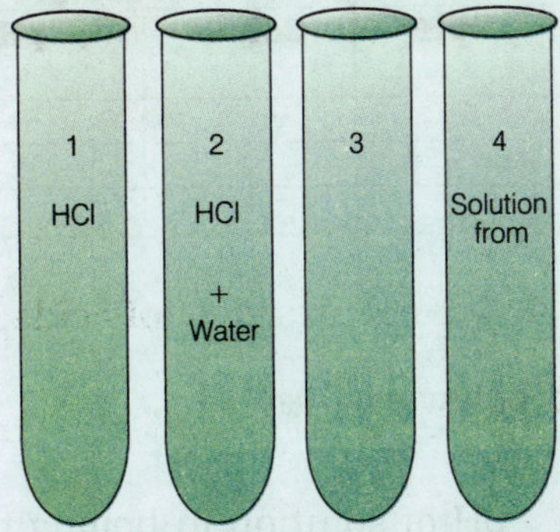

Fig. 3.2 *Set up for experiment*

> ⚠ **ALERT**
> - NaOH *and* HCl *are highly corrosive.*
> - NH_4Cl *is harmful.*
> - *For dilution, add acid slowly into water.*
> - *Never add water to the acid.*

6. Repeat the steps from 1 to 5 for a given solution of base [0.1 M NaOH] and salt [0.1M NH_4Cl].
7. Now, check the pH of all these solutions.

Using pH Paper

(i) Cut a pH paper into small pieces and spread these on the clean glazed tile.
(ii) Take out some solution from boiling tube 1 by using a dropper and pour one drop on one of the pieces of pH paper kept on the glazed tile. Compare the colour of the pH paper with the standard chart.
(iii) Similarly, test the pH of solutions of boiling tubes 2, 3 and 4 one by one and record your observations in a tabular form. (Use table 4.2)
(iv) Repeat the process with different solutions of base and salt (0.1 M NaOH and 0.1 M NH_4Cl) and record the observations.

Using Universal Indicator

(i) Take out 1 mL of solution from each boiling tube and transfer them in separate test tubes and mark them as *A*, *B*, *C* and *D*.
(ii) Add two drops of universal indicator to each of these four test tubes.
(iii) Shake the test tubes well and match the colour of these solutions with the standard pH chart to determine the pH.
(iv) Similarly, observe the change in pH of 0.1 M NaOH and 0.1 M NH_4Cl solution with dilution.
(v) Record your observations in a tabular form. (Use table 4.3)
(vi) Compare the results obtained by pH paper and that obtained by using universal indicator solution for each case.

Observations

Table 3.2 pH change on dilution using pH paper

Boiling tube	0.1 M HCl		0.1 M NaOH		0.1 M NH_4Cl	
	Colour	pH	Colour	pH	Colour	pH
1						
2						
3						
4						

Table 3.3 pH change on dilution using universal indicator

Test tube	0.1 M HCl		0.1 M NaOH		0.1 M NH_4Cl	
	Colour	pH	Colour	pH	Colour	pH
A						
B		-				
C						
D						

Result

(i) The variation of pH with dilution is discussed below as

(a) For HCl solution

pH of solution in boiling tube 1 = ... pH of solution in boiling tube 2 = ...

pH of solution in boiling tube 3 = ... pH of solution in boiling tube 4 = ...

The pH of HCl solutions .... with decrease in concentration or with dilution.

(b) For NaOH solution

pH of solution in boiling tube 1 = ... pH of solution in boiling tube 2 = ...

pH of solution in boiling tube 3 = ... pH of solution in boiling tube 4 = ...

The pH of NaOH solutions .... with decrease in concentration or with dilution.

(c) For NH_4Cl solution

pH of solution in boiling tube 1 = ... pH of solution in boiling tube 2 = ...

pH of solution in boiling tube 3 = ... pH of solution in boiling tube 4 = ...

The pH of NH_4Cl solutions .... with decrease in concentration or with dilution.

(ii) The calculated concentration of solutions of test tube 2,3 and 4 are ..., ... and ... mol L^{-1}, respectively.

PRECAUTIONS

- *Add equal number of drops of the universal indicator to the equal amounts of solution in each of the boiling tubes.*
- *Match the colour of the solution with the standard pH chart carefully.*
- *pH paper should be kept away from acidic or basic impurities.*
- *Always use freshly prepared solution of salt. Make sure that all the salt dissolves in water before testing for the pH of their solution.*

Viva-Voce

Q.1 What happens to the hydrogen ion concentration when an acid is diluted?

Ans. Hydrogen ion concentration decreases per unit volume when an acid is diluted.

Q.2 What safety rule must be followed while diluting acids?

Ans. Always add acid to water slowly and never water to acid.

Q.3 Why are equal volumes of solution used in all test tubes?

Ans. To ensure accurate comparison of pH values and avoid discrepancies.

Q.4 What does a green colour on pH paper indicate?

Ans. It indicates a neutral solution with pH around 7.

Q.5 **Can acetic acid and HCl of the same molarity show the same pH?**

Ans. No, HCl being a strong acid shows lower pH than weak acid like acetic acid at the same molarity.

Q.6 **Why is a universal indicator used instead of a single indicator?**

Ans. Because it gives a complete range of pH values with different colours for accurate estimation.

Q.7 **Why is 0.1 M HCl used in this experiment instead of concentrated HCl?**

Ans. Dilute HCl is safer to handle and allows observation of gradual pH changes with dilution.

Q.8 **Why does the pH of NaOH decrease slightly on dilution, though it remains basic?**

Ans. Because the OH^- ion concentration per unit volume decreases with dilution.

Q.9 **What is the chemical nature of universal indicators?**

Ans. Universal indicators are mixtures of several pH-sensitive dyes, which are weak acids or bases.

Q.10 **Why is it important to test freshly prepared solutions for pH?**

Ans. Because exposure to air can alter the pH due to absorption of CO_2 or evaporation of water.

Questions From NCERT Lab Manual

Q.1 **What trend is observed in the variation of pH with dilution for acidic as well as basic solutions?**

Ans. pH of an acidic solution increases with dilution while pH of a basic solution decreases with dilution.

Q.2 **How do you explain the results of variation in pH with dilution?**

Ans. pH is the negative logarithm of H_3O^+ ion concentration. So, on dilution, the H_3O^+ ion concentration of an acidic solution decreases hence, its pH increases. For basic solution, the pH decreases with dilution due to the increase in H_3O^+ ion concentration.

Q.3 **For each acidic solution, whether we use HCl or H_2SO_4, pH is same to a reasonably good extent, even though HCl is 0.1 M and H_2SO_4 is 0.05 M. How do you explain this result?**

Ans. Both HCl and H_2SO_4 are strong acids and are completely ionised in aqueous solution. 0.1 M HCl and 0.05 M H_2SO_4 produces almost same concentration of H_3O^+ ion on ionisation and hence, have reasonably same pH.

Q.4 **Will the pH of 0.1 M acetic acid be the same as that of 0.1 M hydrochloric acid? Verify your results and explain it.**

Ans. No, the pH of 0.1 M CH_3COOH and 0.1 M HCl will not be the same. Rather ,the pH of CH_3COOH will be higher than that of HCl. This is because CH_3COOH is a weak acid while HCl is a strong acid. Therefore, HCl being a strong acid produces higher concentration of H_3O^+ ions.

Q.5 **If any two acidic solutions (say *A* and *C*) are mixed, what would happen to the pH of the mixture? Verify your answer experimentally.**

Ans. The resulting mixture will have pH value different from the pH values of both the solutions. For an example,

Let pH of solution *A* is 2 and that of *C* is 4. Thus, hydrogen ion concentration, $[H_3O^+]$ in *A* and *C* respectively are 10^{-2} M and 10^{-4} M.

Now, if equal volume of both the solutions are mixed, then final $[H_3O]^+$

$$= \frac{10^{-2}\text{M} + 10^{-4}\text{M}}{2} = 5.05 \times 10^{-5}\ \text{M}$$

Thus, $\text{pH} = -\log(5.05 \times 10^{-3}) = 3 - 0.7033 = 3.3$

This can be verified experimentally by determining the pH of two acidic solutions before mixing and after mixing by using pH paper or universal indicator paper.

Experiment 3.3

AIM

Compare the pH of solutions of strong and weak acids of same concentration.

Theory/Principle

Strong acids are those which get completely ionised in water and has a pH < 3. These acids produce higher concentration of hydrogen ions or hydronium ions for a given concentration of an acid. e.g. HCl, H_2SO_4, HNO_3, HI, etc.

1 mole of H_2SO_4 dissociates to form 2 moles of H_3O^+ whereas, 1 mole of HCl dissociates to form 1 mole of H_3O^+. Their pH can be calculated from their molar concentrations.

Weak acids are those which do not completely dissociates into ions in water. They will have a pH greater than 3 but less than 7, e.g. CH_3COOH, H_3PO_4, H_2S, etc.

Materials Required

- Test tubes : 2
- Dropper : 1
- Pipette : 1
- 0.1 M HCl and 0.1 M CH_3COOH : As per need
- Universal indicator : As per need
- Beakers : 2
- pH chart : 1
- pH paper : As per need

Procedure

Using Universal Indicator

1. Take 5 mL each of 0.1 M HCl and 0.1 M CH_3COOH in two separate test tubes (measure by using a pipette) and label them as *A* and *B*.
2. Add 2-3 drops of universal indicator in each of the test tubes and stir the solutions until the colours are uniform.
3. Compare the colour of the each solutions and match it with standard pH colour chart.
4. Record your observations in the tabular form (Use table 3.4).

ALERT

- HCl *is corrosive and harmful.*
- CH_3COOH *is irritant and corrosive.*

Using pH Paper

1. Take 0.1 M HCl in beaker of 100 mL capacity.
2. Take a strip of pH paper and put a drop of 0.1 M HCl on it.
3. Note down the colour of the pH paper and match it with the standard pH colour chart.
4. Repeat the above process with 0.1 M CH_3COOH solution and find its pH.
5. Record your observations in the tabular form.

Observations

Table 3.4 pH of HCl and CH_3COOH

S. No.	Sample	For Universal Indicator		For pH Papers	
		Colour	pH	Colour	pH
1.	0.1 M HCl	—	—		
2.	0.1 M CH_3COOH	—	—		

Result

(i) pH of 0.1 M HCl solution, i.e. a strong acid is ....

(ii) pH of 0.1 M CH_3COOH solution, i.e. a weak acid is ....

(iii) pH of 0.1 M HCl is .... than that of 0.1 M CH_3COOH.

PRECAUTIONS

- *Use only freshly prepared solutions. Add equal number of drops of universal indicator in each test tube.*
- *Match the colour change with the standard pH chart carefully.*
- *Different pH papers should be used for different solutions.*
- *Store pH papers at a safe and dry place.*

Viva-Voce

Q.1 Which of the following solutions has higher pH 0.1 M HCl or 0.1 M CH_3COOH ?

Ans. 0.1 M CH_3COOH would have higher pH because acetic acid, being a weak acid is only partially ionised and hence, produces lower concentration of H_3O^+.

Q.2 Why a weak acid has higher pH than a strong acid?

Ans. A weak acid is only partially ionised and thus, it produces lower concentration of $H_3O^+(aq)$ ion while a strong acid gets completely ionised and produces higher concentration of $H_3O^+(aq)$ ion. Hence, weak acid has higher pH than that of strong acid.

Q.3 The pH of a solution is 4.2. How does this solution will affect a litmus paper?

Ans. The solution is acidic, hence, it will turn blue litmus paper to red.

Q.4 How pH of a solution can be determined?

Ans. pH of a solution can be determined either by using a pH meter or a pH paper or a universal indicator.

Q.5 Name any two indicators along with their colours in acidic and basic solutions.

Ans.

Indicator	Colour in acidic solution	Colour in basic solution
Phenolphthalein	Colourless	Pink
Methylene yellow	Red	Yellow

Q.6 How will you mix water and acid?

Ans. Always add acid to the water with continuous gentle stirring but never add water to the acid.

Experiment 3.4

AIM

To study the pH change in the titration of a strong acid with a strong base by using universal indicators.

Theory/Principle

The process of adding one solution (generally taken in a burette) to another solution (taken in a conical flask) until the reaction is just complete is called **titration**.

It is assumed that strong acids and bases are completely dissociated in solution. An acid-base titration always results in a **neutralisation reaction** and thus, results in the formation of salt and water.

e.g.

$$\underset{\text{Acid}}{HCl} + \underset{\text{Base}}{NaOH} \longrightarrow \underset{\text{Salt}}{NaCl} + \underset{\text{Water}}{H_2O}$$

Thus, H^+ ions obtained from the acid combine with OH^- ions produced by base and form water. Therefore, when a solution of strong acid is added to a solution of a strong base or *vice-versa*, the pH of the solution changes. As the titration proceeds, initially there is slow change in the pH but in the vicinity of the equivalence point there is very rapid change in the pH of the solution.

Materials Required

- Burette : 1
- Pipette (25 mL) : 1
- Conical flask (100 mL) : 1
- Dropper : 1
- Beakers (250 mL) : 2
- 0.1 M HCl, 0.1 M NaOH and universal indicator : As per need
- pH chart : 1

Procedure

1. Take a clean burette and rinse it with 0.1 M NaOH solution.
2. Now, fill the burette with 0.1 M NaOH solution. Note down the initial reading of the burette.
3. Rinse the pipette with 0.1 M HCl solution. From pipette take out 25 mL of 0.1 M hydrochloric acid (HCl) solution in a 100 mL conical flask.

ALERT

- *Concentrated* HCl *is harmful and corrosive.*
- NaOH *is corrosive.*

4. Add 5 drops of universal indicator solution to the conical flask.
5. Start adding NaOH solution from the burette dropwise into the conical flask. Shake the content of the flask well after each addition of NaOH solution.
6. Note down the colour of the solution carefully in the conical flask after each addition.
7. Find out the pH by comparing its colour with the standard pH chart.
8. Note down your observations in tabular form (use Table 3.5).
9. At the end point, when the amount of HCl has been completely neutralised by NaOH, the extra drop of a strong alkali changes the colour of the solution significantly which matches with the colour of basic pH range. Stop adding more NaOH solution.
10. Plot a graph of pH *versus* total volume of NaOH added.

Observations

Table 3.5 pH change during the neutralisation of 25 mL of HCl (0.1 M) with NaOH (0.1 M) solution

S.No.	Volume of NaOH added in lots (mL)	Total volume of NaOH added to the solution in flask (mL)	Colour produced	pH
1.	0	0		
2.	12.5	12.5		
3.	10.0	22.5		
4.	2.3	24.8		
5.	0.1	24.9		
6.	0.1	25.0		
7.	0.1	25.1		
8.	0.1	25.2		
9.	0.1	25.3		
10.	0.1	25.4		
11.	0.5	25.9		

Result

pH of the solution increases with addition of NaOH solution. Initially change is slow but at the end point, there is a sharp change in the pH of the solution.

PRECAUTIONS

- *To get best results, use solutions of strong acid and strong base of same concentration.*
- *Handle the bottles of acid and base carefully.*
- *Use small amount and equal number of drops of indicator every time.*
- *Lower meniscus of the burette should be observed for colourless solution while measuring volume.*
- *Keep the conical flask over a white paper so that the change in colour is easily visible.*

Viva-Voce

Q.1 What is meant by the equivalence point in a titration?

Ans. The equivalence point is the stage in titration when the amount of acid is completely neutralised by the base, resulting in a neutral solution.

Q.2 What happens to pH after adding NaOH beyond the equivalence point?

Ans. Beyond the equivalence point, excess OH^- ions from NaOH make the solution basic, increasing the pH above 7.

Q.3 Why are strong acids and strong bases of the same molarity used?

Ans. Using equimolar solutions simplifies calculations and ensures the reaction reaches equivalence with equal volumes.

Q.4 How does the graph of pH vs. volume of NaOH added typically look?

Ans. The graph is S-shaped with a slow rise initially, a steep rise near the equivalence point, and a slower rise again beyond the equivalence point.

Q.5 What ionic reaction takes place during the titration?

Ans. The neutralisation reaction is: $H^+(aq) + OH^-(aq) \longrightarrow H_2O(l)$

Q.6 Why is only a small amount of universal indicator used?

Ans. Excess indicator may interfere with the titration by altering the pH slightly and masking the colour change.

Q.7 What is the significance of pH = 7 in this titration?

Ans. It indicates complete neutralisation of a strong acid with a strong base, producing a neutral solution.

Q.8 Is it possible to identify the exact pH by universal indicator?

Ans. Universal indicator gives an approximate pH by colour comparison and for exact pH measurement a pH meter is needed.

Q.9 Why is conical flask used in titration instead of a beaker?

Ans. A conical flask allows easy swirling without risk of spillage during the titration process.

Q.10 What safety precautions should be taken while handling HCl and NaOH?

Ans. Both are corrosive in nature therefore wear gloves, goggles, and handle with care. Always add acid to water and not the reverse.

Questions From NCERT Lab Manual

Q.1 What trend of pH change will you observe in the neutralisation of strong acid with strong base?

Ans. In the beginning, the pH changes gradually but at the end point, there is a sharp change in the pH of the solution.

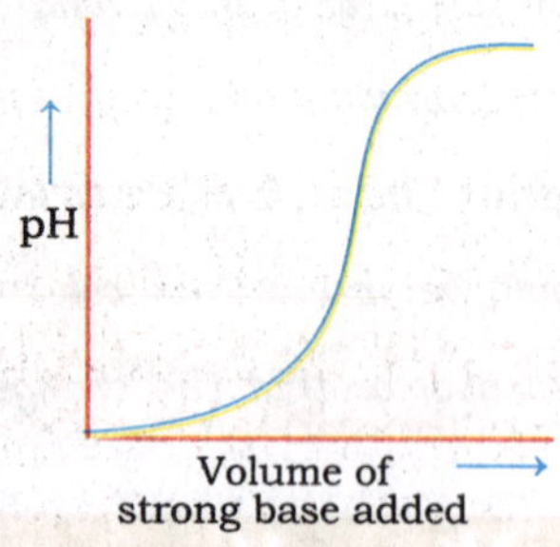

Q.2 In which pH range should the indicator show colour change if HCl is to be neutralised with NaOH? Give answer after looking at the graph of the experiment.

Ans. If HCl is to be neutralised by NaOH, the indicator show a colour change in the pH range approximately 3 to 7. Methyl red (pH range 4.4 to 6.2), methyl orange (pH range 3.1 to 4.4) and bromothymol blue (pH range 6.0 to 7.6) are suitable for such a titration.

Q.3 Do you expect the same trend of pH change for neutralisation of weak acid (acetic acid) with a strong base (sodium hydroxide)?

Ans. No, the trend of pH change for neutralisation is not same as that in the case of HCl *vs* NaOH titration. In case of acetic acid with NaOH titration, initially the pH rises rapidly. As the equivalence point is reached, pH raises gradually because a buffer acid of sodium acetate and acetic acid is formed. After the equivalence point, the graph is same as that in the case of HCl *versus* NaOH.

Q.4 Explain, how does the study of pH change help in choosing the indicator for neutralisation reaction?

Ans. An indicator solution is used to determine when an acid has exactly neutralised a base, or *vice-versa*. A suitable indicator changes colour when equivalent amounts of acid and base is present.

Experiment 3.5

AIM

To study the pH change by common ion effect in case of weak acids and weak bases.

Theory/Principle

The **common ion effect** may be defined as the suppression of degree of dissociation of either a weak acid or a weak base by the addition of small amount of some strong electrolyte having a common ion with that of weak acid or weak base.

e.g., CH_3COOH being a weak acid does not dissociate completely when dissolve in water and thus, an equilibrium exists between its unionised molecules and its ions.

$$CH_3COOH\,(aq) \rightleftharpoons CH_3COO^-\,(aq) + H^+\,(aq) \quad \ldots\text{(i)}$$

When sodium acetate which is an electrolyte is added to it, CH_3COONa dissociates as

$$CH_3COONa(aq) \longrightarrow CH_3COO^-\,(aq) + Na^+\,(aq)$$

Due to the presence of common CH_3COO^- ions, the equilibrium existing in Eq. (i) shifts in the backward direction thereby suppressing the degree of dissociation of CH_3COOH and hence, the concentration of H^+ ions decreases. Thus, the pH of the solution of acetic acid solution increases.

Similarly, NH_4OH a weak base partially dissociates as

$$NH_4OH(aq) \rightleftharpoons NH_4^+(aq) + OH^-\,(aq) \quad \ldots\text{(ii)}$$

When a strong electrolyte, NH_4Cl is added to it, NH_4Cl dissociates as

$$NH_4Cl(aq) \longrightarrow NH_4^+(aq) + Cl^-\,(aq)$$

Due to the presence of NH_4^+ ions, the equilibrium existing in Eq. (ii) shifts in the backward direction and thus, degree of dissociation of NH_4OH is suppressed. Thus, the concentration of OH^- ions decreases and hence, pH of the solution of NH_4OH decreases.

Hence, in case of slightly ionising weak acid or weak base as discussed above, the increase in concentration of common ion [CH_3COO^- and NH_4^+] would shift the equilibrium in the reverse direction, thereby decreasing the concentration of H^+ and OH^- in the respective examples so as to maintain the constancy of equilibrium constants K. This change either in H^+ or OH^- ion concentration is responsible for the change in pH of weak acid or base which can be judged either with the help of a pH paper or by using a universal indicator solution.

Materials Required

- Test tubes : 4
- Test tube stand : 1
- Beakers (100 mL) : 4
- Pipettes (25 mL) : 2
- Ammonia solution (1.0 M) : 50 mL
- Universal indicator and pH paper : As per need
- Ethanoic acid (acetic acid, CH_3COOH 1.0 M) : 50 mL
- Ammonium hydroxide (NH_4OH 1.0 M) : 50 mL
- Ammonium chloride : 2 g
- Sodium acetate or ethanoate (CH_3COONa) : 2 g
- pH chart : 1

Procedure

1. Take four beakers (100 mL each) and mark them as *A*, *B*, *C* and *D*.
2. Transfer 25 mL of 1M ethanoic acid in beakers *A* and *C* and 25 mL of 1M ammonia solution in beakers *B* and *D*.
3. Now, add 2g of sodium ethanoate in beaker *C* and dissolve it.
4. Similarly, add 2g of ammonium chloride in beaker *D* and dissolve it by shaking the content of the beaker thoroughly.
5. Take 2 mL (20 drops) of the solution from beakers *A*, *B*, *C* and *D* respectively into the four separate test tubes and marked them as 1, 2, 3 and 4.
6. Add 2 drops of universal indicator solution in each of the test tubes. Shake the content of the test tubes well and match the colour in each case with the standard pH chart.
7. Record your observations in tabular form. (use Table 3.6)
8. Compare pH of the solution in test tubes 1 and 3 and record the change in pH.
9. Similarly, compare pH of the solution in test tubes 2 and 4 and record the change in pH.

⚠ ALERT

- *Ethanoic acid is corrosive.*
- *Ammonium chloride is harmful.*
- *The concentrated ammonia solution should be supplied in small bottles. Do not keep the bottle of ammonia open for a long period of time. While opening the bottle of ammonia solution, care should be taken because pressure can build up inside the bottle.*

Observation

Table 3.6 Comparison of pH of acid/base and its buffer

S.No.	Composition of the system	Colour of pH paper	pH
1.	CH_3COOH (in water)		
2.	NH_4OH (NH_3 in water)		
3.	CH_3COOH + 2g CH_3COONa		
4.	NH_4OH + 2g NH_4Cl		

Result

(i) pH of acetic acid is ....

(ii) pH of buffer of acetic acid + 2 g sodium acetate is .... than acetic acid.

(iii) pH of ammonium hydroxide is ....

(iv) pH of buffer of ammonium hydroxide + 2 g ammonium chloride is .... than ammonia solution.

(v) Common ion effect .... ionisation of acid/base.

Hence, pH of acetic acid .... on adding sodium acetate to it and pH of ammonium hydroxide .... on adding ammonium chloride to it.

PRECAUTIONS

- *Try only weak acid/base and its salt for the study of the common ion effect.*
- *Add equal number of drops of universal indicators in each of the test tubes.*
- *The compound added should be dissolved completely before noting its pH.*
- *Store pH papers at a safe and dry place.*
- *Handle the bottle ammonium hydroxide with care.*

Viva-Voce

Q.1 Why does pH increase when sodium acetate is added to acetic acid?

Ans. Sodium acetate provides additional acetate ions (CH_3COO^-), which suppress the ionisation of acetic acid by shifting the equilibrium backward, thereby reducing H^+ concentration and increasing the pH.

Q.2 Why does pH decrease on adding ammonium chloride to ammonia solution?

Ans. Ammonium chloride provides extra NH_4^+ ions, which suppress the ionization of ammonia, decreasing OH^- concentration and hence lowering the pH.

Q.3 Which type of substances are selected for studying the common ion effect?

Ans. Weak acids or weak bases along with their salts containing a common ion are used to study the common ion effect.

Q.4 Why is the universal indicator used in this experiment?

Ans. The universal indicator gives a wide pH range and shows different colors for different pH values thus helping to identify and compare the pH changes easily.

Q.5 What is the nature of sodium acetate-acidic, basic or neutral?

Ans. Sodium acetate is a salt of a weak acid and a strong base, and its aqueous solution is basic in nature.

Q.6 What kind of solution is formed when a weak acid and its salt are mixed?

Ans. A buffer solution is formed, which resists drastic pH change.

Q.7 Which salt is added to ethanoic acid to demonstrate the common ion effect?

Ans. Sodium ethanoate (CH_3COONa) is added to ethanoic acid to provide the common acetate ion.

Q.8 What is the significance of the common ion effect in analytical chemistry?

Ans. The common ion effect is used to control the ionisation of weak electrolytes and is important in buffer preparation and salt analysis.

Questions From NCERT Lab Manual

Q.1 Suggest a suitable replacement for CH_3COONa and NH_4Cl in the given experiment.

Ans. Calcium acetate $[(CH_3COO)_2Ca]$ and NH_4Br can be used to replace CH_3COONa and NH_4Cl, respectively.

Q.2 The addition of sodium acetate to acetic acid increases the pH whereas, the addition of NH_4Cl to aqueous NH_3 solution (NH_4OH) decreases the pH of the system. How do you explain these observations?

Ans. In the presence of sodium acetate, CH_3COONa, the concentration of CH_3COO^- ions increases due to which dissociation of CH_3COOH is suppressed because of common ion effect and hence, the concentration of H^+ ions decreases.

$$CH_3COOH \rightleftharpoons CH_3COO^- + H^+$$

$$CH_3COONa \longrightarrow CH_3COO^- + Na^+$$

Similarly, in the presence of NH_4Cl, the concentration of NH_4^+ ions increases which suppresses the dissociation of NH_4OH and hence, concentration of OH^- ions decreases. Thus, to maintain the constancy of equilibrium constant, the concentration of H^+ and OH^- ions decreases in case of acetic acid and ammonium hydroxide, respectively. Therefore, the pH of the system increases/decreases in case of weak acid/base due to common ion effect.

Q.3 In salt/mixture analysis, point out the situations where the variation in pH is carried out by common ion effect.

Ans. On addition of a strong electrolyte i.e. salt of any weak acid/base to either weak acid/base, the concentration of common ion increases.

Thus, in order to maintain equilibrium constant, the concentration of H^+ or OH^- ions decreases which results in the variation in pH.

Q.4 Suggest other pairs of weak acid and its salt and weak base and its salt to carry out the present investigations.

Ans. Pair of weak acid and its salt is benzoic acid (C_6H_5COOH) and sodium benzoate (C_6H_5COONa). Pair of weak base and its salt is aqueous solution of ammonium hydroxide (NH_4OH) and ammonium bromide (NH_4Br).

Q.5 How do buffer solutions resist change in the pH? Explain with a suitable example.

Ans. A buffer solution is able to resist pH change because at equilibrium its two components (conjugate acid and conjugate base) are present in appreciable amounts and are able to neutralise small amount of other acids and bases (in the form of H_3O^+ and OH^-) when they are added to the solution.

An example is a buffer solution of HF and NaF. If we add OH^- ions to the buffer, the conjugate acid, HF will neutralise added amount of base, OH^-. Since, most of the OH^- is neutralised, therefore, a small or no change in pH will occur.

Unit 4

Chemical Equilibrium

Most of the reactions when carried out in a closed vessel do not undergo completion under the given set of conditions of temperature and pressure. As the reaction proceeds, the concentration of reactants decreases and that of products increases. A stage will come when no change in the concentration of reactants and products is observed. This state is called **equilibrium state** or **dynamic** or **chemical equilibrium**.

Equilibrium is attained only in reversible reactions. Reversible reactions take place in the same reaction vessel and can proceed in forward and backward direction simultaneously under the same conditions of temperature and pressure e.g.

$$N_2 + 3H_2 \rightleftharpoons 2NH_3$$

At equilibrium, the rate of forward reaction becomes equal to the rate of backward reaction.

The variation of concentration of reactants and products in a reversible reaction can be seen as.

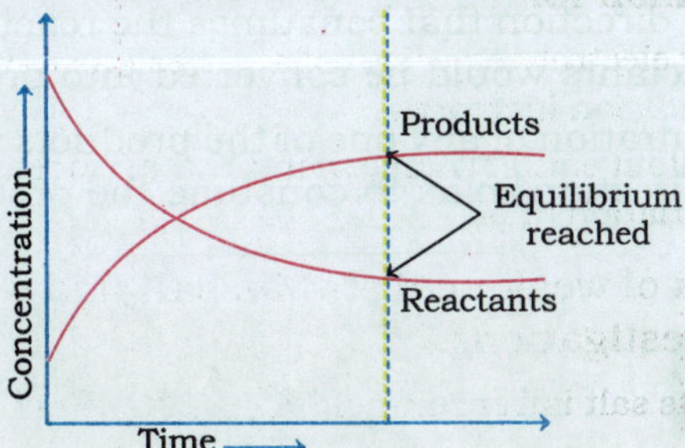

Law of Mass Action

A quantitative relationship has been formulated between the rates of reaction and concentration of the reacting substances on the basis of the observations of many equilibrium reactions. This relationship is called **law of mass action**. It states that,

"the rate of chemical reaction is directly proportional to the product of the molar concentration of the reacting substances with each concentration raised to the power of the number of molecules of that reactant at a constant temperature at any given time (or simply stoichiometric constants)."

Consider the following reversible reaction at a given temperature,

$$aA + bB \rightleftharpoons cC + dD$$

Thus, $r_f = k_f[A]^a\ [B]^b,\ r_b = k_b\ [C]^c\ [D]^d$

where, k_f and k_b are the rate constants for the forward and backward reactions respectively and $[A]$, $[B]$, $[C]$ and $[D]$ are the molar concentrations of A, B, C and D respectively.

The ratio of k_f and k_b, i.e. k_f/k_b is called **equilibrium constant**, K_C. Thus,

$$K_C = \frac{[C]^c [D]^d}{[A]^a [B]^b}$$

This mathematical equation is called **law of chemical equilibrium**. The value of K_C is independent of initial concentration of reactants and is a function of temperature but remains constant at a constant temperature.

At a given temperature, if the concentration of any one of the reactants or products is changed, the equilibrium gets disturbed. Thus, the reaction now proceed in that direction which counteracts the change in concentration so as to maintain the equilibrium.

The state of equilibrium in any reaction is recognised by the constancy of an observable property (macroscopic property) such as colour intensity of the solution.

Le-Chatelier's Principle

The effect of concentration on a reaction in equilibrium can be predicted with the help of Le-Chatelier's principle which states that, "*if a reaction in equilibrium is subjected to a change of concentration (or pressure or temperature), the equilibrium shifts in the direction which tends to undo the effect of the change*".

Thus, on changing the concentration, the equilibrium re-establishes without affecting the equilibrium constant of the reaction. Hence, according to Le-Chatelier's principle, when the concentration of one of the substances in a system at equilibrium is increased, then the equilibrium will shift so as to use up the substance added.

Let us consider at equilibrium, if concentration of any one of the reactants is increased, the equilibrium, will shift in the direction that consumes the reactants, i.e. in the forward direction. As a result, more of the reactants would be converted into products.

On the other hand, if concentration of any one of the products is increased, then the equilibrium will shift in the backward direction so as to consume the products.

Experiment 4.1

AIM

To study the shift in equilibrium in the reaction between ferric ions and thiocyanate ions by increasing/decreasing the concentration of either of the ions.

Theory/principle

To study the effect of change in concentration on equilibrium, consider the equilibrium reaction between ferric chloride (or ferric Fe^{3+} ions) and potassium thiocyanate (or thiocyanate, SCN^- ions) which can be represented as

$$\underset{\text{Pale yellow}}{Fe^{3+}(aq)} + \underset{\text{Colourless}}{SCN^-(aq)} \rightleftharpoons \underset{\text{Blood red}}{[Fe(SCN)]^{2+}(aq)}$$

$$K = \frac{[Fe(SCN)]^{2+}(aq)}{[Fe^{3+}(aq)][SCN^-(aq)]} \quad \text{...(i)}$$

Effect of Increasing the Concentration of Ferric Ions on the Equilibrium

On adding ferric, Fe^{3+} ions in the form of ferric chloride ($FeCl_3$) to the given system, the concentration of Fe^{3+} ions will increase. Thus, in order to maintain the equilibrium, i.e. to keep the value of *K* constant, the concentration of $[Fe(SCN)]^{2+}$ complex should increase so as to oppose the change according to Le-Chatelier's principle. As a result, more SCN^- ions will combine with Fe^{3+} ions to form a blood red complex, $[Fe(SCN)]^{2+}$.

Thus, the equilibrium will shift towards right, i.e. in the forward direction due to increase in the concentration of ferric ions which results in the formation of more $[Fe(SCN)]^{2+}$ ions and hence, the intensity of blood red solution increases. Therefore, the increase in concentration of ferric ions shifts the equilibrium in forward direction.

Effect of Increasing the Concentration of Thiocyanate Ions on the Equilibrium

Similarly, addition of more thiocyanate ions (SCN^-) results in more of the ferric ions to react with thiocyanate ions to yield more $[Fe(SCN)]^{2+}$ complex ions, thereby increasing the intensity of red colour and this also shifts the equilibrium towards right, i.e. in forward direction.

Hence, increase in the concentration of both, Fe^{3+} and SCN^- ions, shifts the equilibrium towards right. In other words, the formation of $[Fe(SCN)]^{2+}$ complex ions is favoured and thus, intensity of blood red colour increases. At equilibrium, colour intensity remains constant.

Materials Required

- Beakers (100 mL) : 2
- Beaker (250 mL) : 1
- Boiling tubes : 6
- Glass droppers : 2
- Test tube stand : 1
- Glass rod : 1
- Burettes : 4
- Ferric chloride : 0.100 g
- Potassium thiocyanate : 0.100 g

Procedure

Preparation of Red Coloured Thiocyanate Solution

1. Dissolve 0.100 g of ferric chloride in 100 mL of water in a beaker and 0.100 g of potassium thiocyanate in 100 mL of water in another beaker, separately.
2. Add 20 mL of ferric chloride solution into 20 mL of potassium thiocyanate solution. Shake it gently. A homogeneous solution of blood red colour will be obtained. Fill this solution in a burette.

⚠ ALERT

Ferric chloride is harmful, avoid contact with skin and eyes and wash your hands after use.

Filling Red Coloured Thiocyanate Solution into Different Tubes and Keeping One of Them for Reference

3. Take five clean boiling tubes of almost similar size and label them as *A*, *B*, *C*, *D* and *E*. Now, add 2.5 mL of the above blood red solution to each of the boiling tubes from burette and place them in a test tube stand. This 2.5 mL solution acts as an **equilibrium mixture**.
4. Add 17.5 mL of water to the boiling tube '*A*' containing red coloured solution so that the total volume of solution in the boiling tube '*A*' is 20 mL.
5. Keep boiling tube *A* with its solution as a reference for the comparison of intensity of the colour until experiment is completed.

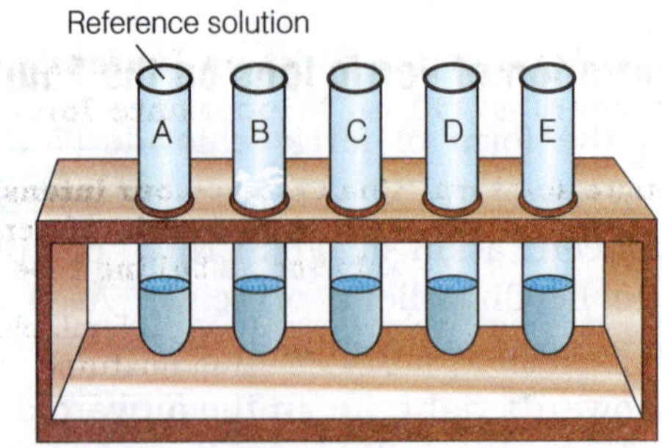

Fig. 4.1 *Set up of experiment for observing equilibrium each boiling tube contains 20 mL solution.*

Increasing the Volume of Ferric Chloride Solution and Water in each Test Tube

6. Now, take three burettes and label them as *a*, *b*, and *c*.
7. Fill the burette '*a*' with ferric chloride solution, burette '*b*' with potassium thiocyanate solution and burette '*c*' with water.
8. Add 1.0 mL, 2.0 mL, 3.0 mL and 4.0 mL of ferric chloride solution to boiling tubes *B, C, D* and *E* respectively from burette '*a*'. Thus, amount of $FeCl_3$ is increasing from *B* to *E*.
9. Now, add 16.5 mL, 15.5 mL, 14.5 mL and 13.5 mL of water to the boiling tubes *B, C, D* and *E* respectively from burette '*c*' so that total volume of solution in each boiling tube is 20 mL.

Compare the Colour Intensity with the Solution in Reference Test Tube

10. Compare the colour intensity of the solution in each boiling tube with the colour intensity of reference solution in boiling tube '*A*'.

Note Colour intensity of the solution will decrease very much on dilution. It will not be of deep red colour.

Increasing the Volume of Potassium Thiocyanate Solution and Water

11. Take another set of four clean boiling tubes and marked them as, *B*′, *C*′, *D*′ and *E*′. Add 2.5 mL of blood red solution to each of the boiling tubes from the burette.
12. Repeat the experiment by adding 1.0 mL, 2.0 mL, 3.0 mL and 4.0 mL of potassium thiocyanate solution from burette '*b*' to the boiling tubes *B*′, *C*′, *D*′ and *E*′ respectively followed by the addition of 16.5 mL, 15.5 mL , 14.5 mL and 13.5 mL of water respectively.
13. Again compare the colour intensity of the solution of these test tubes with reference equilibrium solution in boiling tube *A*.
14. Record your observations in tabular form as in tables 4.1 and 4.2. You may repeat the observations by decreasing the different amounts of given compounds, potassium thiocyanate and ferric chloride solution and compare with the reference solution.

Observations

Table 4.1 Equilibrium Shift on Increasing the Concentration of Ferric Ions

Boiling tube	Volume of ferric chloride solution taken in the system (in mL)	Change in colour intensity as matched with reference solution in boiling tube 'A'	Direction of shift in equilibrium
A	Reference solution for matching colour containing 2.5 mL blood red solution + 17.5 mL water (20 mL equilibrium mixture)		Equilibrium position
B	1.0		
C	2.0		
D	3.0		
E	4.0		

Table 4.2 Equilibrium Shift on Increasing the Concentration of Thiocyanate Ions

Boiling tube	Volume of thiocyanate solution taken in the system (in mL)	Change in colour intensity as matched with reference solution in boiling tube '*A*'	Direction of shift in equilibrium
A	Reference solution for matching colour containing 2.5 mL blood red solution + 17.5 mL water (20 mL equilibrium mixture)		Equilibrium position
B'	1.0		
C'	2.0		
D'	3.0		
E'	4.0		

Result

1. Increase in the concentration of any of the reactants [i.e. Fe^{3+} or SCN^-] shifts the equilibrium in forward direction (towards right), i.e., the intensity of colour increases due to the increase in the concentration of product, $[Fe(SCN)]^{2+}$.
2. Similarly, decrease in the concentration of any of the reactants shifts the equilibrium in the backward direction (towards left).

PRECAUTIONS

- *Use boiling tubes of almost same diameter and thickness, i.e. of same size.*
- *Use very dilute solutions of ferric chloride and potassium thiocyanate.*
- *Compare the intensity of the colour of the solutions by keeping the boiling tubes and the reference boiling tube side by side against a white background.*
- *While measuring the volume, lower meniscus of the burette should be observed in case of colourless solutions.*
- *To judge the change in colour of the solution in an effective manner, note the colour change in diffused sunlight.*

Viva-Voce

Q.1 Why does the solution turn blood red in this reaction?

Ans. The formation of $[Fe(SCN)]^{2+}$. complex gives the blood red colour to the solution, indicating the forward direction of the reaction.

Q.2 Why is the total volume kept constant in all test tubes?

Ans. Keeping the total volume constant ensures that changes in colour intensity are due to shifts in equilibrium and not due to differences in dilution.

Q.3 What will happen to the equilibrium when more Fe^{3+} is added?

Ans. The equilibrium shifts to the right, forming more $[Fe(SCN)]^{2+}$ and increasing the intensity of the blood red colour.

Q.4 Why is the total volume kept constant in all test tubes?

Ans. Keeping the total volume constant ensures that changes in colour intensity are due to shifts in equilibrium and not due to differences in dilution.

Q.5 How does increasing the concentration of thiocyanate ions affect the equilibrium?

Ans. It shifts the equilibrium to the right, forming more $[Fe(SCN)]^{2+}$ and intensifying the blood red colour.

Q.6 What does a constant colour intensity signify at equilibrium?

Ans. It indicates a dynamic equilibrium where the forward and backward reaction rates are equal and the concentration of each species remains constant.

Q.7 What safety precautions should be taken while handling ferric chloride?

Ans. Avoid contact with skin and eyes, as ferric chloride is corrosive and can cause irritation or burns.

Q.8 What kind of reaction is the formation of $[Fe(SCN)]^{2+}$-ionic or molecular?

Ans. It is an ionic reaction involving aqueous ions forming a complex ion.

Questions From NCERT Lab Manual

Q.1 What is the equilibrium constant and how does it differ from the rate constant?

Ans. Equilibrium constant is the ratio of the molar concentrations of products and reactants raised to the power of their stoichiometric coefficients at equilibrium. It tells when the equilibrium is achieved in a chemical reaction, whereas the rate constant tells about the speed of that chemical reaction.

Q.2 It is always advisable to carry out the present experiment with dilute solutions. Why?

Ans. It is always advisable to carry out the given experiment with dilute solutions so that a slight change in concentration of any of the reactants show noticeable difference in the intensity of colour on comparing it with the reference solution.

Q.3 Why boiling tubes of same size are used in the experiment?

Ans. To make the comparison easier and accurate, the boiling tubes of same size should be used.

Q.4 Explain, why representing the ionic reaction between ferric and thiocyanate ions as given in the text *viz.*

$$Fe^{3+}(aq) + SCN^-(aq) \rightleftharpoons [Fe(SCN)]^{2+}(aq)$$

is more appropriate in the following form?

$$[Fe(H_2O)_6]^{3+} + SCN^-(aq) \rightleftharpoons [Fe(H_2O)_5(SCN)]^{2+} + H_2O$$

Ans. In aqueous solution, Fe^{3+} ions are present as hexacoordinate ions with water molecules. In the presence of SCN^- ions, one of the water molecules is replaced by SCN^- as a ligand.

Q.5 Does the constancy in colour intensity indicate the dynamic nature of equilibrium? Explain your answer with appropriate reason.

Ans. No, the colour would remain constant even if the reaction stops altogether at equilibrium.

Q.6 What will be the effect of adding potassium chloride to the system at equilibrium? Verify your answer experimentally.

Ans. Addition of KCl will increase the concentration of K^+ ions which reacts with SCN^- ions to form KSCN leading to a decrease in the concentration of SCN^-. This will shift the equilibrium in the backward direction, i.e., towards left so as to increase the concentration of SCN^- according to Le-Chatelier's principle and as a result of which, the intensity of red colour decreases.

Experiment 4.2

AIM

To study the shift in equilibrium in the reaction between $[Co(H_2O)_6]^{2+}$ ions and Cl^- ions by changing the concentration of either of the ions.

Theory/Principle

Cobalt (II) ions in aqueous medium form a water soluble pink complex, hexaaquacobalt (II), $[Co(H_2O)_6]^{2+}$ ions.

$$\underset{\text{Light pink}}{Co^{2+}} + 6H_2O \rightleftharpoons \underset{\text{Pink complex}}{[Co(H_2O)_6]^{2+}}$$

On gradually replacing water molecules by chloride ions, cobaltous ion, Co^{2+}ion, forms a blue coloured tetrachlorocobaltate (II)ions, $[CoCl_4]^{2-}$complex.

When both the chloride ions and water molecules are present in cobalt(II) salt solution, an equilibrium exists between the hexaaquacobalt(II) ions and the chloride ions as shown below

$$\underset{\text{Pink}}{[Co(H_2O)_6]^{2+}} + 4Cl^- \rightleftharpoons \underset{\substack{\text{Tetrachlorocobaltate (II) ions} \\ \text{(blue)}}}{[CoCl_4]^{2-}} + 6H_2O \quad \text{...(i)}$$

This reaction is called a ligand exchange reaction and its equilibrium constant, K, is expressed as follows

$$K = \frac{[CoCl_4]^{2-}}{[Co(H_2O)_6]^{2+}\ [Cl^-]^4}$$

Note *Since the reaction occurs in the aqueous medium, it is believed that concentration of H_2O is almost constant and is included in the value of K itself and is not shown separately in the expression for K.*

The effect of change in concentration of various ions can be studied as per **Le-Chatelier's principle.**

Effect of Increasing Concentration of Water Molecules

On adding water molecules to the blue solution [i.e. on increasing the concentration of water molecules for Eq. (i)], the equilibrium get shifted to the left hand side and the concentration of $[Co(H_2O)_6]^{2+}$ increases. As a result, the intensity of blue colour decreases and that of pink colour increases.

$$\underset{\text{Pink}}{[Co(H_2O)_6]^{2+}} + 4Cl^- \rightleftharpoons \underset{\substack{\text{Tetrachlorocobaltate (II) ion} \\ \text{(blue)}}}{[CoCl_4]^{2-}} + 6H_2O$$

Thus, the above given reaction shifts towards the backward direction as to maintain the equilibrium constant.

Effect of Increasing Concentration of Cl^- Ions

On adding HCl to the pink coloured complex [i.e., on increasing the concentration of Cl^- ions for Eq.(i)], the equilibrium get shifted towards right hand side, i.e. this would increase the concentration of complex ion $[CoCl_4]^{2-}$ so as to oppose the change (for maintaining the constant value of *K*) thereby, increasing the blue colour intensity and decreasing the pink colour intensity of the solution.

$$\underset{\text{(Pink)}}{[Co(H_2O)_6]^{2+}} + 4Cl^- \rightleftharpoons \underset{\substack{\text{Tetrachlorocobaltate (II) ion} \\ \text{(blue)}}}{[CoCl_4]^{2-}} + 6\ H_2O$$

Thus, the above given reaction shifts towards the forward direction as to maintain the equilibrium constant.

Materials Required

- Conical flask (100 mL): 1
- Beakers (100 mL) : 3
- Burettes : 3
- Test tubes : 6
- Test tube stand : 1
- Glass rod : 1
- Acetone or alcohol : 60 mL
- Concentrated hydrochloric acid : 30 mL
- Cobalt chloride : 0.6000 g

Procedure

Preparation of Blue Coloured Solution

1. Take 60 mL of acetone in a conical flask of 100 mL and dissolve 0.6000 g $CoCl_2$ in it to get a blue solution.
2. Take 5 clean test tubes of same size and mark them as 1, 2, 3, 4 and 5.

⚠ ALERT

- *Acetone and alcohol are highly toxic and inflammable, so keep the bottles away from flames.*
  Do not let the bottles open when not in use.
- *Conc. HCl is corrosive. Wash your hands after use.*
- *Always wear safety goggles.*

Increasing the Volume of Water

3. Add 3.0 mL of cobalt chloride solution in each of the test tubes from 1 to 5, respectively. Now, add 1.0 mL, 0.8 mL, 0.6 mL, 0.4 mL and 0.2 mL of acetone respectively in these test tubes.
4. Add 0.2 mL, 0.4 mL, 0.6 mL and 0.8 mL of water to the test tubes 2, 3, 4 and 5 respectively, so that the total volume of solution in each of the test tubes is 4.0 mL.
5. Note down the gradual change in colour of the mixture from blue to pink with an increase in the amount of water.

Increasing the Volume of Conc. HCl

6. Take 10 mL of cobalt chloride solution in acetone prepared in step (1) and add 5 mL of distilled water to it. A solution of pink colour will be obtained.
7. Take 1.5 mL of pink solution from step (6) in five different test tubes labelled as 1′, 2′, 3′, 4′ and 5′. Add 2.0 mL, 1.5 mL, 1.0 mL and 0.5 mL of water in these test tubes (1′-4′) and 0.5 mL, 1.0 mL, 1.5 mL, 2.0 mL and 2.5 mL concentrated HCl respectively in the test tubes 1′ to 5′ so that the total volume of solution in the test tubes is 4 mL.
8. Note the gradual change in colour of pink solution to light blue with increasing amounts of hydrochloric acid. Record your observations in tabular form [Tables 4.3 and 4.4].

Note *In the first set of experiment, concentration of chloro complex is constant and concentration of water is changing. In the second set of experiment, concentration of aqua complex is constant and concentration of chloride ions is increasing.*

Observations

Table 4.3 Shift in Equilibrium on Adding Water

S. No.	Test tube	Volume of acetone added (in mL)	Volume of $CoCl_2$ solution added (in mL)	Volume of water added (in mL)	Colour of the mixture
1.	1	1.0	3.0	0.0	
2.	2	0.8	3.0	0.2	
3.	3	0.6	3.0	0.4	
4.	4	0.4	3.0	0.6	
5.	5	0.2	3.0	0.8	

Table 4.4 Shift in Equilibrium on Adding Cl^- Ions

S. No.	Test tube	Volume of conc. HCl added (in mL)	Volume of aqua complex solution added (in mL)	Volume of water added (in mL)	Colour of the mixture
1.	1′	0.5	1.5	2.0	
2.	2′	1.0	1.5	1.5	
3.	3′	1.5	1.5	1.0	
4.	4′	2.0	1.5	0.5	
5.	5′	2.5	1.5	0.0	

Result

1. Increase in the concentration of water molecules shifts the equilibrium towards left and hence, intensity of blue colour decreases while that of pink colour increases due to the increase in the concentration of $[Co(H_2O)_6]^{2+}$ ions.
2. Increase in the concentration of Cl^- ions shifts the equilibrium towards right and hence, the intensity of blue colour increases due to the increase in the concentration of $[CoCl_4]^{2-}$ ions.

PRECAUTIONS

- *Use burette or graduated pipette for adding water or solutions.*
- *Use test tubes of same size.*
- *Use only distilled water for the experiment.*
- *Shake the test tubes carefully, so as to avoid the spill of any solution.*
- *While measuring the volume, lower meniscus of the burette should be observed in case of colourless solutions.*

Viva-Voce

Q.1 What observable change indicates a shift in equilibrium in this reaction?

Ans. A change in colour from pink to blue (or vice versa) indicates a shift in equilibrium. The blue colour corresponds to the formation of $[CoCl_4]^{2-}$ and the pink to $[Co(H_2O)_6]^{2+}$.

Q.2 What is the effect of adding water to the equilibrium mixture?

Ans. Adding water dilutes the chloride ion concentration, shifting the equilibrium backward and increasing the concentration of the pink $[Co(H_2O)_6]^{2+}$ complex.

Q.3 Why does the equilibrium shift when chloride ion concentration is increased?

Ans. According to Le Chatelier's Principle, increasing Cl^- concentration favours the forward reaction to consume added ions, forming more blue $[CoCl_4]^{2-}$ complex.

Q.4 What is the role of acetone in this experiment?

Ans. Acetone helps dissolve cobalt chloride and favours the formation of the blue $[CoCl_4]^{2-}$ complex by reducing water content, indirectly reducing the backward shift.

Q.5 What safety precautions should be taken while handling acetone and HCl?

Ans. Use safety goggles and gloves, avoid inhalation or skin contact, keep acetone away from flames as it is flammable, and handle HCl with care due to its corrosiveness.

Q.6 What colours are associated with the two complexes involved in this equilibrium?

Ans. The $[Co(H_2O)_6]^{2+}$ complex is pink, and the $[CoCl_4]^{2-}$ complex is blue.

Q.7 What is observed when more water is added to the blue cobalt chloride solution?

Ans. The solution turns pink as water favours the backward shift, increasing $[Co(H_2O)_6]^{2+}$ concentration.

Questions From NCERT Lab Manual

Q.1 What will be the effect of increasing the temperature of reaction mixture at equilibrium?

Ans. On increasing the temperature, the equilibrium shifts in favour of endothermic reaction.

Q.2 Why should the total volume of the solution in each test tube be kept same?

Ans. To make comparison easier and accurate.

Q.3 Which complex is formed when hydrochloric acid is added to a solution containing cobalt nitrate?

Ans. A blue coloured solution containing $[CoCl_4]^{2-}$ is obtained.

Q.4 Can an aqueous solution of sodium chloride replace concentrated HCl? Verify your answer experimentally.

Ans. No, NaCl cannot replace the concentrated HCl solution. This is because the high concentration of chloride ions in HCl shifts the equilibrium towards right, i.e., towards formation of the blue $[CoCl_4]^{2-}$ complex ion. When NaCl is added instead, the equilibrium does not shift significantly, and the solution remains pink. It can be confirmed by adding a spatula of NaCl which produces a pink colour (and not the blue as expected), this may take sometime because the salt is slow to dissolve completely.

Unit 5

Titrimetric Analysis
(Quantitative Estimation)

The amount of chemical substances in solution can be determined either through titrimetric analysis (Quantitative Estimation) or gravimetric analysis. Titrimetric analysis deals with the measurements of only volumes while gravimetric analysis involves the measurement of volumes as well as mass. Titrimetric analysis is also called **volumetric analysis**.

Titrimetric analysis involves determination of the volume of a solution of accurately known concentration, which is required to react quantitatively with the measured volume of the solution of a substance, concentration of which is to be determined. The solution of accurately known concentration is called **standard solution.** The mass of the substance dissolved in the solution of unknown concentration is calculated from the volume of the standard solution used, the chemical equation and the relative molecular masses of the reacting compounds. The reagent of known concentration is called **titrant** and the substance being titrated is termed as **titrand.**

To carry out titrimetric analysis, standard solution is usually added from the long graduated tube called **burette**. The process of adding the standard solution to the solution of unknown concentration until the reaction is just complete is called **titration**. The point at which reaction is completed is called **equivalence point** or the **theoretical** or **stoichiometric end point.**

Volumetric Apparatus used for Measuring Volume of Liquids

In titrimetric analysis, the volume of the various solutions should be measured accurately. The apparatus used for measuring the volume of liquids are:

1. **Graduated apparatus** These are used to measure the volume of a liquid at a certain temperature. These are not used for very precise measurements. These include volumetric flasks and graduated cylinders.
2. **Calibrated apparatus** These are used to deliver certain specific volume of a liquid at a specified temperature. These include pipettes and burettes. These are used to measure the volume of a liquid accurately. The capacity mark is usually etched on the glass of the equipment.

Aqueous solutions wet the glass surface, therefore these form concave meniscus when filled in these equipments. Central part of the meniscus is rather flat.

The calibration of the apparatus will coincides with the flat portion of the meniscus which gives a measure of the volume of the liquid.

However, if the liquid taken in the apparatus is coloured and opaque like $KMnO_4$ solution or forms a convex meniscus, the reading which coincides with upward surface is noted (or taken).

Note *In flasks and pipettes capacity mark is etched on the narrow part of the equipment to minimise the error in noting the level of meniscus.*

The brief description about their uses and handling of some important glass apparatus are given below

Graduated Cylinder

Before using a graduated cylinder it should be cleaned because dirt may chemically contaminate the substance being measured and it may alter the volume of the liquid. Hence, it may affect the accurate determination of volume. Further, dirty glassware does not drain properly and the volume delivered may not be equal to that indicated by calibration mark. These are available in various capacities of 5 mL, 10 mL, 25 mL, 100 mL, 250 mL, 500 mL, 1000 mL and 2000 mL. Measuring cylinders used for delivering the volume actually contain slightly more than the volume read. This compensates for the film of liquid left on the walls when liquid is poured out.

Burette

A burette is a long, graduated and cylindrical tube of uniform bore. It is fused at the lower end with a stopcock or pinchcock and a fine nozzle. It is used for measuring volume in a quantitative (titrimetric) estimation. It is graduated in millilitres from 0 to 50. Each division is subdivided into ten equal parts. Therefore, each subdivision reads 0.1 mL. The burette is used in the following manner.

Selection of Burette

Before using the burette, its stopcock should be checked. It should not have any leakage.

Cleaning and Rinsing of Burette

Before, filling a burette with the solution, it is thoroughly washed with chromic acid ($K_2Cr_2O_7$ + conc.H_2SO_4) then with distilled water so that no greasy matter remains sticked inside or outside the burette.

After cleaning the burette, it should be rinsed with the solution to be filled. For rinsing the burette, few millilitres of solution are taken into it [Fig. 5.1 (i)]. Close the upper mouth of the burette with the thumb and hold it in horizontal position [Fig. 5.1 (ii)]. The burette is rotated so as to wet the inner walls of the burette with the solution [Fig. 5.1 (iii)]. After rinsing, the solution is drained out from the nozzle of the burette. [Fig. 5.1 (iv)]

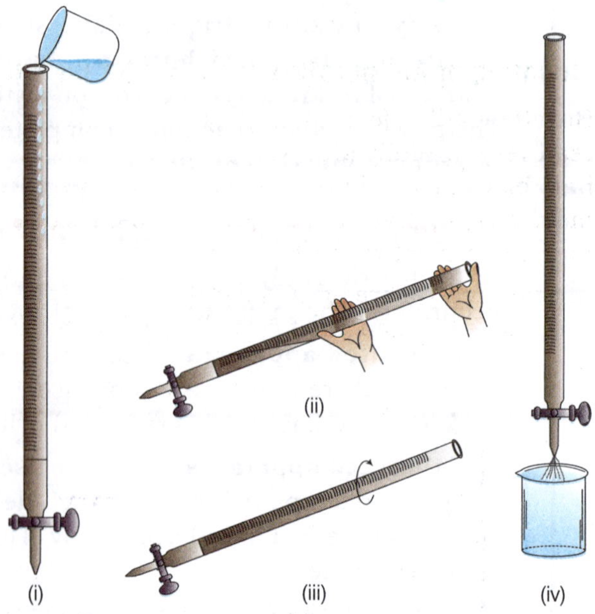

Fig. 5.1 *(i) Filling a small volume of burette with the help of beaker*
(ii) Holding the burette
(iii) Rotating the burette
(iv) Draining of the solution used for rinsing

Fitting and Filling of Burette

After rinsing, fit the burette carefully and properly on the clamp stand at a convenient height which makes you convenient in taking the reading. Then, filled the solution in the burette with the help of a funnel which is inserted at the top of the burette above zero mark [Fig. 5.2 (i)]. The stopcock is opened so that the solution can also be filled in the tip [Fig. 5.2 (ii)].

Remove the Air Bubble

Make sure no air bubbles remain in narrow bottom tip of the burette because they may cause an error at the time of reading. To remove the air bubbles, stopcock is opened wide and the solution is allowed to run through the nozzle into the beaker or flask until there are no air bubbles in it. [Fig 5.2 (iii)]. Remove the funnel from the burette, before noting the reading of the burette and ensure that the nozzle is completely filled [Fig. 5.2 (iv)].

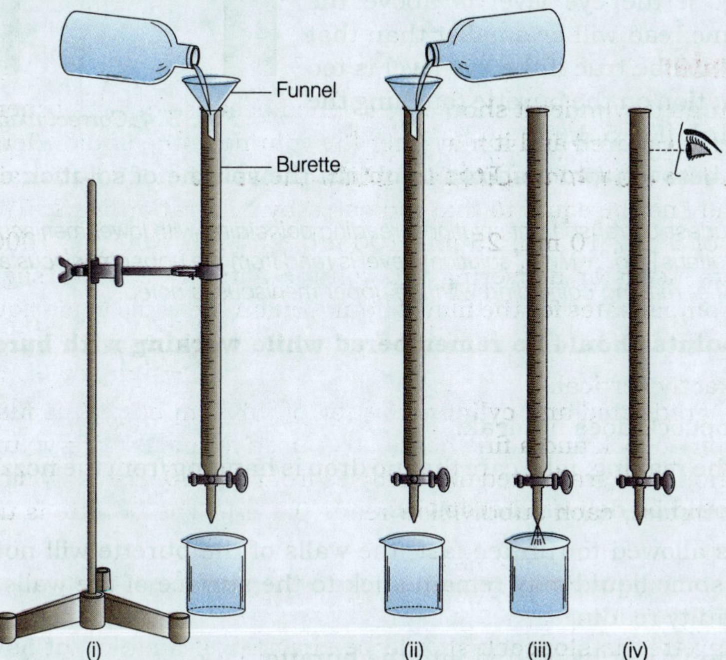

Fig. 5.2 *(i) Filling of solution in burette, (ii) Filling the tip of burette (iii) Remove the air bubbles (iv) To ensure filling of nozzle*

Mounting of Antiparallax Card on the Burette

Burette reading forms the most important aspect of the experiment, therefore, burette should be read very carefully after removing, the parallax. To read the level of a liquid in the burette, hold a half blackened white card called **antiparallax card** behind the burette at the level of the meniscus, so that the black area appears to be just touching the meniscus of the liquid and then note the correct reading [Fig 5.3 (ii)].

In order to prepare an antiparallax card, take a rectangular piece of paper and fold it half. Give two cuts and open the fold to mount it on the burette. [Fig 5.3 (i) a, b, c, d]

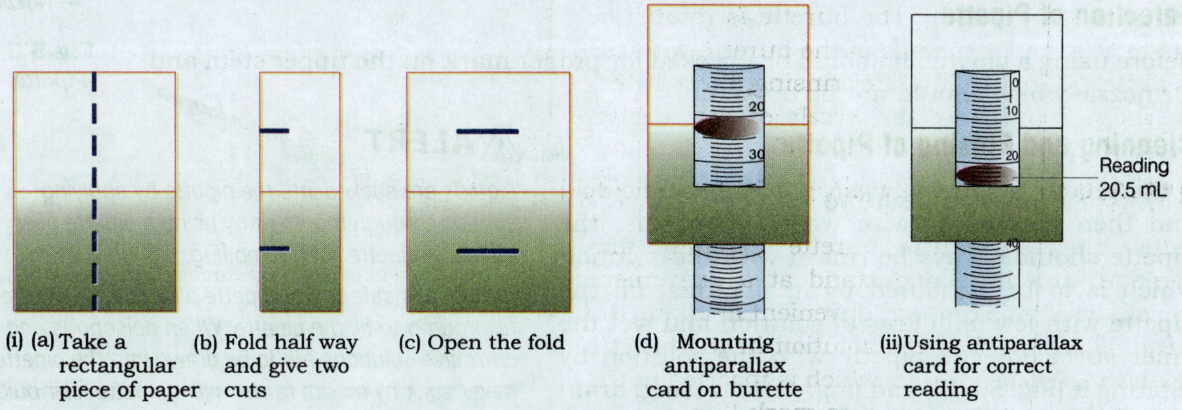

Fig. 5.3 *Use of anti-parallax card*

Reading the Level of Liquid in the Burette

The eye must be levelled with the meniscus of the liquid to eliminate parallax errors for taking initial reading and then final reading at the end. Correct position is with your eye at the same level as the meniscus [Fig 5.4]. If the eye level is above the meniscus, the volume read will be smaller than that taken, the opposite will be true if the eye level is too low. Read the graduation on the burette touching the black part of the card. [Fig 5.3 (ii)]

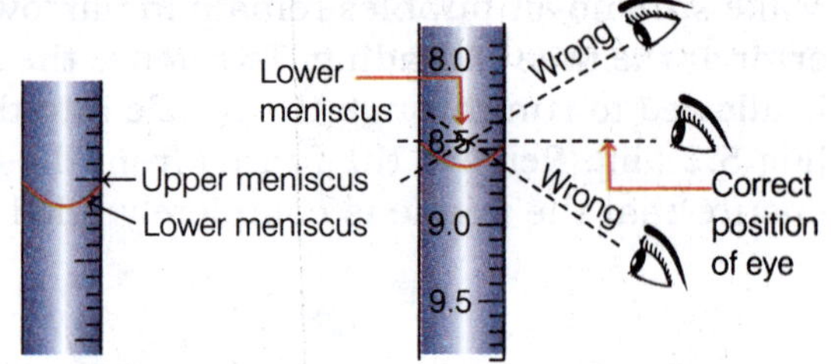

Fig. 5.4 *Correct way of reading burette*

Find the difference between two readings to obtain the volume of solution consumed.

Note *In case of colourless or transparent solutions, reading coinciding with lower meniscus is noted while in case of coloured solutions [e.g. : $KMnO_4$ solution], level is read from the upper meniscus as lower meniscus is not clearly visible, i.e. reading coinciding with the upper meniscus is noted.*

Some important points should be remembered while working with burette

1. Fix burette exactly vertical.
2. Make sure stopcock does not leak.
3. While noting the reading, take care that no drop is hanging from the nozzle of the burette.
4. The liquid should be delivered dropwise.
5. If the liquid is allowed to run too fast, the walls of the burette will not drain properly and some liquid may remain stick to the surface of the walls which may lead to faulty reading.
6. Hot liquids should not be poured into the burette.

Pipette

It is a small and handy apparatus used for accurate measurements of definite volume of solution. It consists of a long narrow tube with cylindrical bulb in the middle and a jet (or nozzle) at its lower end.

On the upper part of the stem, there is an etched circular mark which represents the definite volume upto which the pipette can deliver when filled upto the circular mark. [Fig 5.5]

Pipettes are used for measuring the volumes when these are to be transferred to a flask or some other apparatus. Various capacities of pipettes 1 mL, 2 mL, 5 mL, 10 mL, 20 mL, 25 mL, etc., are available in laboratory.

Fig 5.5 *Pipette*

Selection of Pipette

Before using a pipette, it should be checked for proper mark on the upper stem and for nozzle which should not be broken.

Cleaning and Rinsing of Pipette

If the pipette is greasy, wash it with chromic acid and then thoroughly with water. After this, the pipette should always be rinsed with the solution which is to be measured by it. For this, fill the pipette with few millilitres of solution and wet the inner surface of the pipette with the solution by rotating it [Fig. 5.6 (ii) and (iii)]. After rinsing, drain out the whole amount of solution taken in it

⚠ ALERT

Liquids are sucked into the pipette by applying suction through mouth or by using a pipette filler bulb or a pipette filler pump [Fig. 5.6 (i)].

It is always safe to use pipette filler bulb or pipette filler pump to fill the pipette. When poisonous and corrosive solutions are to be drawn into the pipette, never suck by mouth rather use a pipette filler bulb to draw the liquid up into the pipette.

through the nozzle [Fig. 5.6 (iv)]. Now, it is ready for measuring the solution. Note that while handling the pipette, hands should be dry so that pressure is regulated easily. Also, nozzle of the pipette being used should not be broken.

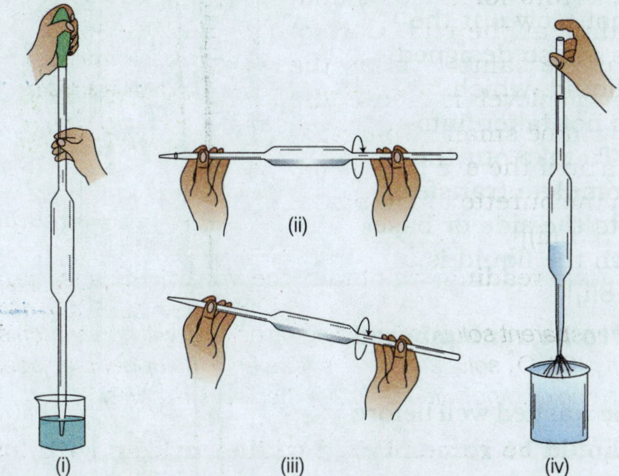

Fig. 5.6 *(i) Filling of pipette through pipette filler pump*
(ii), (iii) Wetting the inner walls by rotating it
(iv) Draining out solution through nozzle

Filling of Pipette

(i) Hold the pipette in one hand tightly, dip the jet of the pipette into the solution to be pipetted out, and squeeze the pipette bulb with the other hand [Fig. 5.7(i)]. But if no filler bulb is provided in the pipette, suck the solution into the pipette by applying action through the mouth as shown in Fig 5.7 (ii).

(ii) Now, loosen your grip on the bulb so that the liquid is sucked into the pipette. When the liquid is above the etched mark on the pipette, remove the bulb, and put the index finger of the hand at its place holding the pipette as shown in Fig 5.7 (iii).

(iii) Loosen the finger carefully to allow the excess liquid to flow out so that the curvature of the meniscus reaches the mark as shown in Fig. 5.7 (iv).

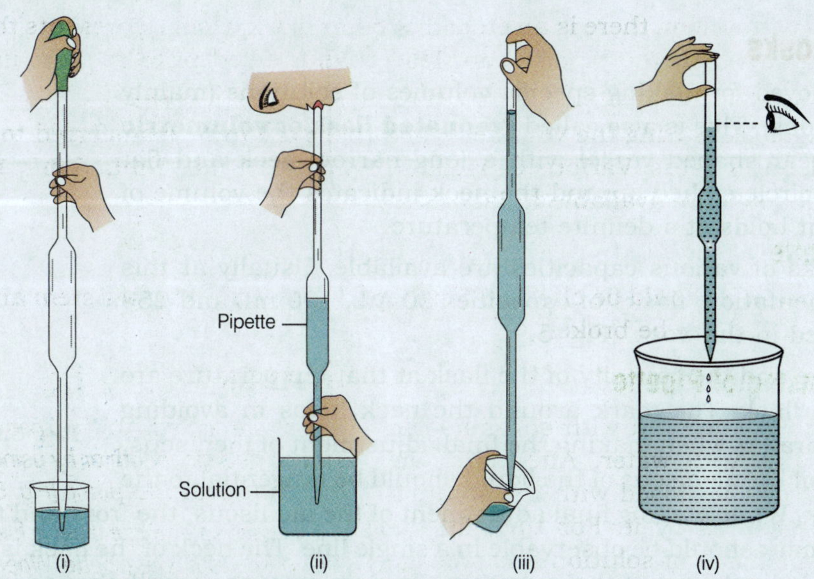

Fig. 5.7 *(i) Filling the pipette using filler bulb*
(ii) Filling the pipette through suction (in case no filler bulb is present)
(iii) Holding the pipette after removing the bulb or suction
(iv) Make sure curvature of the meniscus reaches the mark.

Emptying the Pipette

Now, carefully remove the finger and let the liquid run into the flask [Fig 5.8 (i)]. After emptying the pipette do not blow out the remaining liquid. Pipettes are so designed that the little amount of liquid, which remains untransferred, is not taken into calibration. [Fig. 5.8 (ii)]. To take out the maximum volume after complete transfer, simply touch the pipette to the side or base of the container into which the liquid is being transferred. [Fig. 5.8(i)]

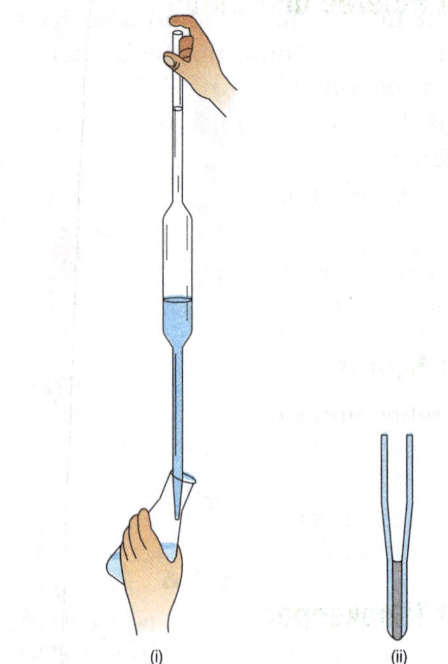

Fig. 5.8 *(i) Transferring the liquid to the flask (ii) Nozzle of the pipette after measuring*

Some important points to be remembered while using a pipette.

1. The pipette should be washed well before use.
2. The pipette should be rinsed before filling it up with the solution to be measured.
3. Always use the fore finger and not the thumb to close the upper end of the pipette.
4. The solution should not be sucked too fast as it may go into the mouth.
5. Do not blow off the last drop remaining in the pipette. Pipettes are so designed that the little amount of liquid, which remains untransferred is not taken into calibration.
6. While handling the pipette, hands should be dry so that the pressure is regulated easily. Also, nozzle of the pipette being used should not be broken.
7. Do not hold the pipette from the bulb because the body heat may expand the liquid inside the pipette.

Measuring Flasks

These are employed for making specific volumes of solutions (mainly standard solutions). This is also called **graduated flask** or **volumetric flask**. It is a pear shaped vessel with a long narrow neck and flat bottom. A thin circle etched around the neck indicates the volume of the liquid that it holds at a definite temperature.

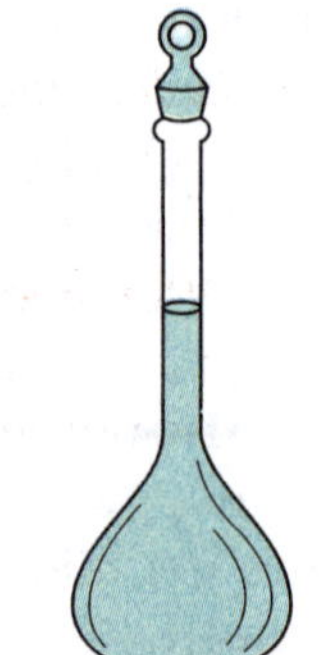

Fig. 5.9 *The measuring flask*

Measuring flasks of various capacities are available. Usually at this level of experimentation, flasks of capacities 50 mL, 100 mL and 250 mL are employed in the work. [Fig. 5.9]

The temperature and the capacity of the flask at that temperature are marked on the flask. The mark around the neck helps in avoiding errors due to parallax when making the final adjustment of meniscus. The lower edge of the meniscus of the liquid should be tangential to the graduated mark. While making final adjustment of the meniscus, the front and the back portion of the circular mark should be observable in a single line. The neck of the flask is made narrow to reduce error in adjustment of the meniscus. In narrow space small change in volume makes large effect on the height of the meniscus.

Duties of Referee and Umpire

Referee

(i) He is responsible for fair play in the match.
(ii) He is the final authority on the rules and regulations from the start to the end of the match.
(iii) Referee performs toss before the start of the match.
(iv) He has the final say on every decision related of the match.

Umpire

(i) He assits the referee by enforcing rules during the match.
(ii) He signals fouls, violations or other rule breaches committed by players.

Duties of Scorer

(i) He takes notes of all the proceedings of the match in a chronological order, alongwith the points gained, time and substitutions made.
(ii) He makes a record of all the fouls made by each player of each team.
(iii) He records personal and technical fouls separately.
(iv) He maintains a score sheet with all the details of each player.

Duties of Timekeeper

(i) He notifies and assists the referee regarding the issues of the game.
(ii) He is responsible for notifying referee about the time at which each part of the match has to begin. This needs to be done atleast three minutes before the actual start of the game.
(iii) He shall start timeout watch for charged timeout.
(iv) The timekeeper also keeps record of the various times and situations when the match was paused and resumed.

Duties of 24 Second Operator

(i) His main duty is to check the 24 Second Rule.
(ii) He keeps a record of every time when possession of ball changes.

Fundamental Skills and Techniques

The brief description of some of the fundamental skills of basketball is given below

1. **Basic Stance**
   (i) *Defensive* There are two types of team defence: zone and man-to-man. In zone defence, each player is assigned a particular area of the court to defend, whereas in man-to-man defence, each player is assigned one of the opposing players.
   (ii) *Offensive* Attacking strategies may involve a number of passes and movement by all attacking players. The fast break is used to score quickly after the attacking team gets the possession of the ball.
2. **Jump Ball** To start the game, the ball is tossed and players jump for collecting the ball. They are not allowed to push or hit the opposing player.
3. **Passing** It is an act of throwing the ball to a teammate.
   (i) *Chest Pass* It is a direct pass to an own teammate at chest level. For performing a two handed chest pass perfectly, the player should hold the ball in front of the chest.
   (ii) *Bounce Pass* Player passes the ball to his teammates after beating defender with a bounce and it reaches the teammate at normal height.
   (iii) *One Hand Pass* After dodging an opponent, the player having the ball passes the ball to his own teammate. It can either be done by one hand or both hands.
   (iv) *Overhead Pass* The two-handed overhead pass is used for taller players. This pass keeps the ball away from defending players; that is why it is more safe.

When the balance is 'arrested', the knife edges do not touch their plates and thereby reducing the wear and tear of the knife edges.

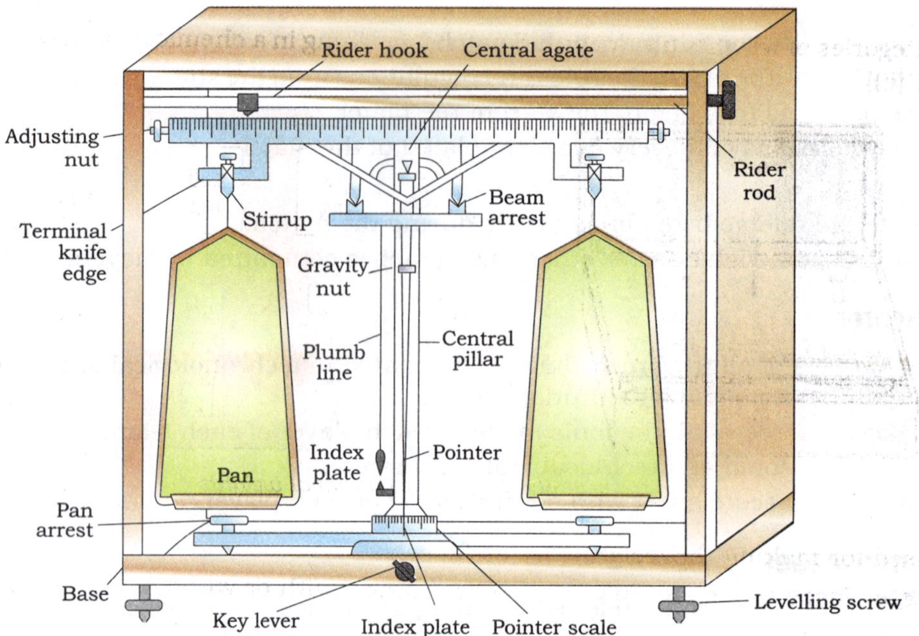

Fig. 5.10 *Chemical or analytical balance*

Rider

Chemical samples less than 10 mg are weighed by rider. Rider is a U-shaped thin wire (usually made up of aluminium or platinum). Its weight itself 10 mg (0.01 g). The rider is placed easily in the grooves (or hooks) of the balance beam with the help of forceps. The hook is fixed to a horizontal rider rod. This rod is rotated or moved to place the rider at any desired point on the beam. The balance beam is divided into 10 equal parts each of which is further sub-divided into 5 parts. One bigger division corresponds to 1 mg (1/10) and one small division reads 0.2 mg (1/5).

B. Weight Box Including Fractional Weights and Riders

Weight box is a special box which contains all the type of weights that are required for measuring the compounds on analytical balance. It is a wooden box having grooves of various sizes containing different types of weights [Fig. 5.11 (i)].

The weight box of a chemical (or analytical) balance generally contains

(a) **Weights for weighing in grams i.e. Gram Weights** These are cylindrical in shape and provided with knobs to pick them up with a forcep. These are arranged in the following order

100 g 50 g 20 g 20 g 10 g
1 g 2 g 2 g 5 g

The value of each weight is stamped on its surface. These are made up of copper and nickel with or without coating of chromium.

(b) **Weights for weighing in milligrams i.e. Milligram Weights** These are made up of different shapes so that small weights can be easily distinguished. These are arranged in three rows

500 mg	200 mg	200 mg	100 mg
50 mg	20 mg	20 mg	10 mg
5 mg	2 mg	2 mg	1 mg

These are made up of aluminium or stainless steel or German silver.

(c) **Rider** A loop made up of aluminium or platinum wire to weigh 0.2 mg to 10 mg.

(d) **Forceps** These are used for lifting the weights and putting them on and off the balance pans.

The three categories of weights (i.e. kg, g and mg) for weighing in a chemical balance are as shown in [Fig. 5.11 (ii)]

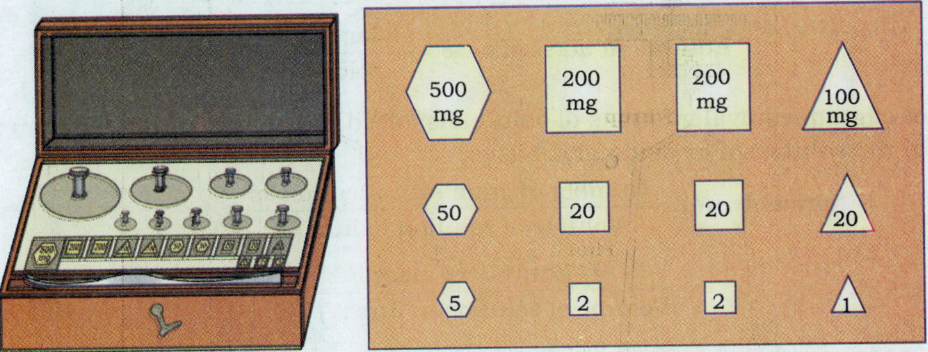

Fig. 5.11 *(i) Weight box (ii) Fractional weights*

Materials used for making the weights are as follows:

Gram weights These are made up of copper and nickel with or without coating of chromium.

Requirement For A Reaction In The Titrimetric Analysis

1. The substance of which amount is to be determined by titrimetric analysis must react completely and rapidly with the other reagent in stoichiometric proportion.
2. The reaction should be fast and there must be alteration in physical or chemical property of the solution at the equivalence point, which can be detected by an indicator.

Acidimetry And Alkalimetry [Acid-Base Titrations]

Titrimetric analysis or titration can be carried out for various types of reactions. But only neutralisation reactions are to be studied in this unit. These involve the titration of base with a standard solution of acid (acidimetry) and the titration of an acid with a standard solution of base (alkalimetry). In quantitative estimation through titrimetric analysis, concentration of solution is expressed in terms of molarity. It is the number of moles of solute dissolved in 1 L of solution.

$$\text{Molarity, } M = \frac{\text{Number of moles of solute}}{\text{Volume of solution in litres}}$$

$$= \frac{\text{Weight of substance in grams/Molecular mass of substance}}{\text{Volume of solution in litre}}$$

$$\text{or} \quad \text{Molarity} = \frac{\text{Strength of solution in gL}^{-1}}{\text{Molecular mass of substance}}$$

Also, Strength of solution = Molarity of solution × Molecular mass of substance

Calculations Used in Acid-Base Titrations

The complete neutralisation is possible only when the amount of base is in equivalent proportion to the amount of acid. Therefore, at the end point equivalent mass of acid dissolved in volume V_1 of solvent shoul be equal to the equivalent mass of the base dissolved in volume V_2 of solvent.

If N_1 and N_2 are the equivalent masses of acid and base respectively dissolved in per litre of solution then, $$N_1V_1 = N_2V_2 \quad \text{...(i)}$$

Equivalent masses of acids and bases is given by the following expression

$$\text{Equivalent mass of acid} = \frac{\text{Molar mass}}{\text{Basicity}} \quad \text{...(ii)}$$

$$\text{Equivalent mass of base} = \frac{\text{Molar mass}}{\text{Acidity}} \quad \text{...(iii)}$$

The number of gram equivalent mass of solute dissolved in one litre of the solution is called the normality of the solution. For acids and bases,

$$\text{Normality } (N) = \frac{\text{Number of gram equivalent mass}}{\text{Volume of solution in litre (V)}}$$

$$= \frac{w / \text{Equivalent mass}}{\text{Volume of solution in litre (V)}} \quad \text{...(iv)}$$

where, w = mass of substance in grams

Also, $$\text{Normality} = \frac{\text{Strength of solution in gL}^{-1}}{\text{Equivalent mass}}$$

Strength of solution = Normality of solution × Equivalent mass.

Equivalent weights of some common acids, common bases and common salts are given in tabulated form below.

Equivalent weight of Common Acids

Acid	Molecular mass	Basicity	Equivalent weight
Hydrochloric acid, HCl	36.5	1	36.5
Oxalic acid, $(COOH)_2 2H_2O$	126	2	63

Equivalent weight of Common Bases

Base	Molecular mass	Acidity	Equivalent weight
Sodium hydroxide (NaOH)	40	1	40
Potassium hydroxide (KOH)	56	1	56

Equivalent weights of Common Salts

Salts	Molecular weight	Valency of metal	Equivalent weight
Sodium carbonate (Na_2CO_3)	106	2	53
Sodium chloride (NaCl)	58.5	1	58.5

Relationship between Normality and Molarity

$$N = a\,M \quad \text{...(v)}$$

Eq. (v) is the expression for the relationship between normality and molarity.

By substituting Eq. (v) in Eq. (i), we have

$$a_1\,M_1V_1 = a_2\,M_2V_2 \quad \text{...(vi)}$$

where, a_1 and a_2 are the basicity and acidity of acid and base respectively and M_1 and M_2 are the molar masses of acid and base respectively. Eq. (vi) can be used for making the solution by dilution for solutions of the same substance, $a_1 = a_2$. Therefore, for using Eq. (vi) for dilution of solution

$$M_1V_1 = M_2V_2 \quad \text{...(vii)}$$

Therefore, to obtain V_2 volume of a solution of molarity M_2 from a solution of molarity M_1, the volume V_1 of the solution of molarity M_1 which is required for dilution, can be calculated from Eq. (vii). $(V_2 - V_1)$ volume of solvent will be required to be added to V_1 volume of the solution of molarity M_1.

Standard Solution

A solution of exactly **known concentration** is called standard solution. Any substance, which is stable at room temperature and does not react with solvent in which it is dissolved, can be directly weighed to prepare its standard solution. Standard solution of an acid or a base is used to determine the unknown concentration of a solution of bases or acids by volumetric analysis. The strength of a standard solution is usually expressed in moles per litre.

Description and preparation of standard solutions is given below

Primary Standard

A primary standard is a compound of sufficient purity in which total amount of impurities does not exceed 0.01-0.02%. The standard solution of these compounds can be prepared by direct weighing of its sample followed by its dissolution in water (or solvent) to obtain a definite volume of solution. This is known as **direct method** of preparing standard solution. Thus, all substances whose standard solutions are prepared by the direct method are known as primary standards.

The substance to be used as a primary standard should also satisfy the following requirements

1. It must be easily available in pure and dry form.
2. It should not undergo any change in air, i.e., it should not be hygroscopic, oxidised by air or affected by gases such as carbon dioxide present in the atmosphere or lose water of crystallisation, so that it can be stored safely.
3. It should be easy to detect the impurities present in it.
4. It should have high **relative molecular mass** so that weighing errors are negligible.
5. Its reaction with another substance should be instantaneous and stoichiometric.
6. The substance should be readily soluble in water.

Note *It is difficult to obtain an ideal primary standard. Therefore, substances having characteristics nearer to the primary standards are usually employed.*

As a rule, unstable hydrated salts should not be used as primary standards. However, sodium carbonate, sodium tetraborate, potassium hydrogenphthalate, oxalic acid, ferrous ammonium sulphate etc., can be used as primary standards because of their sufficient stabilities.

Secondary Standard

The secondary standard solutions are prepared by the **indirect method**. An approximately desired weight of the substance is dissolved in water and the solution made to a known volume. The exact strength of the solution is then determined by titrating it with a suitable standard substance. This is called **standardisation**.

Thus, a solution of secondary standard is the one which may be used for standardisation after finding out its exact concentration by titrating it against a standard solution of primary standard. A secondary standard cannot be used for preparing standard solution by direct weighing. Sodium hydroxide, acetic acid and potassium permanganate are the examples of secondary standards.

Detection of End Point

The end point is detected either by some physical change produced in the reaction mixture itself or by the addition of an auxiliary reagent, known as **indicator**. At the completion of the reaction, the indicator shows a visible change, e.g. (colour change or turbidity) in the solution being titrated. In an ideal titration, the visible end point coincides with the stoichiometric or theoretical end point, but in practice usually some small difference occurs. This represents **titration error**.

Indicator and the experimental conditions selected should be such that the difference between the visible end point and the theoretical end point is minimum.

Indicators In Acid-Base Titration

Acid-base indicators are sensitive to pH change. For most acid-base titrations, it is possible to select indicators which exhibit colour change at pH close to the equivalence point. The two commonly used indicators are mentioned below

Phenolphthalein

Phenolphthalein is a weak acid, therefore it does not dissociate in the acidic medium and remains in the unionised form, which is colourless.

$$\underset{\text{Unionised colourless}}{HPh} \rightleftharpoons \underset{\text{Ionised pink}}{H^+ + Ph^-}$$

Ionised and unionised forms of phenolphthalein are given below

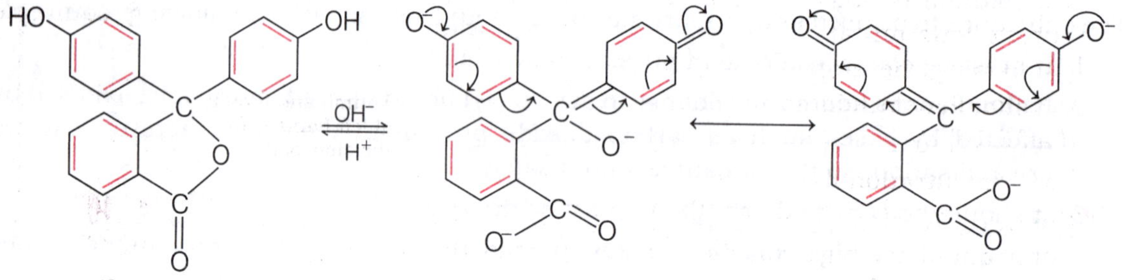

(Colourless in acid)

(Pink in alkali)

Fig 5.12 *Phenolphthalein in acidic and basic medium*

Methyl Orange

Methyl orange is a weak base and is yellow in colour in the unionised form.

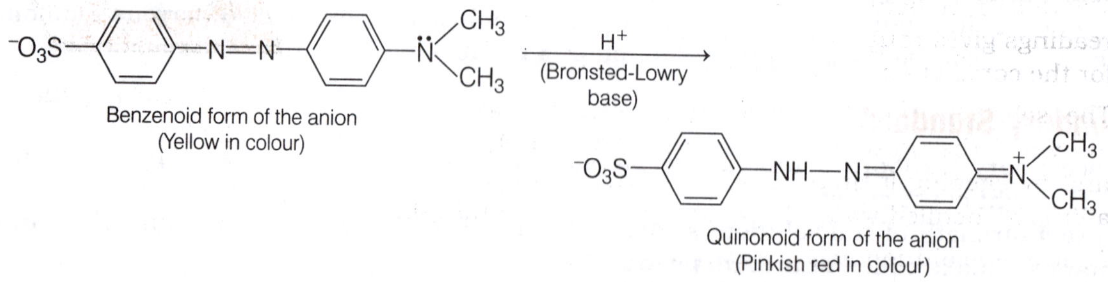

Benzenoid form of the anion (Yellow in colour)

H^+ (Bronsted-Lowry base)

Quinonoid form of the anion (Pinkish red in colour)

Fig. 5.13 *Structures of methyl orange*

Choice of Indicator

In the titration of a **strong acid (HCl, HNO_3, H_2SO_4)** and a **weak base** (Na_2CO_3, K_2CO_3, $NaHCO_3$, $KHCO_3$), methyl orange is chosen as an indicator (End point : Yellow to pink). When titration between **strong base** (NaOH, KOH) and **weak acid** (oxalic acid, acetic acid) is to be performed then phenolphthalein is a good indicator. In this case, alkali is dropped from the burette and acid is taken in the titration flask.

Colour of the solution taken in the titration flask changes from colourless to pink. This change of colour is easily perceptible to the human eye. If alkali is taken in the titration flask, the colour change will be from pink to colourless and accuracy in noting the colour change may be less. In the titration of **strong acid *versus* strong base**, anyone of the above indicators can be used. For the titration of weak acid *versus* weak base no indicator is available.

Procedure for Titration

The process of titration is used to find out the volume of one solution required to react completely with a certain known volume of solution of some other substance. Titration is the most important part of volumetric analysis.

It is carried out in the following steps

1. A glazed tile is placed below the burette and titration flask on the glazed tile below the burette nozzle. The height of the burette is so adjusted that the nozzle tip just enters the mouth of the titration flask.
2. The initial reading of the burette after filling it with the solution is noted down and solution from the burette (one mL at a time) is allowed to run out by opening the stopcock with the left hand. The titration flask is kept in the right hand as shown in [Fig. 5.14].
3. Swirl the titration flask throughout the titration.
4. Continue to run more of the solution from the burette into the titration flask, keeping it all the time shaking. The solution should fall directly into the solution of titration flask. It should not fall on the walls of the flask.
5. Stop adding the solution when the end point is reached and final reading of the burette is taken. The difference between the final and initial readings gives rough volume of the solution used for the completion of the reaction.
6. The solution from the titration flask is thrown away and the titration flask is washed thoroughly first by keeping it under tap water and then with a little of distilled water. Do not rinse the titration flask.
7. Pour more solution into the burette.

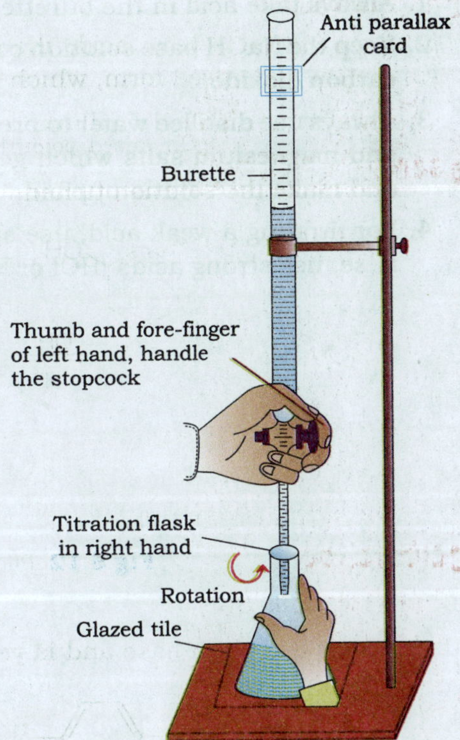

Fig. 5.14 *Handling of a burette in a correct way*

8. Pipette out 15 mL of the solution into the titration flask and add 1-2 drops of the indicator solution.
9. The initial reading of the burette is noted down. Run solution from the burette into the titration flask slowly with constant shaking. Continue to add the solution till the volume added is 1 mL less than the rough volume found out in the first titration. Now add the solution dropwise from the burette.
10. Continue to add the solution dropwise from the burette, till by addition of last single drop, the end point is attained.
11. Note down the final reading of the burette. The difference between the final and initial readings of the burette gives the exact volume of the solution required for the completion of the reaction.
12. Check the correctness of the end point by adding one drop of solution (taken in the titration flask) with the help of a pipette. Restoration of original colour confirms the correctness of the end point.
13. Perform 5 to 6 titrations so that at least three concordant readings (difference not more than 0.05 mL) are obtained.

Precautions in Titration

1. Always take acid in the burette and alkali in the titration flask.
2. Keep the NaOH base solution covered as far as possible to avoid absorption of atmospheric carbon dioxide.
3. Always use distilled water to prepare solution of base as tap water usually contains calcium and magnesium salts which get precipitated as carbonates and hydroxides, respectively and make the solution turbid.
4. For titrating a weak acid, use strong alkali (NaOH or KOH). Similarly, for titrating a weak base, use strong acids (HCl or H_2SO_4).

Experiment 5.1

AIM

Using a chemical balance.

Theory/Principle

The analytical balance is mainly used in volumetric analysis. The accuracy of the quantitative estimations in volumetric estimations depends upon the correct weighing of compounds which can be achieved only by using an analytical balance.

Materials Required

- Chemical balance : 1
- Weight box : 1
- Set of fractional weights along with rider : 1
- Weighing bottle/watch glass : 1

Procedure

Following steps are followed while using a chemical balance

1. Setting the Balance

Before weighing the substance, the balance should be cleaned and set in a proper position. It can be done as:

(i) With the help of leveling screws and plumb line, level the balance.

(ii) Ensure that the beam is horizontal. If it is not then, balance it by using leveling screws.

(iii) Check by raising the beam gently that pointer of the beam oscillates equal divisions on both sides of the zero of the base scale. If it is not so then arrest beam and move the adjusting screws till the pointer oscillates equally on both sides of zero mark.

2. Weighing of the Substance

Remember the following points when weighing a substance

(i) Place a clean and dry watch glass or weighing bottle on the left pan in which weighing material is kept. With the help of forceps, put approximate weights from the weight box on the right pan.

(ii) Note the movement of the pointer on the scale by releasing the beam arrest slowly. If its weight is not appropriate, the pointer will move towards the lighter side.

(iii) According to the requirement, add or remove weights after bringing the pans to rest by arresting the beam with the help of the knob located near the base. When weight on both the pans becomes equal, the pointer moves equal divisions on both sides of the zero of the base scale.

(iv) For adjustment of weight below 10 mg, use the rider.

(v) Arrest the beam and record the correct weight of substance (or compound).

3. Using Rider

For weighing chemicals by using the rider, principle of moment is applied. Weight is equal to the arm length from the centre of the beam multiplied by the weight of the rider. Length of the beam from the centre to one side of the beam is taken as unit length.

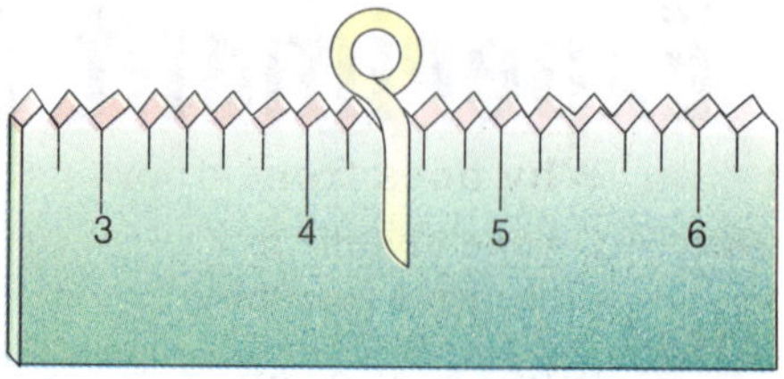

On both sides from the centre, the balance beam is divided into ten equal parts through equidistant marks, each of which corresponds to $\frac{1}{10}$th of the length of the beam. Hence, each big division corresponds to $\frac{1}{10} \times 0.01\,\text{g} = 0.001\,\text{g}$ or 1mg weight. Each big division is further divided into five parts.

Thus, each small division corresponds to only 1/5 milligram, i.e., 0.2 mg or 0.0002 g. Thus, the rider placed at the 4.2 mark will weigh 0.0044 g [i.e. $4 \times 0.001 + 2 \times 0.0002 = 0.0044$ g] [Fig. 5.15].

3 4 5 6

Fig 5.15 *Rider resting on groove of balance beam*

PRECAUTIONS

- *Before and after weighing, pans must be properly cleaned.*
- *Place the gram weights and fractional weights back into the weight box after weighing the substance.*
- *Chemicals should never be placed directly on the pans for weighing. Keep them in a watch glass or weighing bottle or on a paper.*
- *Do not overload the balance as overloading may damage the instrument.*
- *Always keep weights on the right pan and object on the left pan of the balance.*
- *Never weigh a hot or cold object on the balance.*
- *Always transfer the weights by the help of the forceps.*
- *Always release the beam gently.*
- *Do not allow the weights to get spoiled by corrosion.*
- *Hygroscopic substances must be weighed in closed weighing bottles.*
- *Always make necessary adjustments in the balance before weighing.*
- *To insert or remove weights and to keep the object on the pans always use the side doors. Never use the front shutter.*
- *Keep the doors shut while releasing the beam arrest to note the movement of the pointer on the scale.*
- *The balance must always be arrested before the objects or weights are placed or taken off the pans.*
- *Use the same balance and same weight box throughout the experiment. This reduces error in weighing.*

Q.1 Why does front door of the balance kept closed during weighing?

Ans. On opening the front door, vibrations are caused in the pan due to air currents which leads to inaccurate results.

Q.2 What is the minimum weight that can be weighed by the chemical balance?

Ans. 2×10^{-4} g is the minimum weight that can be weighed by the chemical balance using a rider.

Questions From NCERT Lab Manual

Q.1 How is an analytical balance different from a physical balance?

Ans. An analytical balance is more sensitive than physical balance and it can weigh upto 4 places of decimal.

Q.2 On what principle, is weighing by using rider based?

Ans. Principle of moment is applied for weighing of chemicals by using rider.

Q.3 Why are forceps always used for handling the weights?

Ans. Forceps are always used for handling the weights so that no impurity may stick to the weights and we can get more accurate results.

Q.4 Which weights are called fractional weights?

Ans. Milligram (mg) weights are called fractional weights.

Q.5 Can you weigh 0.0023 g using a chemical balance? Give reason for your answer.

Ans. Yes, we can weigh 0.0023 g objects by using a chemical balance with the help of a rider.

Q.6 What is the maximum weight that can be weighed on a chemical balance?

Ans. Chemical or analytical balance can be used to weigh the mass of a substance maximum upto $\pm$ 0.0002 g with great accuracy.

Q.7 The rider rests at a reading of 3.4 on the left side of the beam. What contribution does this make to the weight of the material being weighed when weights are placed on the right pan?

Ans. When the rider rests at a reading of 3.4, this suggests that the object will weigh 0.0038 g ($3 \times 0.001 + 4 \times 0.0002$). Thus, the total weights of 0.0038 g to be placed on the right pan such that the pans comes to rest and pointer moves equal divisions on both sides of the zero of the base scale.

Experiment 5.2

AIM

Preparation of M/10 (or N/5) standard solution of oxalic acid.

Theory/Principle

Oxalic acid is a primary standard and thus, used as a standard solution to determine the unknown concentration of an alkali solution. It is neither deliquescent nor efflorescent. It does not decompose on exposure to air and forms a stable solution. The formula of hydrated crystalline oxalic acid is as follows

$$\begin{array}{l} COOH \\ | \qquad \cdot 2H_2O \\ COOH \end{array}$$

Its molar mass is 126 g/mol and due to the presence of two replaceable hydrogen ions, it has a basicity of 2.

$\therefore$ Equivalent mass of acid $= \frac{\text{Molecular mass}}{\text{Basicity}} = \frac{126}{2} = 63$ g/equivalent.

Calculation of Amount of Oxalic Acid to be Weighed (when molarity is given)

If 126 g of oxalic acid is present in one litre of the solution, it is known as **one molar** (1.0 M) **solution**.

For the preparation of one litre of $\frac{M}{10}$ i.e. 0.1 M oxalic acid solution, we require $\frac{126}{10} = 12.6$ g of hydrated oxalic acid.

Therefore, for preparing 250 mL of 0.1 M oxalic acid solution, we require

$$\frac{12.6\ \text{g} \times 250\ \text{mL}}{1000\ \text{mL}} = 3.1500 \text{ g of hydrated oxalic acid.}$$

In general, for preparing a solution of required molarity, the amount of substance to be weighed can be calculated by using the formula given below

$$\text{Molarity } (M) = \frac{\text{Mass of solute (in g)} \times 1000}{\text{Molar mass of solute} \times \text{volume of solution to be prepared (in mL)}}$$

$\therefore$ Mass of solute (in g)

$$= \frac{\text{Molarity } (M) \times \text{ molar mass of solute} \times \text{ volume of solution to be prepared (in mL)}}{1000}$$

Calculation of Amount of Oxalic acid to be Weighed (when normality is given)

Equivalent mass of oxalic acid $= \frac{\text{Molecular mass}}{\text{Basicity}} = \frac{126}{2} = 63$ g/equivalent

For the preparation of one litre of 0.2 N $\left[\text{or } \frac{N}{5}\right]$ oxalic acid solution, oxalic acid required is $\frac{63}{5}$ g = 12.6g of hydrated oxalic acid.

Therefore, for preparing 250 mL of 0.2 N of oxalic acid solution,

we require $\frac{12.6\ \text{g} \times 250\ \text{mL}}{1000\ \text{mL}} = 3.1500$ g of hydrated oxalic acid.

In general, for preparing a solution of required normality, the amount of substance to be weighed can be calculated by using the formula given below

$$\text{Normality } (N) = \frac{\text{Mass of solute (in g)} \times 1000}{\text{Equivalent mass of solute} \times \text{volume of solution (in mL)}}$$

$$\Rightarrow \text{Mass of solute (in g)} = \frac{\text{Normality } (N) \times \text{Equivalent mass of solute} \times \text{volume of solution (in mL)}}{1000}$$

Materials Required

▪ Measuring flask (250 mL)	:	1	▪ Oxalic acid	:	As per need
▪ Funnel	:	1	▪ Weighing tube/Watch glass	:	1
▪ Wash bottle	:	1	▪ Iron stand with clamp	:	1
▪ Analytical balance and its weight box	:	1	▪ Dropper	:	1

Procedure

Weighing of Oxalic Acid

1. Weigh accurately an empty, clean and dry watch glass or weighing tube (w_1 g) on an analytical balance.
2. Now, weigh w_2 g of oxalic acid by placing it on the above weighed clean and dry watch glass or weighing tube and note weight upto the fourth decimal place, which is equal to 3.1500 g of oxalic acid. This w_2 is the combined mass of watch glass and oxalic acid. Clean the balance before and after weighing the chemicals.

⚠ ALERT

- *Oxalic acid is harmful and dangerous for the environment.*
- *Chemicals should not be spilled on the pan of the weighing balance.*

Transferring of Oxalic Acid

3. Transfer oxalic acid carefully from the watch glass or weighing tube into a clean and dry measuring flask using a funnel placed over it. [Fig. 5.16]
4. Weigh the empty watch glass again (w_3) and find out the mass of oxalic acid transferred to the measuring flask by subtracting this mass (w_3) from the combined mass of watch glass and oxalic acid (w_2). Calculate the exact molarity of the solution from this mass.

Fig. 5.16 *Transferring the oxalic acid into flask*

Diluting Oxalic Acid and Preparing its Solution

5. Use a wash bottle to wash the funnel repeatedly (with small amounts of distilled water) so that sticking particles of oxalic acid if any goes into the measuring flask [Fig. 5.17].
6. While washing the funnel, add water in small amounts so that its volume in the flask does not exceed 1/4th of the measuring flask [Fig 5.17].
7. Swirl the measuring flask slowly till solid oxalic acid dissolves completely.

8. Fill measuring flask with distilled water just below the graduated mark on it along with shaking.
9. Add the last few mL of distilled water dropwise using a dropper until the lower level of the meniscus just touches the graduated mark on the measuring flask [Fig. 5.18 (i)].
10. Place the stopper on the measuring flask and shake it gently to make the solution uniform throughout [Fig 5.18 (ii)]. Label it as $\frac{M}{10}$ (or $N/5$) oxalic acid solution.

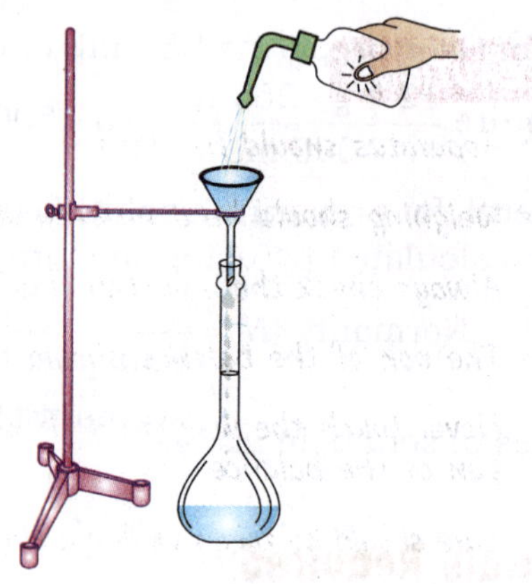

Fig. 5.17 *Washing the funnel (Diluting the solution)*

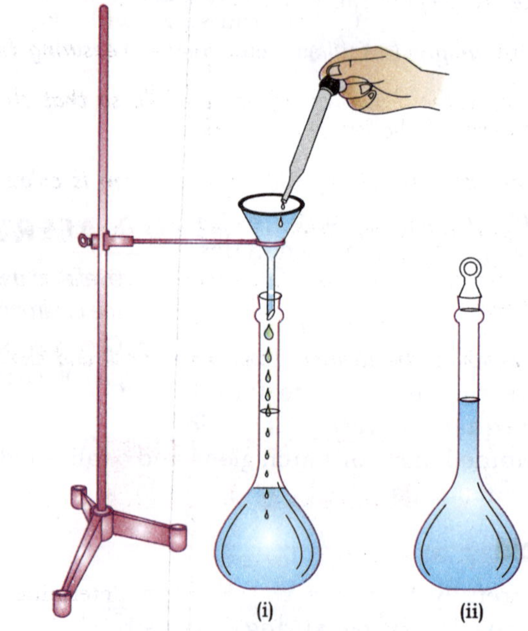

Fig. 5.18 *(i) Adding of distilled water*
(ii) Standard solution of oxalic acid

Calculation

Weight of empty watch glass = w_1 g

Weight of watch glass + oxalic acid = w_2 g

∴ Weight of the oxalic acid = $w_2 - w_1 = w$ g

Volume of the solution to be prepared = 250 mL

Normality of the oxalic acid solution $= \dfrac{w \times 1000}{250 \times 63}$

Molarity of the oxalic acid solution $= \dfrac{w \times 1000}{250 \times 126}$

Result

A standard solution of $M/10$ or $(N/5)$ oxalic acid is obtained.

PRECAUTIONS

- *Apparatus should be clean.*
- *Weighing should be done accurately.*
- *Always check the adjustment of the balance before weighing the substance.*
- *The pan of the balance should be cleaned before and after weighing.*
- *Never touch the weights with hands. Use forceps to transfer weights from the weight box to the pan of the balance.*
- *Care should be taken while weighing the chemicals. These should not be spilled on the pan of the balance.*
- *Always use spatula to transfer the reagent from the bottle on to the watch glass.*
- *Always use distilled water to prepare the standard solution.*
- *Use dropper to fill the last drops of distilled water in the measuring flask.*
- *While making the solution, water should be added carefully so that the lower part of the meniscus just touches the etched mark of the measuring flask.*
- *Lower meniscus should be observed, since, oxalic acid solution is colourless.*
- *Stopper the reagent bottle immediately after withdrawing the substance.*
- *Watch glass/weighing bottle and funnel should be washed several times by using small amounts of distilled water each time.*
- *To ensure uniform composition of the solution, stopper the flask and shake it carefully and thoroughly.*

Viva-Voce

Q.1 What do you mean by a standard solution?

Ans. A standard solution is a solution of known and accurately determined concentration prepared using a known quantity of solute dissolved in a definite volume of solvent.

Q.2 Why is oxalic acid considered a primary standard substance?

Ans. Oxalic acid is a primary standard because it is available in pure and stable form, has high molar mass, is non-hygroscopic, and can be weighed directly to prepare a solution of known concentration.

Q.3 What is meant by molarity of a solution?

Ans. Molarity (M) is defined as the number of moles of solute dissolved per litre of solution.

Q.4 Which apparatus is used for the accurate preparation of a standard solution?

Ans. A volumetric flask is used to prepare a standard solution accurately as it has a precise calibration mark for a fixed volume

Q.5 Why should the oxalic acid be transferred completely from the beaker to the volumetric flask?

Ans. Complete transfer ensures that the entire weighed amount of oxalic acid enters the solution to maintaining accuracy of molarity.

Q.6 Why is it necessary to rinse the funnel and beaker used in transferring oxalic acid?

Ans. Rinsing ensures that no portion of the solute remains behind in the beaker or funnel, ensuring the correct amount is transferred to the volumetric flask.

Q.7 **What is the significance of using a volumetric flask and not a measuring cylinder for this preparation?**

Ans. A volumetric flask provides much greater accuracy in measuring the exact volume required for standard solutions.

Q.8 **How is the final volume of the solution adjusted in a volumetric flask?**

Ans. The final volume is adjusted by carefully adding distilled water drop by drop using a dropper until the bottom of the meniscus touches the calibration mark.

Q.9 **What precautions must be taken while weighing oxalic acid?**

Ans. Weighing should be done on a clean and dry watch glass using an accurate balance, and the mass should be measured to the nearest milligram.

Q.10 **Can oxalic acid be directly used for titration after preparation?**

Ans. Yes, the freshly prepared 0.1 M oxalic acid solution can be directly used as a standard solution in titration.

Q.11 **What is the difference between a primary and secondary standard solution?**

Ans. A primary standard solution is prepared by directly dissolving a known mass of pure substance, while a secondary standard solution is standardised against a primary standard.

Questions From NCERT Lab Manual

Q.1 **What is the formula and the basicity of hydrated oxalic acid and anhydrous oxalic acid?**

Ans. Hydrated oxalic acid has the formula $\begin{array}{c}COOH\\ |\\ COOH\end{array} \cdot 2H_2O$

Its basicity is two. Anhydrous oxalic acid is $\begin{array}{c}COOH\\ |\\ COOH\end{array}$. Its basicity is also two.

Q.2 **What do you mean by 1.0 M solution?**

Ans. A solution containing one mole of solute per litre of solution is called 1.0 M solution.

Q.3 **Why are standard solutions always prepared in a volumetric flask?**

Ans. Volumetric flask is always used to maintain precision while preparing or diluting the standard solution.

Q.4 **Can solid NaOH be used to prepare its standard solution?**

Ans. No, because it is deliquescent or hygroscopic in nature, i.e., it absorbs moisture from air.

Q.5 **What type of substances can be used for preparing standard solution?**

Ans. A substance fulfilling the following criteria can be used for preparing standard solutions

(i) It should be easily available in pure and dry form.

(ii) It should not be hygroscopic, deliquescent or efflorescent in nature.

(iii) It should not be oxidised by air.

(iv) It should be readily soluble and its solution should be stable.

Q.6 **How will you prepare 260 mL of 0.05 M oxalic acid solution?**

Ans. $$\text{Molarity} = \frac{\text{Mass of solute (in g)} \times 1000}{\text{Molecular weight} \times \text{Volume of solution (mL)}}$$

$$0.05\ \text{M} = \frac{\text{Mass of oxalic acid (in g)} \times 1000}{126 \times 250} = 1.575 \text{ g of oxalic acid}$$

Hence, 1.575 g of oxalic acid is dissolved in 250 mL of distilled water to get 0.05 M or $\frac{M}{20}$ oxalic acid solution.

Q.7 **What is meant by 'weighing by transfer'? When is this used?**

Ans. Weighing by transfer means that once the substance is transferred from the watch glass to the measuring flask, weigh the empty watch glass again and find the mass of the substance transferred by subtracting this mass from the weight of combined mass of watch glass and oxalic acid. It is used to calculate the strength of the solution from this mass.

Experiment 5.3

AIM

To determine the strength (concentration) of a given solution of sodium hydroxide by titrating it against a standard solution of oxalic acid.

Theory/Principle

In the titration of a strong acid with a strong base, the amount of acid and base becomes chemically equivalent at the end point and the chemical reaction is called **neutralisation reaction**. Near the end point, there is a sudden change in the pH of the solution. If after end point even a small amount of base/acid is added, the solution would become slightly **alkaline** or **acidic** respectively. Here, oxalic acid (weak acid) is titrated against sodium hydroxide solution (strong base) by using phenolphthalein as an indicator. The reaction between oxalic acid and sodium hydroxide can be depicted as

$$\underset{\text{Hydrated oxalic acid}}{\begin{matrix}COOH\\ |\\ COOH\end{matrix}} \cdot 2H_2O + \underset{\text{Sodium hydroxide}}{2NaOH} \longrightarrow \underset{\text{Sodium oxalate}}{\begin{matrix}COONa\\ |\\ COONa\end{matrix}} + 4H_2O$$

Indicator

In this titration phenolphthalein (HPh) is used as an indicator.

Materials Required

- Burette (50 mL) : 1
- Pipette (10 mL) : 1
- Conical flask (100 mL) : 1
- Burette stand : 1
- Funnel : 1
- White glazed tile : 1
- Measuring flask (100 mL) : 1
- Oxalic acid : As per need
- Sodium hydroxide (NaOH) solution : As per need
- Phenolphthalein indicator : As per need

Procedure

Preparation of 0.1 M Standard Solution of Oxalic Acid

1. To prepare $\frac{M}{10}$ (or $N/5$) standard solution of oxalic acid, follow the same procedure as described in Experiment 5.2.

> **ALERT**
> - *Sodium hydroxide (deliquescent, crystalline solid) is corrosive. It readily attacks on skin and forms a pasty mass.*
> - *Oxalic acid is harmful and irritant.*

Filling of Burette with NaOH Solution and taking Initial Observations

2. Clean and wash the burette thoroughly with distilled water and then finally rinse it with Sodium hydroxide (NaOH) solution (always rinse the burette [Fig. 5.19] with the solution, which is to be taken in it). Clamp the burette vertically in a burette stand.
3. Fill NaOH solution into the burette through a funnel above the zero mark.
4. Run the solution forcefully from the burette nozzle to remove the air gap, if any.
5. Remove the funnel before noting initial reading of the burette. Also while noting the reading, see that no drop of the liquid is hanging at the nozzle of the burette.
6. Note the initial reading by keeping the eye exactly at the same level as the meniscus of the solution.

Titration of NaOH and Oxalic Acid Solution by Using Phenolphthalein as an Indicator

7. Pipette out 10 mL of oxalic acid solution in a clean and dried conical flask. Always wash the pipette with water and rinse with the liquid to be measured before pipetting out the liquid.
8. Add 1-2 drops of phenolphthalein indicator to the conical flask. Adjust the flow of liquid by thumb and two fingers held around the stop cock with a slight inward pressure on the plug to prevent leakage. Place the flask on a glazed tile or white filter paper as shown in [Fig 5.19]. Swirl the liquid during the titration.

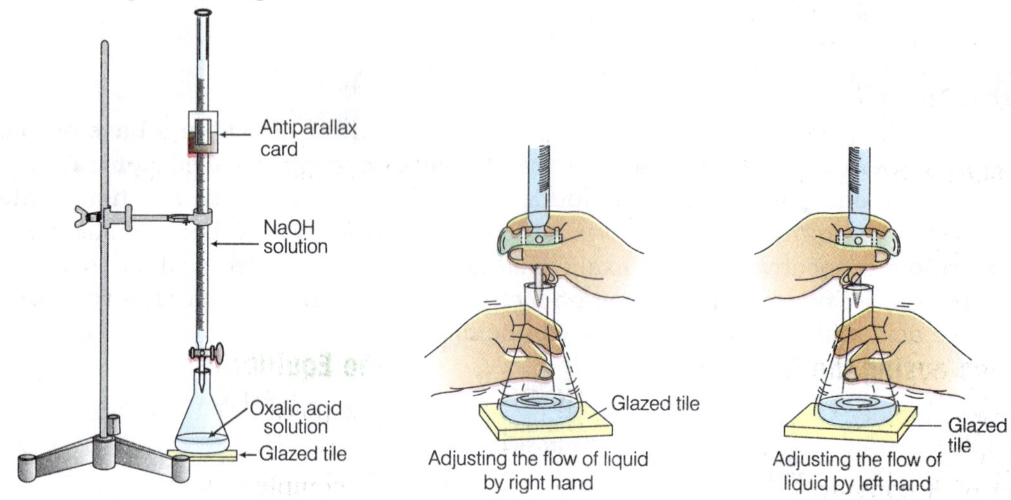

Fig 5.19 *Titrating the solution*

9. Titrate the acid with NaOH solution till a very faint permanent pink colour is obtained. Initially, add the NaOH solution in small quantities after that, add it in a dropwise manner.
10. Read the lower meniscus of the solution in the burette again as the permanent pink colour appears and record it as final reading.
11. Repeat the procedure until three concordant readings are obtained.
12. Record the three concordant readings in the observation table 5.1.

Observation

Solution in burette = NaOH; Solution in conical flask = oxalic acid

Indicator = phenolphthalein; End point = colourless to pink

Table 5.1. Titration of sodium hydroxide *vs* oxalic acid solution

S.No.	Volume of oxalic acid solution taken in conical flask each time (V_1 mL)	Burette readings		Volume of sodium hydroxide solution used V_2 mL = $(y - x)$ mL	Concordant reading (in mL)
		Initial reading (x)	Final reading (y)		
1.					
2.					
3.					

Calculations

When normality is given

$$N_1V_1 = N_2V_2 \quad \Rightarrow \quad N_{\text{oxalic acid}} \times V_{\text{oxalic acid}} = N_{\text{NaOH}} \times V_{\text{NaOH}}$$

$$N_{\text{NaOH}} = \frac{N_{\text{oxalic acid}} \times V_{\text{oxalic acid}}}{V_{\text{NaOH}}}$$

Strength of NaOH solution = N_{NaOH} × Equivalent weight of NaOH= $N_{NaOH} \times 40$ g/L.

When molarity is given $a_1 M_1 V_1 = a_2 M_2 V_2$

$$\Rightarrow a_{\text{oxalic acid}} \times M_{\text{oxalic acid}} \times V_{\text{oxalic acid}} = a_{NaOH} \times M_{NaOH} \times V_{NaOH}$$

$$M_{NaOH} = \frac{a_{\text{oxalic acid}} \times M_{\text{oxalic acid}} \times V_{\text{oxalic acid}}}{a_{NaOH} \times V_{NaOH}}$$

where, a_1 and a_2 are respectively the basicity of oxalic acid and acidity of sodium hydroxide solutions. In this case, $a_1 = 2$ and $a_2 = 1$.

Molar mass of oxalic acid $(M_1) = 126 \text{g/mol}$

Molar mass of sodium hydroxide $(M_2) = 40 \text{g/mol}$

Strength of NaOH solution = M_{NaOH} × Molar mass of NaOH = $M_{NaOH} \times 40$ g/L

Result

The strength of NaOH solution is .... g/L.

PRECAUTIONS

- *All the apparatus used should be cleaned, washed and rinsed thoroughly.*
- *Always rinse the burette with the solution, which is to be taken in it.*
- *Remove the air gap if any, from the burette before titrating the solution. Make sure that the nozzle of burette is also filled.*
- *Never forget to remove the funnel from the burette before noting the readings of the burette and ensure that no drop is hanging from the nozzle of the burette.*
- *Always read the lower meniscus for all transparent solutions and upper meniscus for coloured solutions.*
- *Never suck a strong alkali or acid with the pipette in your mouth. Use pipette sucker or dropper.*
- *Always keep the lower end of the pipette dipped in the liquid while sucking the liquid.*
- *Never hold the pipette at the bulb.*
- *Alkali solution should be added dropwise with constant shaking of the flask.*
- *To note the burette readings, place the eye exactly at the level of the meniscus.*
- *Do not blow out the last drop of the solution from the jet end of the pipette into the flask.*
- *Do not leave the alkali solution in the burette, wash the burette after completing the experiment.*
- *The concentration/strength of the solution must be calculated upto the fourth places of decimal.*
- *Never use the burette and pipette with a broken nozzle.*

Viva-Voce

Q.1 What type of reaction takes place in this titration?

Ans. A neutralisation reaction takes place between oxalic acid (a weak acid) and sodium hydroxide (a strong base).

Q.2 How is the strength (concentration) of NaOH in g/L calculated?

Ans. Strength $\left(\frac{g}{L}\right)$ = Molarity × Molar Mass = $M_2 \times 40$

Q.3 **Why is the burette rinsed with sodium hydroxide before titration?**

Ans. Rinsing with NaOH ensures the solution inside is not diluted or contaminated by residual water, which could affect the accuracy.

Q.4 **Why should the funnel be removed from the burette before starting titration?**

Ans. If the funnel is not removed then extra drops may leak from the funnel into the burette and alter the volume thus affecting the accuracy.

Q.5 **Why is the lower meniscus read for colourless solutions like NaOH?**

Ans. Because colourless solutions do not obscure the curved surface, the lower meniscus gives the correct volume reading.

Q.6 **What precautions should be taken while using a pipette?**

Ans. Never blow out the last drop, always rinse with the solution to be pipetted, and do not hold it at the bulb.

Q.7 **Why is the solution swirled during titration?**

Ans. Swirling helps to mix the acid and base thoroughly thus ensuring complete and uniform neutralisation at every stage.

Questions From NCERT Lab Manual

Q.1 **Why are the burette and the pipette rinsed with the solution with which these are filled?**

Ans. In order to remove any substance sticking to their sides, which otherwise decreases the volume of the liquids to be taken in the burette and the pipette and effect the concentration of the solution.

Q.2 **What is an indicator?**

Ans. It is a chemical substance which exhibits colour change at pH close to equivalence point, gives different colours in different mediums and helps in the detection of the end point.

Q.3 **Which indicator is used in the titration of oxalic acid *versus* sodium hydroxide? Can the titration be performed by using some other indicator?**

Ans. Phenolphthalein. No, the titration cannot be performed by using any other indicator.

Q.4 **Explain the term 'end point'.**

Ans. During titration, the stage at which the reaction is just completed or the point at which the indicator changes its colour is known as 'end point'.

Q.5 **Why should the last drop of the solution not be blown out of a pipette?**

Ans. Because the drops left in the jet end is extra of the volume measured by pipette.

Q.6 **Explain the term basicity of an acid and acidity of a base.**

Ans. Number of replaceable hydroxyl (OH^-) ions furnished by a molecule of the base is known as its acidity. And the basicity of an acid is the number of replaceable hydrogen (H^+) ions furnished by a molecule of an acid.

Q.7 **What is meant by the term concordant readings?**

Ans. The readings in volumetric analysis which differ by less than 0.05 mL are called concordant readings.

Q.8 **Why should one read the lower meniscus in the case of colourless and transparent solutions and the upper meniscus for the solutions of dark colour?**

Ans. It is easy and convenient to read the lower meniscus in case of colourless solution and the upper meniscus in case of coloured solutions.

Q.9 **For titrating NaOH *vs* HCl, phenolphthalein and methyl orange, both are suitable indicators. Why?**

Ans. As, NaOH and HCl are strong base and strong acid respectively, and in their titration, the pH changes rapidly from 3 to 11 range, thus their end point range can be easily detected by these indicators and hence, phenolphthalein and methyl orange, both can be used as indicators.

Q.10 **Can one take oxalic acid solution in the burette and sodium hydroxide solution in the titration flask? Point out the limitations of doing so, if any.**

Ans. No, because generally NaOH solution is taken in the burette and the oxalic acid in the titration flask because the sharperness of the endpoint (colourless to pink) is easier to detect visually.

Experiment 5.4

AIM

To prepare a 0.1 M standard solution of sodium carbonate.

Theory/Principle

Sodium carbonate is used as a primary standard as its characteristics are nearer to primary standards. Therefore, its standard solution can be made by direct weighing. **Anhydrous sodium carbonate** (i.e. a water soluble sodium salt of carbonic acid) has a molecular weight of 106 g/mol.

If 106 g of anhydrous sodium carbonate is present in one litre of the solution, it is known as one **molar** (1.0 M) **solution**. Thus, for the preparation of one litre of 0.1 M anhydrous sodium carbonate, we require $106 \times 0.1 = 10.6000$ g of anhydrous sodium carbonate.

Hence, to prepare 250 mL of 0.1 M Na_2CO_3 solution, anhydrous sodium carbonate required will be $\frac{10.6 \times 250}{1000} = 2.65$ g

Therefore, to prepare 250 mL of 0.1 M Na_2CO_3 solution, 2.65 g of anhydrous carbonate is dissolved in minimum quantity of water and the solution is diluted to exactly 250 mL by adding water to it.

Note *Sodium carbonate commonly occurs as a crystalline heptahydrate* ($Na_2CO_3 \cdot 7H_2O$) *and it readily effloresces to form a white powder, the monohydrate.*

Materials required

- Measuring flask (100 mL) : 1
- Funnel : 1
- Sodium carbonate : As per need
- Watch glass : 1
- Wash bottle : 1
- Dropper : 1

Procedure

Same as in Experiment 5.2.

Calculation

Weight of the empty watch glass $= w_1$ g

Weight of the (watch glass + anhydrous Na_2CO_3) $= w_2$ g

Weight of the anhydrous Na_2CO_3 dissolved $= w_2 - w_1 = w$ g

Volume of the solution prepared = 250 mL

$\therefore$ Molarity of the solution $= \frac{w \times 1000}{250 \times 106}$

ALERT

Sodium carbonate is of low hazard but has irritating odour.

Result

A standard solution of 0.1 M sodium carbonate is prepared.

Note *Precautions for this experiment are same as in experiment 5.2.*

Viva-Voce

Q.1 What type of substance is sodium carbonate with respect to standard solutions?

Ans. Sodium carbonate behaves like a primary standard because it is stable, pure, and has a definite composition.

Q.2 Why is the acidity of sodium carbonate considered to be 2?

Ans. Each molecule of Na_2CO_3 provides two OH^- equivalents because it reacts with two H^+ ions, hence its acidity is 2.

Q.3 What is the first step in preparing a standard solution?

Ans. Accurately weigh the required amount of sodium carbonate on a watch glass.

Q.4 Why is sodium carbonate solution weakly alkaline in nature?

Ans. It undergoes hydrolysis in water forming carbonate ions, which react with water to release OH. ions, making the solution basic.

Q.5 Why should sodium carbonate be dissolved in a minimum quantity of water initially?

Ans. To ensure complete dissolution before transferring it to the measuring flask.

Q.6 What should be done if solid particles are visible in the solution?

Ans. The solution should be shaken or stirred until all particles are completely dissolved.

Q.7 What is the function of the watch glass in this experiment?

Ans. It is used to weigh the required amount of sodium carbonate accurately before transferring it for dissolution.

Questions From NCERT Lab Manual

Q.1 Though, sodium carbonate is a salt yet its aqueous solution is weakly alkaline in nature. Explain why?

Ans. Sodium carbonate is a salt of a strong base (NaOH) and a weak acid (H_2CO_3) and hence releases hydroxide ions in larger concentration than hydrogen ions. Hence, it is alkaline in aqueous solution.

Q.2 How can you determine the acidity of sodium carbonate solution?

Ans. Acidity of salt is equal to the total valency of metal ion. In sodium carbonate (Na_2CO_3), two sodium ions are present, therefore acidity of Na_2CO_3 equals to 2.

Q.3 How will you prepare 250 mL of 0.05 M sodium carbonate solution?

Ans.

$$\text{Molarity} = \frac{w_{Na_2CO_3}}{\text{Molecular weight}} \times \frac{1000}{250}$$

$$\Rightarrow \quad 0.05 = \frac{w_{Na_2CO_3}}{106} \times \frac{1000}{250}$$

$$\Rightarrow \quad w_{Na_2CO_3} = \frac{106}{20 \times 4} = 1.325\,\text{g}$$

$\therefore$ 1.325 g of Na_2CO_3 should be dissolved in 250 mL of distilled water to get 0.05 M solution.

Experiment 5.5

AIM

To determine the strength of a given solution of hydrochloric acid by titrating it against standard sodium carbonate solution.

Theory/Principle

The strength of hydrochloric acid (HCl) is determined by titrating it against a standard solution of sodium carbonate (Na_2CO_3). When Na_2CO_3 reacts with HCl, the following reaction takes place:

$$Na_2CO_3 + 2HCl \longrightarrow 2NaCl + CO_2 + H_2O$$

In this titration, **methyl orange**, a weak base which is yellow in the unionised form, is used as an indicator. In this experiment, the proton furnished by the addition of the acid, first neutralises Na_2CO_3 solution.

Once the entire solution of sodium carbonate is neutralised, the last drop of the acid added from the burette produces the **pinkish red colour** change. This change in colour indicates the end point of titration.

Indicator

Methyl orange and End point Indicator : Methyl orange

End point : Yellow to pinkish-red

Materials Required

- Burette (50 mL) : 1
- Pipette (10 mL) : 1
- Conical flask (100 mL) : As per need
- Burette stand : 1
- Beaker (100 mL) : As per need
- Glazed tile (white) : 1
- Measuring flask (100 mL) : 1
- Dropper : As per need
- Funnel : 1
- Hydrochloric acid : As per need
- Sodium carbonate solution : As per need
- Methyl orange solution : As per need

Procedure

Preparation of $M/10$ (0.1 M) Standard Solution of Sodium Carbonate

1. To prepare $\frac{M}{10}$ [or 0.1 M] standard solution of sodium carbonate, follow the same procedure as described in Experiment 5.2.

⚠ ALERT

- Hydrochloric acid is harmful, corrosive and dangerous for the environment.
- The concentrated HCl should be supplied in small bottles.

Filling the Burette with HCl

2. Wash the burette with distilled water and then rinse and fill the burette with the hydrochloric acid solution above the zero mark. Run the HCl solution to remove the air gap (if any) from the nozzle of the burette.
3. Note down the burette reading which is the initial burette reading.

Addition of Indicator to Na_2CO_3 Solution

4. Rinse the pipette with the given sodium carbonate solution and then pipette out 10 mL of sodium carbonate solution into the conical or titration flask.
5. Add 2-3 drops of methyl orange as an indicator to the conical flask.

Titration of HCl by Standard Na_2CO_3 Solution

6. Place this conical flask under the burette above a glazed tile and start adding HCl solution dropwise to the conical flask until the colour of the solution just changes from yellow to pinkish red.
7. Note down the burette reading which is the final reading.
8. Repeat the experiment until three concordant readings are obtained.
9. Record your observations in table 5.2.

Observation

Solution in burette = HCl　　　Solution in conical flask = Na_2CO_3

Indicator = Methyl orange　　　End point = Yellow to pink-red

Table 5.2 Titration of hydrochloric acid with standard sodium carbonate solution

S.No.	Volume of Na_2CO_3 solution taken in the conical flask each time (V_1 mL)	Burette readings		Volume of HCl solution used V_2 mL = (y – x) mL	Concordant reading (in mL)
		Initial reading (x)	Final reading (y)		

Concordant reading = ... mL

Calculation

The strength of HCl solution is calculated by using the molarity equation

$$a_1 M_1 V_1 = a_2 M_2 V_2$$

$$(Na_2CO_3) \qquad (HCl)$$

where a_1 is the acidity of Na_2CO_3 solution, i.e., the number of $OH^-(aq)$ ions supplied by one mole of the base and a_2 is the basicity of HCl solution, i.e., number of moles of $H^+(aq)$ ions supplied by one mole of the base. M_1 and V_1 are the molarity and volume of Na_2CO_3 solution respectively and M_2 and V_2 are the molarity and volume of HCl solution respectively.

In this case,

$$a_1 = 2 \text{ and } a_2 = 1$$

Molar mass of $Na_2CO_3 (M_1) = 106$ g / mol

Molar mass of HCl $(M_2) = 36.5$ g/mol

Strength (concentration) of HCl solution in g/L = Molarity × Molar mass

= Molarity × 36.5 g/mol

Result

The strength (or concentration) of the given HCl solution is ...... g/L.

PRECAUTIONS

- *Care should be taken while handling the acid and base.*
- *Always rinse the burette and the pipette with the solution which is to be taken in them.*
- *Remove the air gap if any, from the burette before titration.*
- *Never forget to remove the funnel from the burette before noting the initial reading of the burette and ensure that no drop is hanging from the nozzle.*
- *Always read the lower meniscus for all transparent solutions and upper meniscus for the coloured solutions.*
- *Never use burette and pipette with a broken nozzle.*
- *Never suck a strong alkali or an acid with the pipette. Always use a pipette bulb.*
- *Always keep the lower end of the pipette dipped in the liquid while sucking the liquid.*
- *While transferring the solution to the flask, do not blow out the last drop of the solution from the jet of the pipette.*
- *Note down the reading accurately.*
- *The strength of the solution must be calculated upto the fourth decimal place.*

Q.1 Why is methyl orange used as an indicator in the titration of HCl against sodium carbonate?

Ans. Methyl orange is suitable because the titration involves a strong acid (HCl) and a weak base (Na_2CO_3), and methyl orange gives a clear colour change in the acidic pH range.

Q.2 What is the end point in this titration and what is the colour change?

Ans. The end point is when all sodium carbonate has reacted with hydrochloric acid, indicated by a colour change from yellow to pinkish-red due to methyl orange.

Q.3 What is the basicity of hydrochloric acid in this titration?

Ans. The basicity of HCl is 1 because each molecule provides only one H^+ ion in solution.

Q.4 Can you use phenolphthalein instead of methyl orange in this titration? Why or why not?

Ans. No, phenolphthalein is not suitable here because the titration ends in an acidic pH range where phenolphthalein remains colourless. Methyl orange changes colour appropriately in acidic conditions.

Q.5 What is the difference between end point and equivalence point?

Ans. The equivalence point is the theoretical point where equivalent amounts of acid and base have reacted, while the end point is the practical point indicated by a colour change of the indicator.

Q.6 What precaution should be taken while pipetting sodium carbonate solution?

Ans. The pipette should be rinsed with the sodium carbonate solution before use, and one should not blow out the last drop from the pipette into the conical flask.

Q.7 Why is it necessary to record burette readings by placing the eye at the level of the meniscus?

Ans. To avoid parallax error and ensure accurate volume readings.

Q.8 What will happen if sodium carbonate is taken in the burette and HCl in the conical flask?

Ans. It is not recommended because methyl orange changes colour in acidic medium, so the end point may not be visible clearly if acid is not added from the burette.

Questions From NCERT Lab Manual

Q.1 Why is methyl orange not an Arrhenius base?

Ans. An Arrhenius base is one which produces hydroxide ions in aqueous solution. Methyl orange does not furnish OH^- ions in solution. Rather, it accepts proton, thus it is a Bronsted-Lowry base.

Q.2 How can you titrate a solution of Na_2CO_3 and $NaHCO_3$ against HCl?

Ans. By using double indicators-phenolphthalein and methyl orange.

Q.3 What is the difference between an end point and an equivalence point?

Ans. In any titration, end point is the point where the indicator changes its colour while the equivalence point is the point where the chemical reaction is completed stoichiometrically i.e., a stage at which equivalent amounts of acid reacts with equivalent amounts of base. End point may or may not be equal to the equivalence point of the reaction.

Q.4 Which indicator is used in the titration of sodium carbonate against hydrochloric acid and what is the colour change at the end point?

Ans. Methyl orange is used as an indicator. It changes its colour from yellow to light pink at the end point.

Q.5 Can you directly prepare the standard solutions of HCl, HNO_3 and H_2SO_4?

Ans. No, the standard solutions of HCl, HNO_3 and H_2SO_4 cannot be prepared directly because all of these are used as secondary standard solutions.

Unit 6

Systematic Qualitative Analysis

Qualitative analysis of inorganic salts involves the identification of cations and anions present in the salt or mixture of salts. Inorganic salts are obtained either by complete or partial neutralisation of an acid and a base. The positive part of the salt, i.e., cation is contributed by an acid while the negative part, i.e. anion is contributed by a base. e.g.,

Salt	Cation	Anion
NaCl	Na^+	Cl^-
$CuSO_4$	Cu^{2+}	SO_4^{2-}
$FeCl_3$	Fe^{3+}	Cl^-

Qualitative analysis is accomplished by the reactions which are easily perceptible to our senses such as sight and smell. Such reactions involve formation of a precipitate, change in colour, evolution of gas, etc.

The common procedure for testing any unknown sample is to make its solution and then test this solution for the ions present in it. There are separate procedures for detecting cations and anions, therefore qualitative analysis is studied under cation analysis and anion analysis.

Systematic analysis of an inorganic salt involved the steps as follows.

(i) Preliminary tests (dry tests) of solid salt and its solution.

(ii) Identification of anions by reactions carried out in solution (wet tests) and confirmatory tests.

(iii) Identification of cations by reactions carried out in solution (wet tests) and confirmatory tests.

Preliminary test of a salt give useful information which simplifies further course of analysis. These tests give important hints for the presence of certain anions or cations. These involve noting the general appearance and physical characteristics like colour, smell, solubility, etc. of the salt.

Further, gases involved in the preliminary tests with dil. H_2SO_4/dil. HCl and conc. H_2SO_4 also give good indication about the presence of acid radicals. **Preliminary tests** are also known as **dry tests.**

The following points are advised to note by the students in order to make the detection of radicals accurate and easy.

(i) Strictly adhere to the systematic scheme of analysis.

(ii) Keep your apparatus clean and do not pour back the reagents into stock bottle once it is taken out.

(iii) Use distilled water for analysis.

(iv) Use your own glass nozzle for passing (H_2S) gas and always wash it with water before and after starting experiment.

(v) Record all observations neatly during experimentation in a notebook.

In contrast to inorganic compounds the atoms in an organic compound are linked to each other by covalent bonds. Hence, organic compounds don't furnish ions in solution. Thus, in order to test the presence of above elements in an organic compound, it is fused with sodium metal to form ionisable sodium salts. Though we may also fuse the organic compounds with potassium, we prefer sodium (Na) because it is easily available and its reaction is easily controllable as compared to potassium (K).

Experiment 6.1

AIM

To detect one anion and one cation in a given salt.

Anions CO_3^{2-}, S^{2-}, SO_3^{2-}, SO_4^{2-}, NO_2^-, NO_3^-, Cl^-, Br^-, I^-, PO_4^{3-}, $C_2O_4^{2-}$, CH_3COO^- (insoluble salts excluded)

Cations Pb^{2+}, Cu^{2+}, As^{3+}, Al^{3+}, Fe^{3+}, Mn^{2+}, Ni^{2+}, Zn^{2+}, Co^{2+}, Ca^{2+}, Sr^{2+}, Ba^{2+}, Mg^{2+}, NH_4^+

Theory/Principle

Preliminary examination of the salt is based upon the observations obtained by observing the general appearance and physical properties like colour, smell, solubility of the salt as we have already discussed. In contrast, the identification of cations and anions it is based upon two basic principles

(i) the solubility product and

(ii) the common ion effect.

When ionic product of a salt exceeds from its solubility product, precipitation takes place. Common ion effect is used to control the ionic product of a salt. The nature of the ions present in the salt can also be found by its solubility in water and the pH of its aqueous solution.

- If the salt solution is acidic or basic in nature, this suggests that it is being **hydrolysed** in water.
- If the salt solution comes out to basic, the salt may be of **carbonate** or **sulphide**. But, if the solution shows acidic nature, it may be a salt of **weak base** or you can say it is an **acidic salt**. Thus, in case of acidic salt, it is recommended to neutralise the solution with sodium carbonate before carrying out the test for anions.

> **ALERT**
> - *Alcohol, H_2S are inflammable and toxic.*
> - *Potassium permanganate is harmful.*
> - *Manganese dioxide, lead chromate and oxalate are harmful.*
> - *Nitric acid and silver nitrate are corrosive.*
> - *Chromyl chloride is oxidising, corrosive, use minimum amount to avoid pollution by Cr^{3+} ions.*
> - *Bromine is corrosive, very toxic by inhalation.*
> - *Iodine is harmful on inhalation and when comes in contact with skin.*
> - *Chlorine, chloroform are toxic by inhalation.*
> - *Disposal of iodine is done by adding sodium thiosulphate solution to dissolve the iodine.*

Thus, the preliminary tests should always be performed before carrying out the confirmatory tests for ions.

Materials Required

Boiling tubes	: As per need	Test tubes	: As per need
Measuring cylinder	: 1	Test tube stand	: 1
Test tube holder	: 1	Delivery tube	: 1
Corks	: As per need	Filter paper	: As per need
Reagents	: As per need for a particular test	Spatula	: 1
Funnel	: 1	Dropper	: As per need

SYSTEMATIC ANALYSIS OF ANIONS
(OR ACIDIC RADICALS)

The acidic radicals are analysed on the basis of preliminary tests which involves the dry heating of the salt in a test tube. These tests are based upon the fact that :

- Salts containing CO_3^{2-}, S^{2-}, NO_2^-, SO_3^{2-} and CH_3COO^- ions react with dil. H_2SO_4 to give out CO_2, H_2S, NO_2, SO_2 and CH_3COOH gas or vapours, respectively which can be identified by their confirmatory tests.
- Salts containing Cl^-, Br^-, I^-, NO_3^- and $C_2O_4^{2-}$ reacts with conc. H_2SO_4 but not with dil. H_2SO_4 to produce characteristic gases.
- Salts containing SO_4^{2-} and PO_4^{3-} reacts neither with dil. H_2SO_4 nor with conc. H_2SO_4. These are therefore identified by individual tests.

Hence, the acidic radicals may be identified by performing the following tests in the order given below :

Step I Preliminary Test with Dilute Sulphuric Acid

In this test, the action of dilute H_2SO_4 on the salt is noted at room temperature and on warming, carbonate (CO_3^{2-}), sulphide (S^{2-}), sulphite (SO_3^{2-}), nitrite (NO_2^-) and acetate ions (CH_3COO^-) react with dil. H_2SO_4 to evolve different gases. The different characteristics of the gases evolved gives the information about the anions.

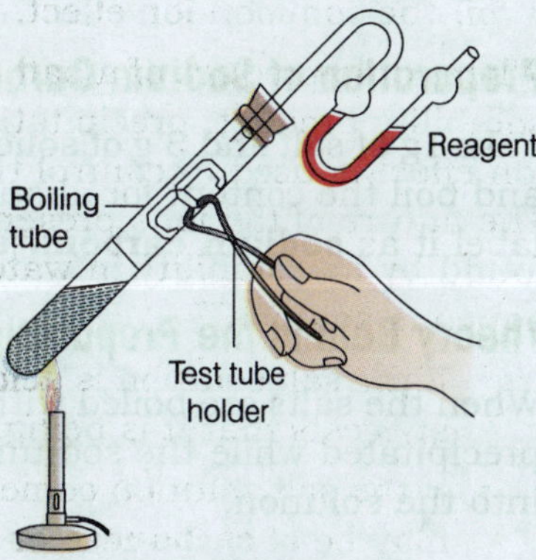

Fig. 6.1 *Testing a gas by heating*

Procedure

1. Take 0.1 g of the salt in a clean and dry test tube and add 1-2 mL of dil. H_2SO_4.
2. Observe the change, if any at room temperature.
3. If no gas is evolved, warm the contents of the test tube.
4. If any gas is evolved, test it by using the apparatus as shown in Fig 6.1.

Observation

Table 6.1. Observations of Preliminary test with dilute H_2SO_4

S.No.	Observation	Gas evolved	Possible acidic radicals or anions
1.	Brisk effervescence with the evolution of colourless and odourless gas which turns lime water milky.	CO_2	CO_3^{2-} (carbonate)
2.	Evolution of colourless gas with the smell of rotten eggs (H_2S like smell) which turns lead acetate paper black.	H_2S	S^{2-} (sulphide)
3.	Brown fumes are evolved which turns acidified potassium iodide (KI) solution containing starch solution blue.	NO_2	NO_2^- (nitrite)

S.No.	Observation	Gas evolved	Possible acidic radicals or anions
4.	Colourless gas with pungent smell of burning sulphur which turns acidified potassium dichromate solution green.	SO_2	SO_3^{2-} (sulphite)
5.	Solution gives colourless vapours with smell of vinegar which turns blue litmus red.	CH_3COOH vapours	CH_3COO^- (acetate)

Note *Like CO_2, SO_2 also turns lime water milky but CO_2 is odourless gas and SO_2 has a characteristic smell.*

Confirmatory Tests for CO_3^{2-}, S^{2-}, NO_2^-, SO_3^{2-} and CH_3COO^-

Depending upon the solubility of the given salts in water, either water extract (original solution) or sodium carbonate extract is used for performing the confirmatory or wet tests.

1. **Water Extract** It is prepared when salt is completely soluble in water. Dissolve the salt in water taken in a test tube. Shake the test tube to make a clear solution. This aqueous solution is used for confirmatory tests of acid radicals. This water extract is also called **original solution** of salt.
2. **Sodium Carbonate Extract** It is prepared when salt is insoluble in water.

Preparation of Sodium Carbonate Extract

Take 1g of salt and 3 g of solid carbonate in a boiling tube. Add 15 mL of distilled water to it. Stir and boil the content for about 10 minutes. Cool, filter and collect the filtrate in a test tube and label it as **sodium carbonate extract.**

Theory Behind the Preparation of Sodium Carbonate Extract

When the salts are boiled with sodium carbonate extract, the carbonates of metallic radicals are precipitated while the sodium salts of corresponding acid radicals being soluble in water pass into the solution.

$$ZnS + Na_2CO_3 \longrightarrow ZnCO_3 \downarrow + Na_2S$$

Note *Sodium carbonate extract contains unreacted sodium carbonate in solution, which has to be destroyed before using the extract for various tests. To do this, the extract is acidified with some suitable acid and is boiled to expel CO_2. The selection of acid used for destroying excess Na_2CO_3 depends upon the radical [or anion] to be identified.*

Confirmatory tests for CO_3^{2-}, S^{2-}, NO_2^-, SO_3^{2-} and CH_3COO^- are listed below

Confirmatory tests	Procedure	Observation	Inference	Chemistry involved
1 CONFIRMATION OF CARBONATE ION (CO_3^{2-})				
(i) **Dilute acid test**	Add dil. H_2SO_4 [or dil. HCl] to dissolve 0.1 g of salt taken in a test tube.	Brisk effervescence with colourless and odourless CO_2 gas is evolved, which turns lime water milky. But on passing the gas for some more time, through lime water milkiness disappears.	Brisk effervescence of evolution of CO_2 and appearance of milkiness in lime water indicates the presence of CO_3^{2-} ion in the given salt.	$Na_2CO_3 + H_2SO_4 \longrightarrow Na_2SO_4 + H_2O + CO_2\uparrow$ $CO_2 + Ca(OH)_2 \longrightarrow CaCO_3\downarrow + H_2O$ (White ppt.) Gas turns lime water milky due to formation of $CaCO_3$. $CaCO_3 + CO_2 + H_2O \longrightarrow Ca(HCO_3)_2$ (Soluble) Milkiness disappears due to the formation of soluble calcium hydrogen carbonate.

Confirmatory tests	Procedure	Observation	Inference	Chemistry involved
(ii) **Barium chloride test**	Add barium chloride or calcium chloride solution to 2 mL of original solution taken in a test tube.	White precipitate of calcium or barium carbonate is formed which is soluble in carbonic acid and mineral acids.	The formation of white precipitate confirms the presence of CO_3^{2-} in the given salt.	$CO_3^{2-} + Ca^{2+} \longrightarrow \underset{\text{White ppt.}}{CaCO_3}\downarrow$ $CO_3^{2-} + Ba^{2+} \longrightarrow \underset{\text{White ppt.}}{BaCO_3}\downarrow$
(iii) **Silver nitrate test**	Add silver nitrate solution to the original solution. Shake the solution and then add excess of $AgNO_3$.	White precipitate of silver carbonate is produced which is soluble in HNO_3 and NH_3. In excess of $AgNO_3$, white precipitate turns yellow.	This change of white precipitate into yellow precipitate in the presence of $AgNO_3$ confirms the presence of CO_3^{2-}.	$CO_3^{2-} + 2Ag^+ \longrightarrow \underset{\text{White ppt.}}{Ag_2CO_3}\downarrow$ This white precipitate turns yellow in the presence of $AgNO_3$ due to the formation of precipitate Ag_2O which is of yellow colour. $\underset{\text{White}}{Ag_2CO_3} \longrightarrow \underset{\text{Yellow}}{Ag_2O}\downarrow + CO_2\uparrow$
2 CONFIRMATION OF SULPHIDE ION(S^{2-})				
(i) **Sodium nitroprusside solution test**	Add NH_4OH, Na_2CO_3 to 1 mL of water extract. Shake it well then add few drops of sodium nitroprusside solution.	A hydrogen sulphide gas with rotten egg smell is evolved when H_2SO_4 is added to salt solution. On addition of sodium nitroprusside, violet or purple colouration is obtained.	Purple or violet colouration due to the formation of complex compound $Na_4[Fe(CN)_5NOS]$ confirms the presence of S^{2-} ion in the salt.	$Na_2S + H_2SO_4 \longrightarrow Na_2SO_4 + H_2S\uparrow$ $Na_2S + \underset{\text{Sodium nitroprusside}}{Na_2[Fe(CN)_5NO]} \longrightarrow$ $\underset{\text{Violet or purple colour complex}}{Na_4[Fe(CN)_5NOS]}$
Note *If salt is insoluble in water use sodium extract of salt.*				
(ii) **Lead acetate test**	Add dil. H_2SO_4 to 1 mL water extract and warm the solution. Add lead acetate solution to the above solution.	Gas with rotten egg smell is evolved. Black precipitate of PbS is formed which is insoluble in CH_3COOH.	Gas evolved is H_2S, S^{2-} may be present. The black precipitate confirms the presence of S^{2-} ion.	$Na_2S + H_2SO_4 \longrightarrow Na_2SO_4 + H_2S\uparrow$ $(CH_3COO)_2Pb + H_2S \longrightarrow$ $\underset{\text{Lead sulphide (Shining black)}}{PbS}\downarrow + 2CH_3COOH$
3 CONFIRMATION OF NITRITE ION (NO_2^-)				
(i) **Dilute acid test**	Add dil. H_2SO_4 to a solid nitrite and warm the solution.	Reddish brown fumes are evolved.	Reddish-brown fumes indicate the presence of NO_2^- ion.	Reddish-brown fumes are of NO_2. $2NaNO_2 + H_2SO_4 \longrightarrow Na_2SO_4 + 2HNO_2$ $3HNO_2 \longrightarrow HNO_3 + 2NO + H_2O$ $2NO + O_2 \longrightarrow \underset{\text{Brown gas}}{2NO_2}\uparrow$

Confirmatory tests	Procedure	Observation	Inference	Chemistry involved
(ii) **Starch-iodide test**	Add 1 mL of KI solution to the salt solution or water extract followed by addition of freshly prepared starch solution and acetic acid to acidify the solution. Alternatively, a filter paper moistered with potassium iodide, starch solution and few drops of acetic acid can be exposed to evolved brown gas.	Deep blue colour appears.	The deep blue colouration confirms the presence of NO_2^- ion in the given salt.	$NO_2^- + CH_3COOH \longrightarrow HNO_2 + CH_3COO^-$ $2KI + 2HNO_2 + 2CH_3COOH \longrightarrow 2CH_3COOK + I_2\uparrow + 2NO + 2H_2O$ When liberated iodine interacts with starch, a blue colour solution is formed. I_2 + starch $\longrightarrow$ Blue complex
(iii) **Silver nitrate test**	Add $AgNO_3$ to water extract of salt.	White crystalline ppt. of $AgNO_3$ is obtained.	The white ppt. confirms the presence of NO_2^- ions.	$NO_2^- + Ag^+ \longrightarrow \underset{\text{White ppt.}}{AgNO_2\downarrow}$
(iv) **Ferrous sulphate test**	Add a few drops of dil. acetic acid and few drops of $FeSO_4$ to a salt solution.	Dark brown or black ppt. is formed.	NO_2^- ions confirmed.	$KNO_2 + CH_3COOH \longrightarrow CH_3COOK + HNO_2$ $3HNO_2 \longrightarrow HNO_3 + 2NO + H_2O$ $FeSO_4 + NO \longrightarrow \underset{\text{Dark brown}}{FeSO_4\cdot NO}$
(v) **Sulphanilic acid-1-naphthylamine reagent test (Griss-Ilosvay test)**	Acidify 1 mL of water extract with acetic acid. Add 2-3 drops of sulphanilic acid solution followed by 2-3 drops of 1-naphthylamine reagent	Appearance of red colour due to formation of red azo-dye.	NO_2^- ion confirmed.	$NO_2^- + CH_3COOH \longrightarrow HNO_2 + CH_3COO^-$ 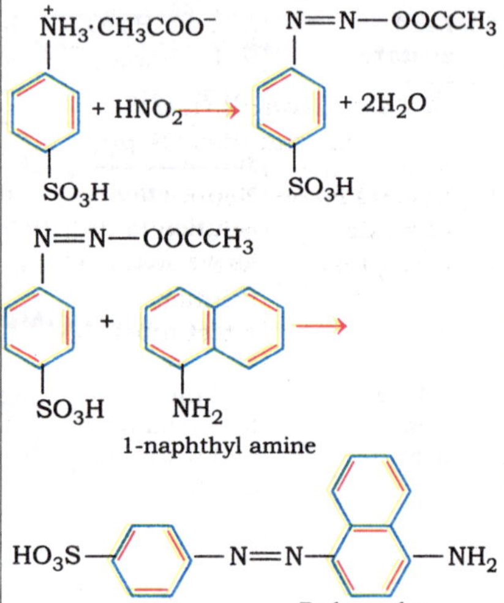 $\overset{+}{N}H_3\cdot CH_3COO^-$ (on benzene ring with SO_3H) + HNO_2 $\longrightarrow$ $N{=}N{-}OOCCH_3$ (on benzene ring with SO_3H) + $2H_2O$ $N{=}N{-}OOCCH_3$ (on benzene ring with SO_3H) + 1-naphthyl amine (NH_2) $\longrightarrow$ $HO_3S{-}C_6H_4{-}N{=}N{-}C_{10}H_6{-}NH_2$ Red azo-dye $+ CH_3COOH$

Note *The test solution should be very dilute. In concentrated solutions reaction does not proceed beyond diazotisation.*

Confirmatory tests	Procedure	Observation	Inference	Chemistry involved
4 CONFIRMATION OF SULPHITE ION (SO_3^{2-})				
(i) **Barium chloride, $BaCl_2$ test**	Take 1 mL of water extract or sodium extract of salt in a test tube and add $BaCl_2$ solution. Further, add dil. HCl to the above solution.	White ppt. of $BaSO_3$ is obtained which is soluble in dil. HCl with the evolution of SO_2 gas.	This confirms the presence of SO_3^{2-} ions.	$Na_2SO_3 + BaCl_2 \longrightarrow 2NaCl + \underset{\text{White ppt.}}{BaSO_3} \downarrow$ $BaSO_3 + 2HCl \longrightarrow \underset{\text{Soluble}}{BaCl_2} + H_2O + SO_2\uparrow$ The precipitate of $BaSO_3$ dissolves due to decomposition of sulphite by dil. HCl.
Note *The white precipitate of sulphite obtained above decolourises acidified potassium permanganate solution.* $BaSO_3 + H_2SO_4 \longrightarrow BaSO_4 + H_2O + SO_2$ $2KMnO_4 + 3H_2SO_4 \longrightarrow K_2SO_4 + 2MnSO_4 + 3H_2O + 5[O]$ $SO_2 + H_2O + [O] \longrightarrow H_2SO_4$				
(ii) **Potassium dichromate, $K_2Cr_2O_7$ test**	Add dil. H_2SO_4 to a water extract of salt. Then, dip $K_2Cr_2O_7$ paper to this solution.	Solution turns green due to the reduction of $K_2Cr_2O_7$ to Cr^{3+} ions.	This confirms the presence of SO_3^{2-} ions.	On treating sulphite with warm dil. H_2SO_4, SO_2 gas with smell of burning sulphur is obtained. $Na_2SO_3 + H_2SO_4 \longrightarrow Na_2SO_4 + H_2O + SO_2$ SO_2 turns $K_2Cr_2O_7$ paper dipped with dil. H_2SO_4 to green. $K_2Cr_2O_7 + H_2SO_4 + 3SO_2 \longrightarrow K_2SO_4 + \underset{\text{Chromium sulphate (green)}}{Cr_2(SO_4)_3} + H_2O$
5 CONFIRMATION OF ACETATE ION (CH_3COO^-)				
(i) **Ethanol test**	Take a salt (0.1 g) in a China dish. Add 1 mL ethanol and 0.2 mL conc. H_2SO_4 and heat.	Fruity odour is observed.	Fruity odour of ethyl acetate indicates the presence of CH_3COO^- ions.	$2CH_3COONa + H_2SO_4 \longrightarrow Na_2SO_4 + 2CH_3COOH$ $CH_3COOH + C_2H_5OH \xrightarrow{H^+} \underset{\text{Ethyl acetate (Fruity odour)}}{CH_3COOC_2H_5} + H_2O$
Note *You can also test the presence of acetate ions by treating it with dil. H_2SO_4. If vinegar smell is obtained, this indicates the presence of acetate ions.*				
(ii) **Neutral ferric chloride, $FeCl_3$ test**	Neutral $FeCl_3$ solution is added to the salt solution taken in a test tube.	Blood red colouration is obtained.	Blood red colour of $Fe(CH_3COO)_3$ confirms the presence of acetate ion.	Acetate gives deep red colour on reaction with neutral $FeCl_3$ solution due to the formation of complex ion which decomposes on heating to give iron (III) dihydroxyacetate as brown-red ppt. $6CH_3COO^- + 3Fe^{3+} + 2H_2O \longrightarrow [Fe_3(OH)_2(CH_3COO)_6]^+ + 2H^+$ $[Fe_3(OH)_2(CH_3COO)_6]^+ + 4H_2O \longrightarrow 3[Fe(OH)_2(CH_3COO)] + 3CH_3COOH + H^+$ Iron (III) dihydroxyacetate (Brown-red ppt.)

Note Preparation of neutral $FeCl_3$ *Add dilute NaOH solution to $FeCl_3$ solution drop by drop along with shaking until a precipitate of $Fe(OH)_3$ is obtained. Filter the precipitate and use the filtrate for analysis.*

Step II Preliminary Test with Concentrated Sulphuric Acid

Procedure

1. If no positive result is obtained from dil. H_2SO_4 test, take 0.1 g of salt in a test tube. Add 3-4 drops of conc. H_2SO_4 .
2. Observe the change in the reaction mixture.
3. If no gas is evolved, then warm the mixture.
4. Identify the gas evolved on heating [as given in table 6.2].

Table 6.2 Observation with concentrated H_2SO_4

S.No.	Observation	Gas evolved	Possible acidic radical or anions	Reactions involved
1.	Colourless, pungent smelling gas giving dense white fumes when a rod dipped in NH_4OH is brought near the mouth of the test tube.	HCl	Cl^- (chloride)	$NaCl + H_2SO_4 \longrightarrow \underset{\text{Sodium hydrogen sulphate}}{NaHSO_4} + \underset{\text{(Colourless gas)}}{HCl\uparrow}$ $HCl + NH_4OH \longrightarrow \underset{\text{White fumes}}{NH_4Cl} + H_2O$ or $HCl + NH_{3}(aq) \longrightarrow \underset{\text{Ammonium chloride White fumes}}{NH_4Cl\uparrow}$
2.	Reddish brown fumes with a pungent odour. The fumes get intensified on heating the reaction after addition of solid MnO_2 to the reaction mixture. Brown vapours turn starch paper yellow.	Br_2 vapours	Br^- (bromide)	$2NaBr + 2H_2SO_4 \longrightarrow \underset{\text{Brown fumes}}{Br_2} + SO_2 + Na_2SO_4 + 2H_2O$ $2NaBr + MnO_2 + 2H_2SO_4 \longrightarrow$ $Na_2SO_4 + MnSO_4 + 2H_2O + Br_2$
3.	Violet pungent vapours which turn starch paper blue and a layer of violet sublimate is formed on the sides of test tube. The violet vapours get intensified on addition of MnO_2 to the reaction mixture.	I_2 vapours	I^- (iodide)	$2NaI + 2H_2SO_4 \longrightarrow Na_2SO_4 + SO_2 + 2H_2O + \underset{\text{Violet vapours}}{I_2}$ $I_2 + \text{Starch solution} \longrightarrow \text{Blue colour}$ Some HI, SO_2, H_2S and S are also formed due to the following reactions. $NaI + H_2SO_4 \longrightarrow NaHSO_4 + HI$ $2HI + H_2SO_4 \longrightarrow 2H_2O + I_2 + SO_2$ $6NaI + 4H_2SO_4 \longrightarrow 3I_2 + 4H_2O + S + 3Na_2SO_4$ $8NaI + 5H_2SO_4 \longrightarrow 4I_2 + H_2S + 4Na_2SO_4 + 4H_2O$ On adding MnO_2, the violet vapours become dense. $2NaI + MnO_2 + 2H_2SO_4 \longrightarrow$ $I_2 + MnSO_4 + Na_2SO_4 + 2H_2O$
4.	Brown pungent fumes are evolved on heating salt with conc. H_2SO_4 which gets intensified by the addition of Cu turnings and the solution acquires blue colour.	NO_2	NO_3^- (nitrate)	$NaNO_3 + H_2SO_4 \longrightarrow NaHSO_4 + HNO_3$ $4HNO_3 \longrightarrow \underset{\text{Brown fumes}}{4NO_2} + O_2 + 2H_2O$ $2NaNO_3 + 4H_2SO_4 + 3Cu \longrightarrow$ $\underset{\text{Blue}}{3CuSO_4} + Na_2SO_4 + 4H_2O + 2NO$ The solution turns blue due to the formation of $CuSO_4$. The evolved NO oxidise to give excess of brown fumes. $2NO + O_2 \longrightarrow 2NO_2$ (Dark brown fumes)

S.No.	Observation	Gas evolved	Possible acidic radical or anions	Reactions involved
5.	Colourless and odourless gas is evolved which turns lime water milky and the gas coming out of lime water if ignited burns with a blue flame.	CO and CO_2	$C_2O_4^{2-}$ (oxalate)	$(COONa)_2 + H_2SO_4(conc.) \longrightarrow Na_2SO_4 + H_2O + \underbrace{CO_2\uparrow + CO\uparrow}_{\text{Colourless gases}}$

Confirmatory Tests for Cl^-, Br^-, I^-, NO_3^- and $C_2O_4^{2-}$

Confirmatory tests for Cl^-, Br^-, I^-, NO_3^- and $C_2O_4^{2-}$ which reacts with concentrated sulphuric acid are listed below.

Tests	Procedure	Observation	Inference	Chemistry involved
1 CONFIRMATION OF CHLORIDE ION (Cl^-)				
(i) **Silver nitrate ($AgNO_3$) test**	To 1-2 mL of sodium carbonate extract of salt add dil. HNO_3 to acidify it or take water extract and add $AgNO_3$ solution.	A curdy white precipitate of AgCl soluble in NH_4OH solution is formed.	This confirms the presence of Cl^- ions in the salt.	$NaCl + AgNO_3 \longrightarrow NaNO_3 + \underset{\text{White curdy ppt.}}{AgCl\downarrow}$ $AgCl + 2NH_4OH \longrightarrow \underset{\text{Diammine silver (II) chloride (Soluble)}}{[Ag(NH_3)_2]\ Cl} + 2H_2O$
	Warm the salt with some solid $K_2Cr_2O_7$ taken in a test tube and add conc. H_2SO_4 to it. Heat the test tube and pass the vapours through NaOH, yellow solution is obtained. Divide the solution into two parts : Add few drops of dil. CH_3COOH solution and lead acetate solution in the first part.	Red vapours of chromyl chloride (CrO_2Cl_2) are formed, which on passing through NaOH forms a yellow solution of Na_2CrO_4. This Na_2CrO_4 produces a yellow precipitate of $PbCrO_4$ when added to lead acetate solution.	Yellow precipitate confirms the presence of Cl^- ions.	$4NaCl + K_2Cr_2O_7 + 6H_2SO_4 \longrightarrow 4NaHSO_4 + 2KHSO_4 + 3H_2O + \underset{\text{Chromyl chloride}}{2CrO_2Cl_2}$ $CrO_2Cl_2 + 4NaOH \longrightarrow Na_2CrO_4 + 2H_2O + 2NaCl$ $\underset{\text{Sodium chromate}}{Na_2CrO_4} + (CH_3COO)_2Pb \longrightarrow \underset{\text{Lead chromate (Yellow precipitate)}}{PbCrO_4} + 2CH_3COONa$
(ii) **Chromyl chloride test**	If the second part of yellow solution so obtained above is acidified with dil. H_2SO_4 and small amounts of amyl alcohol and 1 mL of 10% H_2O_2 solution is added to it.	On gentle shaking, the organic layer turns blue due to the formation of $CrO_5.CrO_4^{2-}$ ion formed in the reaction of chromyl chloride with NaOH reacts with H_2O_2 to form CrO_5 which dissolves in amyl alcohol to give blue colour.	This test is also used for detecting Cl^- ions.	$CrO_4^{2-} + 2H^+ + 2H_2O_2 \longrightarrow \underset{\text{Chromium pentoxide}}{CrO_5} + 3H_2O$

Tests	Procedure	Observation	Inference	Chemistry involved
(iii) **Manganese dioxide test**	Take 0.1 g of salt in a test tube, add a pinch of MnO_2 and 3-4 drops of conc. H_2SO_4. Heat the reaction mixture. Bring a moist starch iodide paper near the mouth of test tube.	Greenish-yellow pungent gas of Cl_2 is liberated which turns moist starch iodide paper blue.	Greenish-yellow pungent gas confirms the presence of Cl^- ions.	$MnO_2 + 2H_2SO_4 + 2NaCl \longrightarrow MnSO_4 + \underset{\text{Greenish-Yellow}}{Cl_2\uparrow} + Na_2SO_4 + 2H_2O$
2 CONFIRMATION OF BROMIDE ION (Br^-)				
(i) **Silver nitrate, $AgNO_3$ test**	To 1-2 mL of sodium carbonate extract of the salt, add dil. HNO_3 (to acidify the extract) and $AgNO_3$ solution. Shake the test tube.	Pale yellow precipitate of AgBr partially soluble in NH_4OH is obtained.	A pale yellow precipitate confirms the presence of Br^- ions.	$NaBr + AgNO_3 \longrightarrow \underset{\text{Pale yellow ppt.}}{AgBr\downarrow} + NaNO_3$ $AgBr + 2NH_4OH \longrightarrow \underset{\text{Sparingly soluble complex}}{[Ag(NH_3)_2Br]} + 2H_2O$
Note *Water extract can also be used to perform this test.*				
(ii) **Carbon disulphide, CS_2 or chlorine water test**	Add freshly prepared Cl_2 water and few drops of carbon disulphide (CS_2) to the salt solution or sodium carbonate extract neutralised with dil. HCl. Shake it well and allow to stand. In place of CS_2, carbon tetrachloride (CCl_4) or chloroform ($CHCl_3$) or dichloromethene can also be used.	An orange-brown coloured layer in CS_2 is obtained due to the liberation of Br_2.	Orange-brown colouration confirms the presence of bromide ions.	$2NaBr + Cl_2 \longrightarrow 2NaCl + Br_2$ $Br_2 + CS_2 \longrightarrow$ Orange-brown layer of Br_2 gas
3 CONFIRMATION OF IODIDE ION (I^-)				
(i) **Silver nitrate, $AgNO_3$ test**	Sodium carbonate extract of solution. Take 1 mL of sodium carbonate extract, acidify it with dil. HNO_3 [or simply take water extract Add $AgNO_3$ solution to it.]	Yellow precipitate of silver iodide AgI (insoluble in NH_4OH) is obtained.	Appearance of yellow precipitate confirms the presence of iodide ions.	$NaI + AgNO_3 \longrightarrow \underset{\text{Yellow ppt.}}{AgI\downarrow} + NaNO_3$
(ii) **Lead acetate test**	To the salt solution [or sodium extract], add lead acetate solution.	A yellow crystalline ppt. of lead iodide (soluble in hot water) is obtained.	Presence of I^- ions is confirmed.	$2I^- + Pb^{2+} \longrightarrow \underset{\text{Yellow ppt.}}{PbI_2\downarrow}$
(iii) **$CHCl_3$ or Cl_2 water test**	Add 1 mL of $CHCl_3$ (or CCl_4) and chlorine water in excess to the salt solution in water [or sodium carbonate extract] and shake the test tube vigorously.	Violet colouration in organic ($CHCl_3$) layer is observed.	Violet colouration confirms the presence of I^- ions.	$2NaI + Cl_2 \longrightarrow 2NaCl + I_2$, I_2 dissolves in organic solvent and solution becomes violet.

Tests	Procedure	Observation	Inference	Chemistry involved
4 CONFIRMATION OF NITRATE ION (NO_3^-)				
Ring test $FeSO_4$ Dark brown ring	Add 2 mL of conc. H_2SO_4 to 1 mL of an aqueous salt solution and shake well. Cool the test tube under tap water. Now, add freshly prepared ferrous sulphate solution dropwise along the sides of the test tube, so that it forms a layer on the top of the liquid already present in the test tube.	A dark brown ring of nitrosoferrous sulphate, $[Fe(NO)]SO_4$ is formed at the junction of two solutions.	Presence of NO_3^- ion is confirmed.	$NaNO_3 + H_2SO_4 \longrightarrow NaHSO_4 + HNO_3$ $2HNO_3 + 6FeSO_4 + 3H_2SO_4 \longrightarrow 3Fe_2(SO_4)_3 + 2NO + 4H_2O$ $FeSO_4 + NO \longrightarrow [Fe(NO)]SO_4$ Nitrosoferrous sulphate (Brown ring)
5 CONFIRMATION OF OXALATE ION $C_2O_4^{2-}$				
(i) **Calcium chloride test**	1 mL sodium carbonate extract of salt acidified with acetic acid taken in a test tube. Boil off (CO_2) and add $CaCl_2$ solution.	A white ppt of calcium oxalate insoluble in ammonium oxalate and oxalic acid solution but soluble in dil. HCl and dil. HNO_3 is obtained.	White ppt confirms the presence of oxalate ions.	$CaCl_2 + Na_2C_2O_4 \longrightarrow CaC_2O_4 \downarrow + 2NaCl$ Calcium oxalate (White ppt.)
(ii) **$KMnO_4$ test**	Filter the white precipitate of calcium oxalate formed in calcium chloride test. The white precipitate is dissolved in dil. H_2SO_4 and then 1 mL of dil. $KMnO_4$ is added and warm the solution.	Pink colour of $KMnO_4$ is discharged. Pass the gas through lime water. It turns milky. White precipitate is formed which dissolves on passing the gas for some more time.	Presence of oxalate ions is confirmed.	$CaC_2O_4 + H_2SO_4 \longrightarrow CaSO_4 + H_2C_2O_4$ $2KMnO_4 + 3H_2SO_4 + 5H_2C_2O_4 \longrightarrow 2MnSO_4 + K_2SO_4 + 8H_2O + 10CO_2$

Step III Test for Sulphate and Phosphate

If no positive test is obtained in steps I and II, then tests for the presence of sulphate and phosphate ions are performed. These tests are listed below:

Confirmatory Tests for SO_4^{2-} and PO_4^{3-}

Tests	Procedure	Observation	Inference	Chemistry involved
1 CONFIRMATION OF SULPHATE (SO_4^{2-})				
(i) **Barium chloride test**	Add $BaCl_2$ solution to 1 mL salt solution or sodium extract followed by the addition of dil. HCl.	White precipitate of $BaSO_4$ is obtained which is insoluble in HCl (conc.) or HNO_3 (conc.).	White precipitate confirms the presence of SO_4^{2-} ions.	$Na_2SO_4 + BaCl_2 \longrightarrow BaSO_4 \downarrow$ White ppt. $+ 2NaCl$

Tests	Procedure	Observation	Inference	Chemistry involved
(ii) **Lead acetate test**	Acidify the aqueous solution or sodium carbonate extract with acetic acid and add lead acetate solution.	White precipitate of lead sulphate is formed which is soluble in hot ammonium acetate solution.	Presence of SO_4^{2-} ions is confirmed.	SO_4^{2-} ions give white ppt. of lead sulphate when aqueous solution or sodium carbonate extract neutralised with acetic acid is treated with lead acetate solution. $Na_2SO_4 + (CH_3COO)_2Pb \longrightarrow \underset{\text{White ppt.}}{PbSO_4} \downarrow + 2CH_3COONa$
2 CONFIRMATION OF PHOSPHATE (PO_4^{3-})				
(i) **Ammonium molybdate test**	Acidify the original solution with conc. HNO_3 and add ammonium molybdate solution. Heat to boiling.	A canary yellow precipitate of ammonium phospho-molybdate is obtained.	A yellow ppt confirms the presence of PO_4^{3-} ions.	$Na_2HPO_4 + 12(NH_4)_2MoO_4 + 23HNO_3 \longrightarrow \underset{\text{Canary yellow ppt.}}{(NH_4)_3[P(Mo_3O_{10})_4]} \downarrow + 2NaNO_3 + 21NH_4NO_3 + 12H_2O$
(ii) **Magnesia mixture test**	Add magnesia mixture to 1-2 mL of aqueous salt solution and allow to stand. (Magnesia mixture is formed by adding NH_4Cl to $MgCl_2$ solution and boil the solution. Then, add NH_4OH till a strong smell of ammonia is obtained)	A white precipitate is obtained.	Presence of PO_4^{3-} ions is confirmed.	$Na_2HPO_4 + MgCl_2 + NH_4OH \longrightarrow \underset{\text{(White ppt.)}}{Mg(NH_4)PO_4} \downarrow + 2NaCl + H_2O$

SYSTEMATIC ANALYSIS OF CATIONS

(Group Analysis for Basic Radicals)

The systematic qualitative analysis of cations can be done with the following steps

Step I Preliminary Examination of the Salt for the Identification of Cations

Preliminary examination of a salt furnishes important information and it simplifies further course of analysis. Although, these tests are not conclusive yet sometimes, they provide important hints/clues for the presence of certain cations. These tests are also named as **dry tests.**

Dry test involves the following tests

1. Physical observation of salt or mixture
2. Dry heating test
3. Flame test
4. Charcoal cavity test
5. Cobalt nitrate test
6. Borax bead test
7. Microcosmic salt bead test

1. Physical Observation of Salt or Mixture

In physical examination, colour, smell and density of a given mixture are observed. To check the smell, take a pinch of the salt between your fingers and rub with a drop of water.

S.No.	Observation	Inference
1.	**Colour of the substance**	
	(i) Blue and if its aqueous solution is also blue.	Salts of cupric (Cu^{2+})
	(ii) Bright green and if its aqueous solution is also green.	Salts of nickel (Ni^{2+})
	(iii) Dark green and if its aqueous solution is also dark green but becomes light on dilution.	Salts of chromium (Cr^{3+})
	(iv) Violet-pink and if its aqueous solution is pink.	Salts of cobalt (Co^{2+})
	(v) Light pink and if its aqueous solution is colourless.	Salts of manganese (Mn^{2+})
	(vi) Reddish brown	Fe_2O_3
	(vii) Red	HgO, HgI_2, Pb_3O_4, Cu_2O
	(viii) Orange-red	Sb_2S_3
	(ix) Black	CuO, NiO, SnO, FeS, CuS, HgS, PbS, CoS, FeO, Co_3O_4, Ni_2O_3, Cu_2S, $CuBr_2$, NiS, etc.
	(x) Yellow	As_2S_3, CdS, Bi_2O_3, As_2S_5, PbI_2, AgI, Chromates, etc.
	(xi) Yellow-green and if its aqueous solution is light green or almost colourless.	Salts of Fe^{2+}
	(xii) Yellow-brown and if its aqueous solution is yellow.	Salts of Fe^{3+}
	(xiii) Colourless	Transition metals absent except some salts of Mn^{2+}.
	(xiv) Purple	Some Cr^{3+} salts and permanganates.
2.	**Density**	
	(i) Mixture of salts is too light (fluffy powder).	Salts of Zn^{2+}, Bi^{+}, Al^{3+}, Sr^{2+}, Ca^{2+} and Mg^{2+}.
	(ii) Mixture of salts is too heavy.	Salts of Hg^{2+}, Ba^{2+} and Pb^{2+}.
3.	**Deliquescence**	
	(i) Salts absorbs moisture and becomes pasty or like liquid.	If coloured, then $FeCl_3$, $Cu(NO_3)_2$ and $Fe(NO_3)_3$. If colourless, then $ZnCl_2$, $MgCl_2$ and $AlCl_3$.

2. Dry Heating Test

Take the given salt around 0.1 g in a clean and dry test tube. Heat the test tube first gently and then strongly. Observe the changes taking place upon heating.

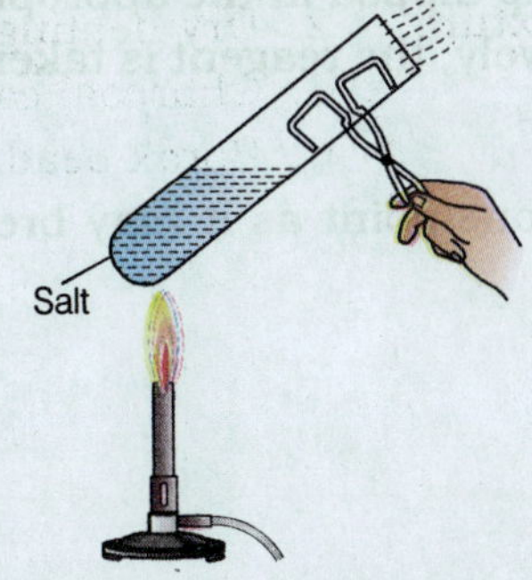

Fig 6.2 *Heat the salt present in the test tube*

It is to be noted that on heating, some salts undergo decomposition, therefore, some characteristic changes in the colour of residue may be obtained.

S.No.	Observation	Inference
1.	**Substance melts**	Salts of alkali metals, chlorides of Hg, Ag and Pb and salts having water of crystallisation.
2.	**Substance cracks**	$Pb(NO_3)_2$, $Ba(NO_3)_2$, NaCl and KI.
3.	**Substance swells**	Alums, salts of phosphate and borate.
4.	**Substance sublimes** on heating and the colour of sublimate is	
	• White	$HgCl_2$, As_2O_3, Hg_2Cl_2, $AlCl_3$, Sb_2O_3, halides of NH_4^+.
	• Yellow	As_2S_3 and HgI_2
	• Black	Sulphides of Hg, Sb and As
	• Blue, yellow or violet vapours	Iodides
	• Grey (having garlic odour)	As^{3+}
5.	**Colour of residue** obtained after heating (mainly metallic oxides)	
	• White and non-fusible.	Oxides of Ca, Ba, Sr, Mg, Zn and Al.
	• Initially, green but becomes dirty white or yellow on heating.	Salts of Fe^{2+}
	• Yellow-brown when hot, on cooling, it is brown.	SnO_2
	• Black and infusible.	NiO, MnO_2 and CuO
	• Dark orange-red in heating state and sublimes.	HgO
	• White infusible and becomes yellow on heating.	Salts of Zn^{2+}
	• Initially, blue or green but becomes white on heating.	Salts of Cu^{2+}
	• Initially, pink but becomes blue on heating.	Salts of Co^{2+}
	Colourless, odourless gas NH_3, turns red litmus to blue and Nessler's reagent brown.	Ammonium salts (NH_4^+)

Some points to be remembered while performing the heating test

1. Use a perfectly dry test tube for performing this test. While drying a test tube, keep it in slanting position on the flame with its mouth slightly downwards so that the drops of water which condense on the upper cooler parts, do not fall back on the hot bottom, as this may break the tube.
2. For testing a gas, a filter paper strip dipped in the appropriate reagent is brought near the mouth of the test tube or alternatively, the reagent is taken in a gas detector and the gas is passed through it.
3. Do not heat the tube strongly at one point as it may break, so rotate it continuously to ensure uniform heating.

3. Flame Test

Salt to be analysed is treated with conc. HCl to form metal chlorides which are **volatile** in non-luminous flame and their vapours impart characteristic colour to the flame.

Theory

Metal chlorides formed are thermally ionisable and cations formed absorb heat energy from the flame such that the valence electrons get excited to higher energy levels.

On coming back to their original/stable state, they transmit energy in the form of light of characteristic wavelength. Since, different metal ions emit light of different wavelengths, hence, different colours are imparted by different metal ions.

Procedure

1. To perform flame test, take a platinum wire and make a small circular loop at its one end by winding it around the tapered end of a pencil. [Fig. 6.3 (ii)]
2. Clean the platinum loop by dipping it into conc. HCl and then heating it strongly in the non-luminous flame. Repeat this procedure until the wire imparts no colour to the flame.
3. Make a paste of about 0.1-0.2 g of the well powdered sample of the salt with 2-3 drops of conc. HCl on a clean watch glass.
4. Dip the clean loop of the platinum wire in the paste [Fig. 6.3 (iv)]. Introduce the loop into the lower oxidising or non-luminous flame [Fig 6.3 (v)]. First, observe the colour of the flame with the naked eye and then through a blue glass. Salts particularly of group V (Ba^{2+}, Ca^{2+} and Sr^{2+}) are identified by the colours of the flame.

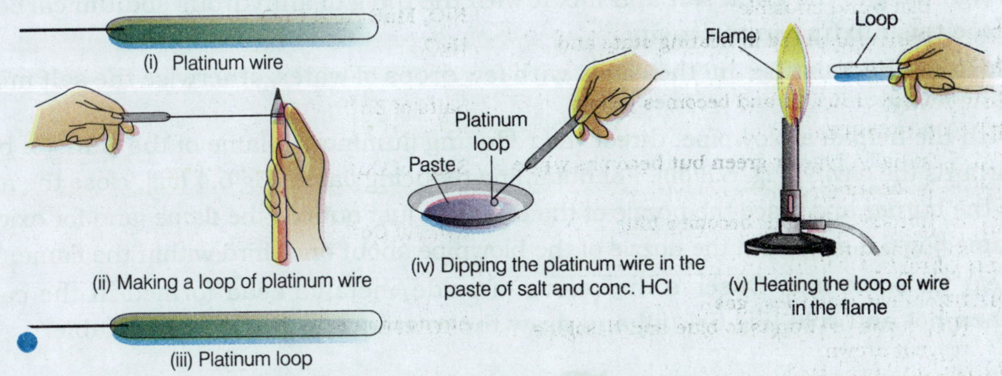

Fig. 6.3 *Performing the flame test*

Observation

S.No.	Colour (with naked eye)	Colour (through blue glass)	Cation(s)
1.	Golden yellow	Invisible	Na^+
2.	Violet	Pink	K^+
3.	Carmine red	Crimson red or pink	Li^+
4.	Brick-red	Light yellowish-green	Ca^{2+}
5.	Apple-green	Bluish-green	Ba^{2+} and Mo^{2+}
6.	Green	Same	Cu^{2+} and Tl^{3+}
7.	Crimson red	Purple	Sr^{2+}
8.	Blue	Same	Cu^{2+}, As^{3+}, Sb^{3+} and Bi^{3+}

Note *Blue colour of Cu^{2+} ion is observed when present with certain complex ions or other elements are present.*

4. Charcoal Cavity Test

Theory

When a salt is fused with anhydrous Na_2CO_3 or oxidising mixture in a cavity on charcoal block in reducing flame, first metallic carbonates and finally, metallic oxides are formed. The metallic oxides so formed appear as coloured residue in the cavity.

(i) $Pb(NO_3)_2 + Na_2CO_3 \xrightarrow{\Delta} PbCO_3 + 2NaNO_3$

$PbCO_3 \xrightarrow{\Delta} PbO + CO_2\uparrow$

(Brown when hot, Yellow when cold)

(ii) $CuSO_4 + Na_2CO_3 \xrightarrow{\Delta} CuCO_3 + Na_2SO_4$

$CuCO_3 \xrightarrow{\Delta} CuO + CO_2\uparrow$

(iii) $ZnSO_4 + Na_2CO_3 \xrightarrow{\Delta} ZnCO_3 + Na_2SO_4$

$ZnCO_3 \xrightarrow{\Delta} ZnO + CO_2\uparrow$

(Yellow when hot white when cold)

Sometimes, these metallic oxides reduced to metals by the action of carbon present in reducing flame. On cooling, these metals form **beads**.

$$PbO + C \longrightarrow \underset{\text{Greyish-white beads}}{Pb} + CO\uparrow$$

$$CuO + C \longrightarrow \underset{\text{Reddish beads}}{Cu} + CO\uparrow$$

Procedure

1. Make a small cavity in a charcoal block with the help of a knife or a charcoal borer. Do not apply a large pressure, otherwise it will break. [Fig 6.4(i)].
2. Weigh 0.2 g of the given salt and mix it with the 0.5 g of anhydrous sodium carbonate and place this mixture in the cavity.
3. Moisten the mixture in the cavity with few drops of water, otherwise the salt mixture will blow away.
4. With the help of a blowpipe, direct the reducing (luminous) flame of the Bunsen burner towards the cavity [Fig. 6.3 (ii)]. For obtaining reducing flame [Fig 6.4 (iii)], close the air holes of the burner and place the nozzle of the blowpipe just outside the flame (and for oxidising flame [Fig 6.3 (iv)]), hold the nozzle of the blowpipe about one-third within the flame.
5. Heat for sometime. Observe the colour of oxide/metallic bead formed in the cavity both when hot and cold [Fig 6.4 (ii)] and draw the inference as per the given table.

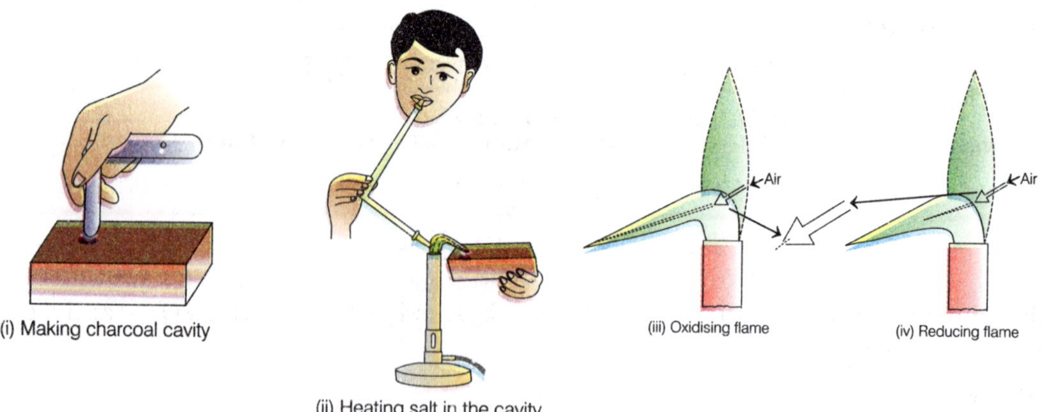

Fig 6.4 *Charcoal cavity test*

Note *To obtain oxidising flame hold the nozzle of the blow pipe about one third within the flame. To obtain reducing flame place nozzle of the blow pipe just outside the flame.*

Observation

Colour in charcoal cavity test

S. No.	Bead	Crust (Residue)	Inference
1.	Greyish-white soft metallic bead	Brown which turns yellow on cooling.	Pb^{2+}
2.	Lustrous white bead	—	Ag^{+}
3.	White-brown bead	Orange which turns yellow on cooling.	Bi^{3+}
4.	—	Garlic like smelly fumes with white residue.	As^{3+}
5.	—	Red-brown precipitate which easily turns into vapour.	Cd^{2+}
6.	—	Red crust with smell of ammonia	NH_4^+
7.	—	Black precipitate	Fe^{3+}, Co^{2+} and Mn^{2+}
8.	Red bead	—	Cu^{2+}
9.	—	White residue which glows.	Al^{3+}, Ba^{2+}, Ca^{2+} and Mg^{2+}
10.	—	Yellow when hot, white when cold.	Zn^{2+}

Note *Some points to be remembered while performing charcoal cavity test.*

(i) Always make a fresh cavity for a new test.

(ii) Do not bore a deep cavity.

(iii) Thoroughly clean the mouth of blow pipe before use.

5. Cobalt Nitrate Test

Theory

This test is applied to those salts which leave white residue in the charcoal cavity test. Thus, we can say that this test is performed only when infusible mass (contains metallic oxides like CaO, Al_2O_3, MgO and ZnO) is obtained in charcoal cavity test.

In this test, cobalt nitrate decomposes on heating and form cobalt (II) oxide, CoO, that combines with the metal oxides (white residue of charcoal cavity test) to form double oxides which gives characteristic colours. e.g.

$$2Co(NO_3)_2 \xrightarrow{\Delta} 2CoO + 4NO_2\uparrow + O_2\uparrow$$

$$CoO + ZnO \longrightarrow \underset{\text{Green}}{CoO \cdot ZnO}$$

$$CoO + MgO \longrightarrow \underset{\text{Pink}}{CoO \cdot MgO}$$

$$CoO + Al_2O_3 \longrightarrow \underset{\text{Blue}}{CoO \cdot Al_2O_3}$$

Similarly, phosphates and borates react with cobalt oxide to form $Co_3(PO_4)_2$ and $Co_3(BO_3)_2$ which is blue in colour.

Procedure

1. Add 1-2 drops of cobalt nitrate solution to infusible mass or white residue obtained in charcoal cavity and heat the mixture with the help of blowpipe in oxidising flame (non-luminous flame).
2. Observe the colour of the residue.

Observation

Colour shown in cobalt nitrate test

S.No.	Colour of the residue	Inference
1.	Green	Zn^{2+}
2.	Pink	Mg^{2+}
3.	Bluish-green	Sn^{2+}
4.	Blue	Al^{3+}
5.	Black	Co^{2+}, Fe^{2+}, Mn^{2+}, Ni^{2+}

Note *Cobalt nitrate should not be used in excess otherwise black coloured cobalt oxide (Co_3O_4) may be formed and it is difficult to identify other colours in the presence of black colour. Always use dilute solution of cobalt nitrate.*

6. Borax Bead Test

Borax bead test is performed only for coloured salts because borax reacts with metal salts to form metal borates of metaborates which have characteristic colours.

Theory

On heating borax, $Na_2B_4O_7 \cdot 10H_2O$ on the platinum loop loses its water of crystallisation. It swells upto fluffy white porous mass. On further heating, the fluffy mass melts into a colourless liquid which later forms a transparent, colourless, glass like beads of sodium metaborate ($NaBO_2$) and boric anhydride (B_2O_3).

$$Na_2B_4O_7.10H_2O \xrightarrow[-10H_2O]{\Delta} Na_2B_4O_7 \xrightarrow{\Delta} \underset{\text{Sodium metaborate}}{2NaBO_2} + \underset{\text{Boric anhydride}}{B_2O_3}$$

Boric anhydride is non-volatile. When it reacts with coloured metallic salt, a characteristic coloured bead of metal metaborate is formed. Beads of characteristic colours are produced with salts of Cu, Fe, Cr, Mn, Co and Ni The colour of the bead depends upon the flame (luminous or non-luminous) in which it has been heated. e.g., Copper forms blue coloured bead in oxidising flame.

$$CuSO_4 + B_2O_3 \xrightarrow{\text{Non-luminous flame}} \underset{\substack{\text{Cupric (II) metaborate}\\ \text{(green when hot, blue}\\ \text{when cold)}}}{Cu(BO_2)_2} + SO_3 \text{ (Oxidising and non-luminous flame)}$$

In reducing flame, two reactions may take place :

(i) The blue $Cu(BO_2)_2$ is reduced to colourless cuprous metaborate.

$$\underset{\text{Blue}}{2Cu(BO_2)_2} + 2NaBO_2 + C \xrightarrow{\text{Luminous flame}} \underset{\substack{\text{Cuprous}\\ \text{metaborate}}}{2CuBO_2} + Na_2B_4O_7 + CO\uparrow$$

(ii) Cupric metaborate may be reduced to metallic copper and the bead appears red and opaque.

$$\underset{\text{Blue}}{2Cu(BO_2)_2} + 4NaBO_2 + 2C \xrightarrow{\text{Luminous flame}} \underset{\text{Red and opaque}}{2Cu\downarrow} + 2Na_2B_4O_7 + 2CO\uparrow$$

Procedure

1. Make a small circular loop at the end of a clean platinum wire. Heat the loop in Bunsen flame until it becomes red hot and then dip it in a heap of powdered borax.
2. Heat it again. The borax will first swell up and then get fused giving a colourless, transparent glass like bead. If the bead is coloured, it means that the platinum wire is not clean. Then, repeat the above procedure till a colourless bead is formed but only after cleaning the wire.

3. Dip the hot bead with a small quantity of dry salt and fuse it in the oxidising flame again shown in [Fig. 6.5 (ii)].
4. Note down the colour of the bead while it is hot and when it is cold in both the flames. [Fig 6.5].

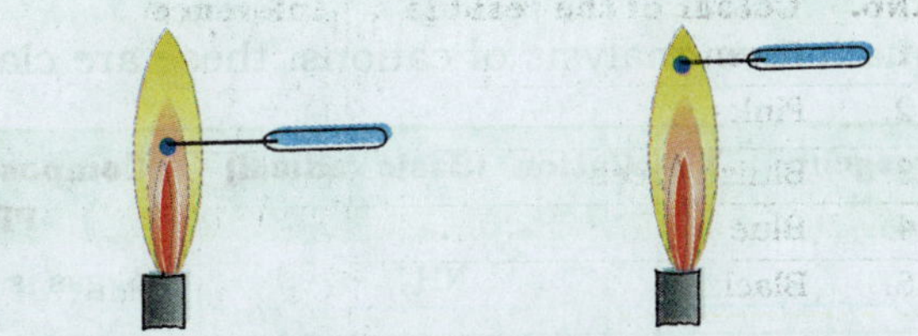

(i) Heating in reducing flame (ii) Heating in oxidising flame

Fig 6.5 *Borax bead test*

5. Now, heat the bead in the reducing (luminous) flame as shown in [Fig. 6.5 (i)].
6. Note down the colour of the bead observed, once again while it is hot and then cold.
7. To remove the bead from the platinum wire, heat it to redness and tap the platinum wire with your finger. [Fig 6.6].

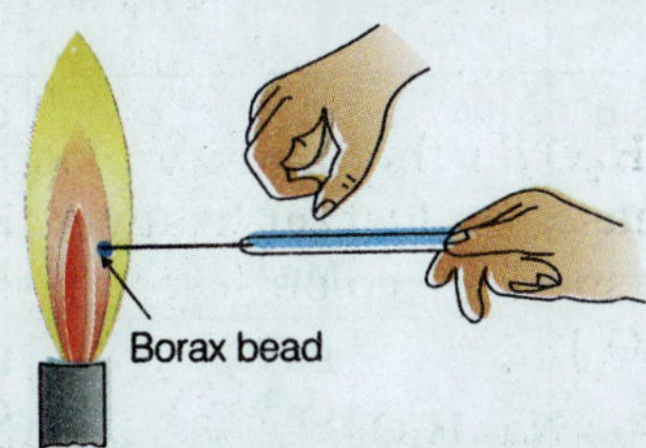

Fig. 6.6 *Removing borax bead from platinum wire*

Observation

Colour in borax bead test

S.No.	Oxidising (non-luminous) flame		Reducing (luminous) flame		Inference
	Hot	Cold	Hot	Cold	
1.	Green	Blue	Colourless	Opaque red	Cu
2.	Yellowish-brown	Yellow	Green	Green	Fe
3.	Yellow	Yellowish-green	Green	Green	Cr
4.	Light-violet	Light violet	Colourless	Colourless	Mn
5.	Blue	Blue	Blue	Blue	Co
6.	Violet	Reddish brown	Grey	Grey	Ni
7.	Yellow	Colourless	Brown	Brown	Mo
8.	Rose-violet	Rose-violet	Red	Violet	Au
9.	Yellow	Colourless	Yellow	Yellowish-brown	W
10.	Yellow	Pale yellow	Pale green	Pale green to nearly colourless	U
11.	Yellow	Greenish-yellow	Dirty green	Emerald green	V
12.	Yellow	Colourless	Grey	Pale violet	Ti
13.	Orange-red	Yellow	Colourless	Colourless	Ce

Confirmatory/Wet Tests for The Identification of Cations

The basic radicals or cations indicated in the dry or preliminary test are confirmed by the wet tests.

For convenience of the qualitative analysis of cations, these are classified into six groups:

Group	Group reagent	Cation (Basic radical)	Composition of ppt	Colour of ppt
Zero	NaOH	NH_4^+	NH_3 gas is evolved	—
I	Dil. HCl	Pb^{2+}	$PbCl_2$	White
II	H_2S in the presence of dil. HCl	Pb^{2+} Cu^{2+} As^{3+}	PbS CuS As_2S_3	Black Black Yellow
III	Conc. HNO_3 and NH_4OH in the presence of excess of NH_4Cl.	Fe^{3+} Al^{3+}	$Fe(OH)_3$ $Al(OH)_3$	Brown white gelatinous ppt.
IV	H_2S in the presence of NH_4OH.	Co^{2+} Ni^{2+} Zn^{2+} Mn^{2+}	CoS NiS ZnS MnS	Black Black Bluish-white Flesh colour
V	$(NH_4)_2CO_3$ in the presence of NH_4OH.	Ba^{2+} Ca^{2+} Sr^{2+}	$BaCO_3$ $CaCO_3$ $SrCO_3$	White White White
VI	Na_2HPO_4	Mg^{2+}	$Mg(NH_4)PO_4$	White

Preparation of Original Solution

The first essential step for the identification of cations is to prepare a clear and transparent solution of the salt. This is called **original solution.**

To prepare the original solution, following solvents are tried one after the other in the systematic order, i.e. if the salt does not dissolve in a particular solvent, even on heating, try the next one. The solution must be transparent and should not have any suspended particles. List of the solvents is given below:

1. **Distilled water** (cold, hot) Take a little amount of the salt in a clean boiling tube and add a few mL of distilled water and shake it. If the salt does not dissolved, heat the content of the boiling tube till the salt completely dissolves.
2. **Dilute HCl** If salt is insoluble in water, take fresh salt in a clean boiling tube and add a few mL of dil. HCl to it. If the salt is insoluble in cold, heat the boiling tube till the salt is completely dissolved.
3. **Concentrated HCl** If the salt does not dissolve either in water or dilute HCl even on heating try to dissolve it in few mL of conc. HCl by heating.

Note Dil. HNO_3 *or* H_2SO_4 *cannot be used in place of* HCl *because* H_2SO_4 *causes the precipitation of* Pb^{2+}, Ba^{2+}, Sr^{2+} and Ca^{2+} *as insoluble sulphates while* HNO_3 *is an oxidising agent and can bring about the oxidation of* H_2S *to give yellow precipitate of S in the second group.*

Group Analysis

Analysis of Zero Group Cation, NH_4^+

Experiment and Procedure	Observation	Inference	Chemistry involved
The given salt around 0.1 g is heated with 1-2 mL of conc. NaOH solution.	A pungent smell of ammonia is obtained.	NH_4^+ cations may be present.	Ammonia gas is evolved by the action of sodium hydroxide on ammonium salts like NH_4Cl, $(NH_4)_2SO_4$, etc. $NH_4Cl + NaOH \longrightarrow NaCl + NH_3 + H_2O$ $(NH_4)_2SO_4 + 2NaOH \longrightarrow Na_2SO_4 + 2NH_3 + 2H_2O$
Bring a glass rod dipped in HCl near the mouth of the test tube.	White dense fumes are observed.	NH_4^+ cations are present.	The evolved gas reacts with HCl to give visible white fumes of NH_4Cl. $NH_3 + HCl \longrightarrow \underset{\text{White fumes}}{NH_4Cl\uparrow}$
Pass the gas through Nessler's reagent.	Brown precipitate is obtained.	Presence of NH_4^+ ions is confirmed.	On passing the gas through Nessler's reagent, a brown colouration or a precipitate of basic mercury (II) amido iodine is formed. $\underset{\text{Nessler's reagent}}{2K_2HgI_4} + NH_3 + 3KOH \longrightarrow \underset{\text{Basic mercury(II) amido-iodine brown ppt.}}{HgO\cdot Hg(NH_2)I} + 7KI + 2H_2O$

Analysis of Cations Belonging to Group I-VI

For the detection of cations belonging to groups I to VI, the cations are precipitated from the original solution by using the group reagents according to the scheme given below :

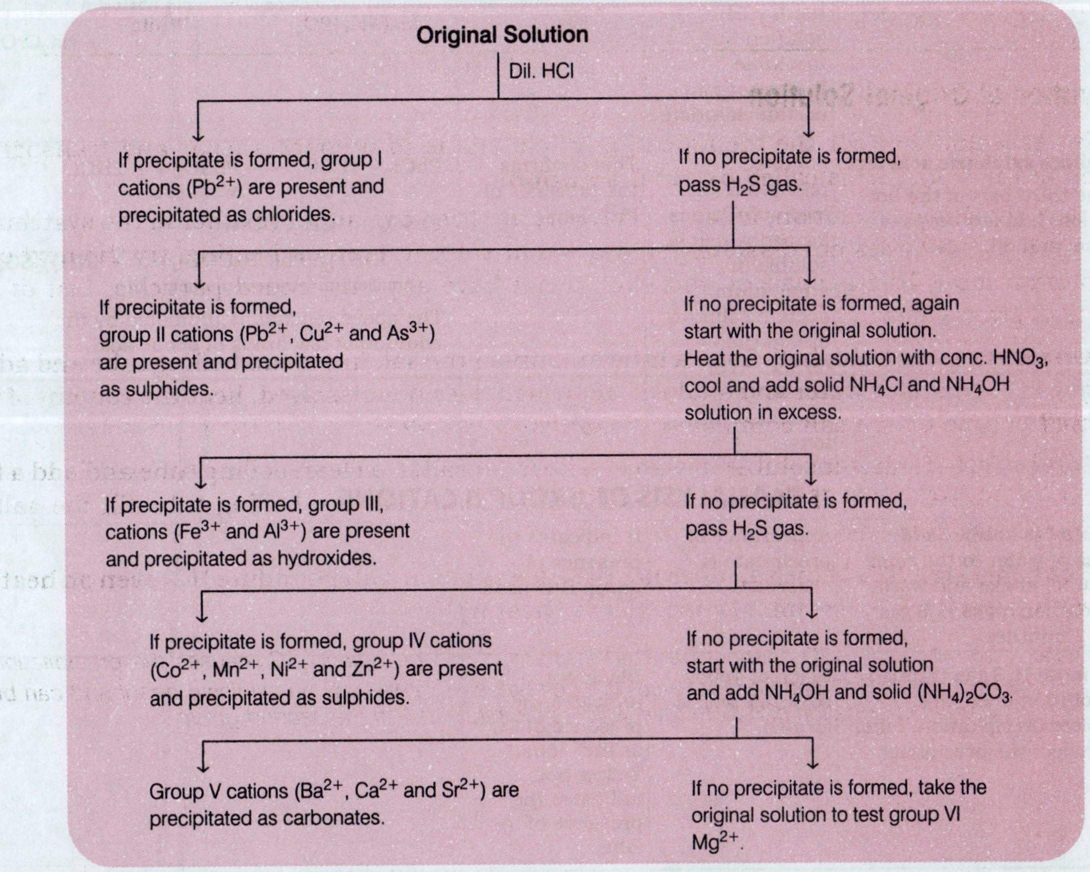

Various tests are used to analyse and confirm the basic radicals or cations belonging to a particular group. These are listed below :

Experiment and Procedure	Observation	Inference	Chemistry involved
❶ ANALYSIS OF GROUP I CATIONS			
To the original solution prepared in water, add dil. HCl.	A white precipitate is formed.	Group I, Pb^{2+} may be present.	Lead is precipitated as lead chloride. $\underset{\text{Present in a given salt}}{Pb^{2+}} + 2Cl^- \longrightarrow \underset{\text{White ppt.}}{PbCl_2\downarrow}$
Note *In case the original solution is prepared in conc. HCl, dilute the solution with cold water and cool the test tube under tap water.*			
Confirmatory Tests for Pb^{2+} Dissolve the white precipitate in hot water and divide the solution into three parts:			
(i) **Potassium iodide test** Add KI (potassium iodide) solution to the first part of the hot solution.	A yellow precipitate of lead iodide is formed which is soluble in boiling water and on cooling, shiny crystals are formed.	Presence of Pb^{2+} ions is confirmed.	$\underset{\text{(Hot solution)}}{PbCl_2} + 2KI \longrightarrow \underset{\text{Yellow ppt.}}{PbI_2\downarrow} + 2KCl$
(ii) **Potassium chromate test** Add potassium chromate (K_2CrO_4) solution to the second part of the solution.	A yellow precipitate of lead chromate is formed which is soluble in hot NaOH solution but insoluble in ammonium acetate solution.	This confirms the presence of Pb^{2+} ions.	$\underset{\text{Hot solution}}{PbCl_2} + K_2CrO_4 \longrightarrow \underset{\text{Lead chromate (Yellow precipitate)}}{PbCrO_4\downarrow} + 2KCl$ $PbCrO_4 + 4NaOH \rightleftharpoons \underset{\text{Sodium tetrahydroxo plumbate (III)}}{Na_2[Pb(OH)_4]} + Na_2CrO_4$
(iii) **Dilute sulphuric acid test** To the third part of the hot solution, add few drops of alcohol and dil. H_2SO_4.	A white precipitate of lead sulphate is formed which is soluble in ammonium acetate solution due to the formation of tetraaceto plumbate (II) ions.	This confirms the presence of Pb^{2+} ions.	$PbCl_2 + H_2SO_4 \longrightarrow \underset{\text{White ppt.}}{PbSO_4\downarrow} + 2HCl$ $PbSO_4 + 4CH_3COONH_4 \longrightarrow \underset{\text{Ammonium tetraacetoplumbate (II)}}{(NH_4)_2[Pb(CH_3COO)_4]} + (NH_4)_2SO_4$ The above reaction is promoted by the addition of few drops of acetic acid.
❷ ANALYSIS OF GROUP II CATIONS			
If group I is absent, add excess of water to the same test tube, shake and warm the solution, pass H_2S gas for 1-2 minutes.	Appearance of precipitate is observed.	It indicates the presence of group II cations.	
Pass more H_2S gas through the solution to ensure complete precipitation. Filter and collect the precipitate.	Black or yellow coloured ppt. is formed.	Black ppt. indicates the presence of Cu^{2+} or Pb^{2+} ions. Yellow ppt. indicates the presence of As^{3+} ions.	

<table>
<tr><th colspan="2">Experiment and Procedure</th><th>Observation</th><th>Inference</th><th colspan="2">Chemistry involved</th></tr>
<tr><td colspan="2">Dissolve the collected precipitate in excess of yellow ammonium sulphide solution and shake the test tube.</td><td>Precipitate may be soluble or insoluble in ammonium sulphide solution.</td><td>If black precipitate is insoluble, group II A (copper or lead group) is present and if yellow precipitate is soluble, group II B (arsenic group) is present.</td><td colspan="2"></td></tr>
<tr><td colspan="2">Confirmatory Tests for Group II A Cations (Pb^{2+} and Cu^{2+})
Boil the black precipitate with (1-2 mL) dilute nitric acid and add few drops of alcohol and dil. H_2SO_4.</td><td>Either white ppt. or no ppt. is formed.</td><td>White ppt indicates the presence of Pb^{2+} ions and no ppt indicates the presence of Cu^{2+} ions.</td><td colspan="2">For Pb^{2+} ions
Lead sulphide precipitate dissolves in dilute HNO_3. On adding dilute H_2SO_4 and few drops of alcohol to this solution, a white precipitate of lead sulphate appears.
$\underset{\text{Black ppt. (Soluble in } HNO_3)}{3PbS} + 8HNO_3 \longrightarrow 3Pb(NO_3)_2 + 4H_2O + 2NO + 3S$
$Pb(NO_3)_2 + H_2SO_4 \longrightarrow 2HNO_3 + \underset{\text{White ppt.}}{PbSO_4\downarrow}$
For Cu^{2+} ions
Copper sulphide dissolves in nitric acid due to the formation of copper nitrate.
$\underset{\text{Black ppt.}}{3CuS} + 8HNO_3 \longrightarrow 3Cu(NO_3)_2 + 4H_2O + 2NO + 3S$</td></tr>
<tr><td>Tests for Pb^{2+} ions
Dissolve the white ppt. in ammonium acetate solution and acidify it with acetic acid. Divide the solution into two parts:</td><td>Tests for Cu^{2+} ions
If no ppt. is formed, then add NH_4OH solution in excess.</td><td>For Pb^{2+}
No colouration or ppt. is formed in case of Pb^{2+} ions.
For Cu^{2+}
Blue colouration is observed.</td><td>For Cu^{2+}
Blue colouration indicates the presence of Cu^{2+} ions.</td><td>For Pb^{2+} ions
$\underset{\text{White ppt.}}{PbSO_4} + 4CH_3COONH_4 \rightarrow (NH_4)_2[Pb(CH_3COO)_4] + (NH_4)SO_4$</td><td>For Cu^{2+} ions
A small amount of NH_4OH precipitates basic $CuSO_4$ which is soluble in excess of NH_4OH due to the formation of tetra amminocopper (II) complex.
$S + 2HNO_3 \longrightarrow H_2SO_4 + 2NO$
$2Cu^{2+} + SO_4^{2-} + 2NH_3 + 2H_2O \longrightarrow Cu(OH)_2 \cdot CuSO_4 + 2NH_4^+$
$Cu(OH)_2 \cdot CuSO_4 + 8NH_3 \longrightarrow \underset{\text{Deep blue}}{2[Cu(NH_3)_4]SO_4} + 2OH^- + SO_4^{2-}$</td></tr>
</table>

Experiment and Procedure		Observation	Inference	Chemistry involved	
For Pb^{2+} ions	**For Cu^{2+} ions**				
(i) **Potassium chromate, K_2CrO_4 test** To the first part, add K_2CrO_4 solution, a yellow ppt. is formed.	(i)**Potassium ferrocyanide test** Add acetic acid (to acidify the solution) and potassium ferrocyanide solution.	**For Pb^{2+} ions** A yellow ppt. is observed in potassium chromate test. **For Cu^{2+} ions** A chocolate brown ppt is observed in potassium ferrocyanide test.	**For Pb^{2+} ions** A yellow ppt. confirms Pb^{2+} ions. **For Cu^{2+} ions** A brown ppt. confirms the presence of Cu^{2+} ions.	**Potassium chromate test** $(NH_4)_2[Pb(CH_3COO)_4] + K_2CrO_4 \longrightarrow$ $PbCrO_4\downarrow$ Yellow ppt. $+ 2CH_3COOK + 2(NH_4)_2SO_4$	**Potassium ferrocyanide test** $[Cu(NH_3)_4]SO_4 + 4CH_3COOH \longrightarrow$ $CuSO_4 + 4CH_3COONH_4$ $2CuSO_4 + K_4[Fe(CN)_6]$ Potassium hexacyano ferrate (II) $\rightarrow Cu_2[Fe(CN)_6]\downarrow$ Copper hexacyano ferrate (II) Chocolate brown colour $+ 2K_2SO_4$
(ii) **Potassium iodide test** To the second part, add KI solution, a yellow ppt. is formed.	(ii) **Potassium iodide test** To second part, add acetic acid and KI solution.	**For Pb^{2+} ions** A yellow ppt. is formed in KI test **For Cu^{2+}** A white ppt. is formed in KI test.	**For Pb^{2+} ions** Yellow ppt. confirms the presence of Pb^{2+} ions. **For Cu^{2+} ions** A white ppt. confirms the presence of Cu^{2+} ions.	**Potassium iodide test** $Pb^{2+} + 2I^- \longrightarrow PI_2$	**Potassium iodide test** White precipitate is due to formation of Cu_2I_2 and the brown colour is due to liberation of I_2 $2CuSO_4 + 4KI \longrightarrow$ $Cu_2I_2\downarrow + I_2 + 2K_2SO_4$ White ppt. Brown colouration
Confirmatory test for group II B Cations [As^{3+} ions] Dissolve the yellow precipitate in yellow ammonium sulphide solution and acidify the solution with dilute HCl.		A yellow precipitate is formed.	As^{3+} ions are present.	Ammonium thioarsenides formed on dissolution of As_2S_3 decomposes with dilute HCl and a yellow precipitate of As_2S_5 is formed. $As_2S_3 + 3(NH_4)_2S_2 \longrightarrow 2(NH_4)_3AsS_4 + S$ $2(NH_4)_3AsS_4 + 6HCl \longrightarrow As_2S_5\downarrow + 3H_2S + 6NH_4Cl$	
Heat the yellow precipitate with conc. HNO_3 and add ammonium molybdate solution.		A canary yellow precipitate is formed.	Presence of As^{3+} ions is confirmed.	As_2S_5 dissolves in conc. HNO_3 on heating due to arsenic acid formation which gives a canary yellow precipitate on addition of ammonium molybdate solution. $As_2S_5 + 10HNO_3 \xrightarrow{+4H_2O}$ (Yellow ppt.) $6H_3AsO_4 + 10NO + 15\,S$ (Soluble) $H_3AsO_4 + 12(NH_4)_2MoO_4$ Arsenic acid Ammonium molybelate $+ 21HNO_3 \longrightarrow$ $(NH_4)_3[As(Mo_3O_{10})_4]\downarrow + 21NH_4NO_3 + 12H_2O$ Yellow ppt. of ammonium arsinomolybdate	

Experiment and Procedure	Observation	Inference	Chemistry involved
3 ANALYSIS FOR GROUP III CATIONS			
If group II is absent, take the original solution and add 2-3 drops of conc. HNO_3 to oxidise Fe^{2+} to Fe^{3+}, ions. Boil the solution for few minutes and cool it. Add 2 g of NH_4Cl and boil again, cool the solution under tap water. Add excess of NH_4OH solution till it smells of NH_3 and shake the test tube.	Either brown or white precipitate is formed.	Brown precipitate indicates the presence of Ferric Fe^{3+} ions while white gelatinous precipitate indicates the presence of Aluminium Al^{3+} ions.	Original solution when heated with nitric acid, ferrous ions are oxidised to ferric ions. $2FeCl_2 + 2HCl + [O] \longrightarrow 2FeCl_3 + H_2O$ The group III cations are precipitated as hydroxides on the addition of excess of ammonium hydroxide, NH_4OH. $FeCl_3 + 3NH_4OH \longrightarrow 3NH_4Cl + Fe(OH)_3\downarrow$ (Reddish brown ppt.) $AlCl_3 + 3NH_4OH \longrightarrow 3NH_4Cl + Al(OH)_3\downarrow$ White ppt. These precipitates dissolve in dilute HCl due to the formation of corresponding chlorides.

Note *Add sufficient quantity of* NH_4Cl, *otherwise the hydroxides of higher group may be precipitated alongwith the radicals of third group. Sometimes, the addition of conc.* HNO_3 *in the analysis of group III serves to oxidise* Fe^{2+} *to* Fe^{3+} *ions. Thus, before confirming* Fe^{3+} *ions, first confirm* Fe^{2+} *ions.*

Experiment & Procedure	Observation	Inference	Chemistry involved
Confirmatory test for Fe^{2+} ions Add conc. HNO_3 to the original solution and few drops of potassium ferricyanide solution.	A deep blue colouration is obtained.	This deep blue colouration confirms Fe^{2+} ions.	Turnbull's blue precipitate is formed $3Fe^{2+} + 2K_3[Fe(CN)_6] \longrightarrow Fe_3[Fe(CN)_6]_2 + 6K^+$
Confirmatory Tests for Fe^{3+} and Al^{3+} ions			
Brown Precipitate Fe^{3+}			
Dissolve the brown precipitate in dil. HCl and divide into two parts :			Reddish brown precipitate of $Fe(OH)_3$ dissolves in Cl and $FeCl_3$ is formed. $Fe(OH)_3 + 3HCl \longrightarrow FeCl_3 + 3H_2O$
(i) **Potassium ferrocyanide test** Add potassium ferrocyanide solution to the first part.	A blue colour precipitate appears when solution containing $FeCl_3$ is treated with potassium ferrocyanide solution.	Prussian blue colouration confirms the presence of Fe^{3+} ions.	Prussian blue precipitate is due to ferric ferrocyanide. $4FeCl_3 + 3K_4[Fe(CN)_6] \longrightarrow$ (Potassium ferrocyanide) $Fe_4[Fe(CN)_6]_3\downarrow + 12KCl$ Prussian blue ppt. If potassium hexacyanoferrate II is added in excess then $KFe[Fe(CN)_6]$ is formed which tends to form a colloidal solution and cannot be filtered. $FeCl_3 + K_4[Fe(CN)_6] \longrightarrow KFe[Fe(CN)_6] + 3KCl$ Soluble prussian blue

Experiment & Procedure	Observation	Inference	Chemistry involved
(ii) Potassium thiocyanate test To the second part, add potassium thiocyanate (potassium sulphocyanide) solution.	A blood red colouration appears.	Blood red colouration confirms the presence of Fe^{3+} ions.	$FeCl_3 + 3KSCN \longrightarrow 3KCl + [Fe(SCN)_3]$ (KSCN: Potassium thiocyanate; $[Fe(SCN)_3]$: Blood red colour)
White Precipitate Al^{3+} Dissolve the white precipitate in dilute HCl and divide it into two parts :			$Al(OH)_3 + 3HCl \longrightarrow AlCl_3 + 3H_2O$
(i) Lake test Add blue litmus solution to the first part and add ammonium hydroxide solution drop by drop along the sides of the test tube till blue colour develops.	A blue mass floating in the colourless solution appears.	Blue mass formation confirms the presence of Al^{3+} ions.	When blue litmus is added to the solution, a red colouration is obtained due to acidic nature of the solution. On addition of NH_4OH solution drop by drop, the solution becomes alkaline and $Al(OH)_3$ is precipitated which adsorbs blue colour from the solution and forms insoluble adsorption complex named lake. $AlCl_3 + 3NH_4OH \longrightarrow 3NH_4Cl + Al(OH)_3\downarrow$ ($Al(OH)_3$: Blue colour adsorbs by this ppt.)
(ii) To the second part, add NaOH solution and warm.	A gelatinous white precipitate is obtained soluble in excess NaOH.	A white precipitate confirms the presence of Al^{3+} ions.	When the solution containing $AlCl_3$ is treated with NaOH, a white gelatinous precipitate of $Al(OH)_3$ is formed which is soluble in excess of NaOH due to the formation of sodium aluminate. $AlCl_3 + 3NaOH \longrightarrow Al(OH)_3\downarrow + 3NaCl$ $Al(OH)_3 + NaOH \longrightarrow NaAlO_2 + 2H_2O$ ($Al(OH)_3$: White gelationous ppt.; $NaAlO_2$: Sodium aluminate)

4 ANALYSIS OF GROUP IV CATIONS

Experiment & Procedure	Observation	Inference	Chemistry involved
If group III cations are absent, pass H_2S gas in the solution taken for group III for a few minutes.	Either white, black or flesh coloured precipitate appears.	Group IV cations Zn^{2+}, Mn^{2+}, Ni^{2+} or Co^{2+} may be present.	On passing H_2S gas through group III solution, cations Zn^{2+}, Mn^{2+}, Ni^{2+} and Co^{2+} precipitates as their sulphides. $Zn(OH)_2 + H_2S \longrightarrow 2H_2O + ZnS\downarrow$ (White ppt.) $Mn(OH)_2 + H_2S \longrightarrow 2H_2O + MnS\downarrow$ (Buff or flesh coloured ppt.) $Ni(OH)_2 + H_2S \longrightarrow 2H_2O + NiS\downarrow$ (Black ppt.) $Co(OH)_2 + H_2S \longrightarrow 2H_2O + CoS\downarrow$ (Black ppt.)
Confirmatory Test for Zn^{2+} ions Dissolve the precipitate in dil. HCl. Boil off H_2S and divide the solution into two parts:			ZnS dissolves in HCl to form $ZnCl_2$. $ZnS + 2HCl \longrightarrow ZnCl_2 + H_2S\uparrow$
(i) Sodium hydroxide test To the first part, add NaOH solution.	A white precipitate is obtained soluble in excess of NaOH solution.	This confirms the presence of Zn^{2+} ions.	On addition of NaOH, white precipitate of $Zn(OH)_2$ is formed which is soluble in excess of NaOH solution on heating. $ZnCl_2 + 2NaOH \longrightarrow Zn(OH)_2\downarrow + 2NaCl$ (White ppt.) $Zn(OH)_2 + 2NaOH \longrightarrow Na_2ZnO_2 + 2H_2O$ (Na_2ZnO_2: Sodium zincate)

Experiment & Procedure	Observation	Inference	Chemistry involved
(ii) **Potassium ferrocyanide test** Neutralise the second part with NH_4OH and add potassium ferrocyanide solution.	A bluish-white ppt. appears.	This confirms the presence of Zn^{2+} ions.	When potassium ferrocyanide $K_4[Fe(CN)_6]$ solution is added to the solution after neutralisation by NH_4OH, a bluish-white precipitate of zinc ferrocyanide appears. $2ZnCl_2 + K_4[Fe(CN)_6] \longrightarrow \underset{\text{Bluish-white}}{Zn_2[Fe(CN)_6]} \downarrow + 4KCl$
Confirmatory test for Mn^{2+} ions. Dissolve the precipitate in dil. HCl by boiling off H_2S gas. Then, add NaOH solution in excess.	A white precipitate is formed which turns brown on keeping.	The presence of Mn^{2+} ions is confirmed.	MnS precipitate dissolves in dil. HCl by boiling and forms a white precipitate of $Mn(OH)_2$ with NaOH solution when added in excess. $MnS + 2HCl \longrightarrow MnCl_2 + H_2S\uparrow$ $MnCl_2 + 2NaOH \longrightarrow \underset{\text{White ppt.}}{Mn(OH)_2} \downarrow + 2NaCl$ $Mn(OH)_2$ turns brown due to atmospheric oxidation into hydrated manganese dioxide. $Mn(OH)_2 + [O] \longrightarrow \underset{\text{(Brown colour)}}{MnO(OH)_2}$
Confirmatory test for Ni^{2+} and Co^{2+} ions Dissolve the precipitate in *aqua-regia*. Now, evaporate the solution to dryness and cool. Dissolve the residue water and divide the solution in two parts :			$3NiS + 2HNO_3 + 6HCl \longrightarrow 3NiCl_2 + 2NO + 3S + 4H_2O$ $CoS + HNO_3 + 3HCl \longrightarrow CoCl_2 + NOCl + S + 2H_2O$
For Ni^{2+} ions **Dimethyl glyoxime test** Add NH_4OH solution to the first part and then few drops of dimethyl glyoxime are added and shake the test tube.	A brilliant red precipitate is obtained.	The red precipitate confirms the presence of Ni^{2+} ions.	When dimethyl glyoxime is added to the aqueous solution of nickel chloride and made alkaline by adding NH_4OH solution, a brilliant red precipitate is obtained. $NiCl_2 + 2NH_4OH + \underset{\text{Dimethyl glyoxime}}{\begin{matrix} H_3C-C=N-OH \\ \vert \\ H_3C-C=N-OH \end{matrix}} \longrightarrow$ $\underset{\text{Bright red ppt.}}{\begin{matrix} OH\cdots\cdots O \\ CH_3-C=N \quad N=C-CH_3 \\ Ni \\ CH_3-C=N \quad N=C-CH_3 \\ O\cdots\cdots HO \end{matrix}} + 2NH_4Cl + 2H_2O$
For Co^{2+} ions **Potassium nitrite test** Add NH_4OH solution to the second part and then add acetic acid and a crystal of potassium nitrite.	A yellow coloured complex or precipitate is obtained.	A yellow precipitate confirms the presence of Co^{2+} ions.	When potassium nitrite is added to an aqueous solution of salt containing cobalt and the solution is neutralised with dil. CH_3COOH, a yellow precipitate of cobalt complex named potassium hexanitritocobaltate (III) is formed. $CoCl_2 + 7KNO_2 + 2CH_3COOH \longrightarrow \underset{\text{Potassium hexanitritocobaltate (III) (Yellow precipitate)}}{K_3[Co(NO_2)_6]} + 2KCl + 2CH_3COOK + H_2O + NO$

Note *Pass H_2S gas only through a test portion. If no precipitate results, reject the test portion and proceed for group V with the remaining solution. In case a dirty white precipitate results, then tests for Mn^{2+} or Zn^{2+}. Also note the colour of the original salt.*

Experiment & Procedure	Observation	Inference	Chemistry involved
5 ANALYSIS OF GROUP V CATIONS			
If group IV cations are absent, then proceed for detection of group V cations. For this, add 2-3 g of solid NH_4Cl to the original solution. Boil and cool the contents. Add an excess of NH_4OH solution till it smells of ammonia and then add solid $(NH_4)_2CO_3$.	A white precipitate is observed.	The appearance of white precipitate indicates the presence of group V cations.	When $(NH_4)_2CO_3$ is added to the salt solution containing NH_4Cl and NH_4OH, the carbonates of Ba^{2+}, Sr^{2+} and Ca^{2+} are precipitated. $BaCl_2 + (NH_4)_2CO_3 \longrightarrow \underset{\text{White ppt.}}{BaCO_3 \downarrow} + 2NH_4Cl$ $SrCl_2 + (NH_4)_2CO_3 \longrightarrow SrCO_3 \downarrow + 2NH_4Cl$ $CaCl_2 + (NH_4)_2CO_3 \longrightarrow CaCO_3 \downarrow + 2NH_4Cl$
Preserve the small amount of precipitate for flame test. Then, dissolve the remaining white precipitate by boiling with dilute acetic acid and divide the solution into three parts one each for Ba^{2+}, Sr^{2+} and Ca^{2+} ions.	White precipitate dissolves.	The insoluble carbonates of Ba, Sr and Ca dissolves in acetic acid due to the formation of soluble acetate.	$BaCO_3 + 2CH_3COOH \longrightarrow (CH_3COO)_2Ba + H_2O + CO_2 \uparrow$ $SrCO_3 + 2CH_3COOH \longrightarrow (CH_3COO)_2Sr + H_2O + CO_2 \uparrow$ $CaCO_3 + 2CH_3COOH \longrightarrow (CH_3COO)_2Ca + H_2O + CO_2 \uparrow$
Confirmatory Tests for Ba^{2+} ions			
(i) **Potassium chromate test** To the first part, add potassium chromate solution.	A yellow precipitate is obtained.	The yellow precipitate indicates the presence of Ba^{2+} in the salt.	K_2CrO_4 gives yellow precipitate of $BaCrO_4$ with barium acetate, $(CH_3COO)_2Ba$. $(CH_3COO)_2Ba + K_2CrO_4 \longrightarrow \underset{\text{Yellow ppt.}}{BaCrO_4 \downarrow} + 2CH_3COOK$
(ii) **Flame test** Heat the preserved precipitate in the non-luminous flame of Bunsen burner taken on a platinum wire which is dipped in conc. HCl to observe the colour of the flame produced.	A grassy green flame is obtained which is visible through blue glass.	A grassy green colour of the flame confirms the presence of Ba^{2+} ions.	
Confirmatory test for Sr^{2+} ions			
(i) **Ammonium sulphate test** To the second part of the solution, add ammonium sulphate solution. Heat and scratch the sides of the test tube with a glass rod and cool.	A white precipitate is obtained.	The white precipitate indicates the presence of Sr^{2+} ions.	Ammonium sulphate gives a white precipitate of strontium sulphate with strontium acetate. $(CH_3COO)_2Sr + (NH_4)_2SO_4 \longrightarrow \underset{\text{White ppt.}}{SrSO_4 \downarrow} + 2CH_3COONH_4$
(ii) **Flame test** Heat the precipitate taken on the platinum wire directly on the non-luminous flame.	A crimson red flame is produced.	A crimson red flame confirms the presence of Sr^{2+} ions.	—

Experiment & Procedure	Observation	Inference	Chemistry involved
For Ca^{2+} ions			
(i) **Ammonium oxalate test** To the third part of the solution, add ammonium oxalate solution and shake well.	A white precipitate of calcium oxalate is obtained.	The white precipitate indicates the presence of Ca^{2+} ions.	Ammonium oxalate gives a white precipitate with calcium acetate. $(CH_3COO)_2Ca + (NH_4)_2C_2O_4 \longrightarrow \underset{\text{White ppt.}}{(COO)_2Ca} \downarrow + 2CH_3COONH_4$
(ii) **Flame test** Heat the precipitate taken on the platinum wire directly on the non-luminous flame.	A brick red flame which looks greenish yellow through blue glass.	A brick red flame confirms the presence of Ca^{2+} ions.	—

Note *The radicals of group V should be tested in the order* Ba^{2+}, Sr^{2+}, Ca^{2+} *[Easy to remember as Bata shoe company]. If* Ba^{2+} *is confirmed, do not proceed to test for* Sr^{2+} *and* Ca^{2+}. *Similarly, if* Sr^{2+} *is confirmed do not test for* Ca^{2+} *ions.*

Experiment and Procedure	Observation	Inference	Chemistry involved
6 ANALYSIS OF GROUP VI CATION, Mg^{2+}			
If group V is absent, test for the group VI cation. To a part of the original solution, add 2-3 g of solid NH_4Cl and NH_4OH solution in excess. Warm and cool the solution and then add solution of disodium hydrogen phosphate till white crust formation takes place in the inner walls of the test tube.	A white crystalline precipitate is obtained on the inner walls of the test tube which is scratched with a glass rod.	A white precipitate indicates the presence of Mg^{2+} ions.	$Mg^{2+} + 2NH_4Cl \longrightarrow MgCl_2 + 2NH_4^+$ $MgCl_2 + NH_4OH + Na_2HPO_4 \longrightarrow \underset{\text{White ppt.}}{Mg(NH_4)PO_4} \downarrow + 2NaCl + H_2O$

Note *Sometimes precipitate of magnesium ammonium phosphate appears after sometime. So warm the solution and scratch the sides of test tube after adding sodium hydrogen phosphate solution.*

Result

(i) The cation(s) present in the salt/salt mixture is/are ...

(ii) The anion(s) present in the salt/salt mixture is/are ...

PRECAUTIONS

- Always use an apron, eye protector and hand gloves while working in the chemistry laboratory.
- Before using any reagent or chemicals, read the labels on the bottles carefully. Do not use unlabelled reagent.
- Never mix chemicals and reagents unnecessarily. Never taste any chemical.
- Be careful in smelling chemicals or vapours. Fan the vapours gently towards your nose. Do not put your nose directly above the test tube or beakers for smelling.
- Wash your hands immediately after touching any salt as it may be corrosive.
- Do not add sodium metal to water or do not throw it in the sink or dustbin.
- Be careful while heating the test tube. The test tube should never point towards a person while heating or adding a reagent.
- Always use the reagents in minimum quantity. Use of reagents in excess, not only lead to wastage of chemicals but also cause damage to the environment.
- Always pour acid into water for dilution. Never add water to acid.
- Be very careful while dealing with the explosive compounds, inflammable substances, poisonous gases, electric appliances, glass wares, flame and the hot substances.
- Always wash your hands after the completion of the laboratory work.
- Keep your working surrounding clean. Never throw papers and glass in the sink. Always use dustbin for this purpose.

Viva-Voce

Q.1 What is the first step performed in systematic qualitative salt analysis?

Ans. The first step is the preliminary examination of the salt which includes noting the colour, smell, solubility, and physical appearance.

Q.2 Which type of anions can be detected with dilute sulphuric acid test?

Ans. Dilute sulphuric acid helps in identifying carbonate, nitrite, acetate, sulphite and sulphide radicals by the evolution of characteristic gases.

Q.3 How does the presence of carbonate ion in salt get confirmed?

Ans. Carbonate ion is confirmed by the brisk effervescence of carbon dioxide gas which turns lime water milky.

Q.4 What is the characteristic smell observed if ammonium ion is present?

Ans. Ammonium ion gives a pungent smell of ammonia gas on heating with alkali like sodium hydroxide.

Q.5 What is the significance of using group reagents in cation analysis?

Ans. Group reagents help in classifying cations into different analytical groups for systematic detection.

Q.6 What is the confirmatory test for Pb^{2+} ion?

Ans. Pb^{2+} ion is confirmed by formation of yellow precipitate with potassium iodide solution.

Q.7 How are Group II cations precipitated?

Ans. Group II cations are precipitated as sulphides by passing hydrogen sulphide gas through salt solution in presence of dilute hydrochloric acid.

Q.8 Which radical turns acidified potassium dichromate paper green?

Ans. Sulphite radical (SO_3^{2-}) turns acidified potassium dichromate paper green due to formation of sulphur dioxide gas.

Q.9 **What is the observation if sulphide ion is present in the salt?**

Ans. Sulphide ion gives rotten egg smell due to evolution of hydrogen sulphide gas in reaction with dilute acid.

Q.10 **How is the nitrate ion confirmed in salt analysis?**

Ans. Nitrate ion is confirmed by the brown ring test formed between ferrous sulphate and concentrated sulphuric acid in the presence of nitrate.

Q.11 **What confirms the presence of chloride ions in the salt?**

Ans. Formation of a white curdy precipitate of silver chloride with silver nitrate solution confirms the chloride ion.

Q.12 **Which observation indicates the presence of ferrous ions in salt?**

Ans. Ferrous ions give dirty green precipitate with ammonium hydroxide and turn brown on standing due to oxidation.

Q.13 **Which gas turns lead acetate paper black?**

Ans. Hydrogen sulphide gas turns lead acetate paper black due to formation of lead sulphide.

Q.14 **Why is filtration required after each group precipitation?**

Ans. Filtration separates the precipitate from the solution so that the subsequent group analysis can be done on the filtrate.

Q.15 **What is the importance of systematic procedure in salt analysis?**

Ans. It ensures that no radical is missed or wrongly identified and helps in confirming the presence of only one cation and one anion in the given salt.

Q.16 **Why is a platinum wire used in the flame test and borax bead test?**

Ans. Platinum wire is inert thus does not interfere with the test and withstands high temperatures without reacting or corroding.

Q.17 **What precautions should be taken before using platinum wire in the bead test?**

Ans. The platinum wire should be cleaned by dipping in HCl and heating until it imparts no colour to the flame, ensuring accurate results.

Q.18 **Which colour confirms the presence of zinc oxide in the cobalt nitrate test?**

Ans. A green residue after heating with cobalt nitrate confirms the presence of zinc oxide.

Q.19 **What colour residue indicates the presence of Zn^{2+} in the charcoal cavity test?**

Ans. Yellow when hot and white when cold residue in the cavity indicates zinc oxide, confirming the presence of Zn^{2+}.

Q.20 **Why are oxidising and reducing flames used separately in borax bead test?**

Ans. Different metal ions show characteristic colours in oxidising and reducing flames, helping distinguish between oxidation states or elements.

Q.21 **What flame colour confirms the presence of Ba^{2+} ions?**

Ans. Barium ions give an apple green flame that appears bluish green through a blue glass.

Questions From NCERT Lab Manual

Q.1 **What is the difference between a qualitative and a quantitative analysis?**

Ans. Qualitative analysis deals with the identification of the constituents, i.e., acidic or basic radicals of a compound. On the other hand, quantitative analysis helps to estimate the concentration/amount/percentage of these elements present.

Q.2 **Why is platinum metal preferred to other metals for the flame test?**

Ans. Platinum does not react with acids and also does not impart any characteristic colour to the flame. Thus, it is preferred for the flame test.

Q.3 **Name the anions detected with the help of dilute H_2SO_4.**

Ans. NO_2^-, S^{2-}, SO_3^{2-} and CO_3^{2-}.

Q.4 **Name the anions detected by conc. H_2SO_4.**

Ans. Cl^-, Br^-, I^-, CH_3COO^- and NO_3^-.

Q.5 **How is sodium carbonate extract prepared?**

Ans. The salt is mixed with double the amount of solid Na_2CO_3 and about 20 mL of distilled water is added. It is then boiled till its volume is reduced to one-third and then filtered. The filtrate is sodium carbonate extract.

Q.6 **What is lime water and what happens on passing carbon dioxide gas through it?**

Ans. Lime water is a solution of calcium hydroxide $[Ca(OH)_2]$. It turns milky on passing CO_2 gas through it due to the formation of white precipitate of insoluble calcium carbonate

$$Ca(OH)_2 + CO_2 \longrightarrow \underset{\substack{\text{Milkiness} \\ \text{(Calcium carbonate)}}}{CaCO_3 \downarrow} + H_2O$$

Q.7 **How will you test the presence of carbonate ion?**

Ans. On treating the mixture with dil. HCl , CO_2 gas is evolved. When the gas is passed through lime water, it turns milky due to the formation of insoluble precipitate of calcium carbonate.

$$CO_2(g) + \underset{\text{Limewater}}{Ca(OH)_2(aq)} \longrightarrow \underset{\text{Milkiness}}{CaCO_3(s)} + H_2O(s)$$

$$Na_2CO_3 + 2HCl \longrightarrow 2NaCl + H_2O + CO_2 \uparrow$$

Q.8 **What is the composition of dark brown ring which is formed at the junction of two layers in the ring test for nitrates?**

Ans. $[Fe(NO)]SO_4$ (nitroso ferrous sulphate)-brown ring

Q.9 **Name the radical confirmed by sodium nitroprusside test.**

Ans. Sulphide (S^{2-}).

Q.10 **Describe the layer test for bromide and iodide ions.**

Ans. To the salt solution, dil. HCl and 1-2 mL of CS_2 is added and mixed well. Then, add chlorine water and shake it well. Orange and violet colour in CS_2 layer appears in case of bromide and iodide ions, respectively.

$$2KBr + Cl_2 \longrightarrow 2KCl + Br \qquad 2KI + Cl_2 \longrightarrow 2KCl + I_2$$

$$Br + Cl_2 \longrightarrow \text{Yellow or orange colour} \qquad I_2 + Cl_2 \longrightarrow \text{Violet coloured layer}$$

Q.11 **Why is silver nitrate solution stored in dark coloured bottles?**

Ans. If $AgNO_3$ is kept in light coloured/transparent bottles, it breaks down to give black/brown silver oxide and nitric acid.

$$2AgNO_3(aq) + H_2O(l) \longrightarrow Ag_2O(s) + 2HNO_3(aq)$$

If stored in dark bottles, this reaction is minimised and the reagent can be kept for quite a long time.

Q.12 **How do you test the presence of sulphide ion?**

Ans. Add ammoniacal sodium nitroprusside to the aqueous salt solution, a violet colouration occurs which confirms the presence of S^{2-} ion.

$$\underset{\substack{\text{Sodium} \\ \text{sulphide}}}{Na_2S} + \underset{\substack{\text{Sodium} \\ \text{nitroprusside}}}{Na_2[Fe(CN)_5NO]} \longrightarrow \underset{\text{Violet colour}}{Na_4[Fe(CN)_5NOS]}$$

Q.13 **Why does iodine give a blue colour with starch solution?**

Ans. The blue colour is due to the formation of inclusive complex between iodine and amylose unit of starch.

Q.14 **What is Nessler's reagent?**

Ans. Nessler's reagent is $K_2[HgI_4]$, potassium tetraiodomercurate (II).

Q.15 **How can one prevent the precipitation of group IV radicals with the second group radicals?**

Ans. HCl is added to the solution in group II before passing H_2S gas to avoid the precipitation of group IV radicals.

Q.16 Why is it essential to boil off H_2S gas before precipitation of radicals of group III?

Ans. If H_2S would not be boiled off, group IV cations will also get precipitated along with the group III radicals.

Q.17 Why is heating with conc. HNO_3 done before precipitation of group III?

Ans. It is done to oxidise ferrous salts to ferric salts and also helps in the removal of H_2S gas.

Q.18 Why is NH_4OH added before $(NH_4)_2CO_3$ solution while precipitating group V cations?

Ans. $(NH_4)_2CO_3$ contains some NH_4HCO_3 in it. NH_4OH is added to convert NH_4HCO_3 to $(NH_4)_2CO_3$ so that Ba^{2+}, Sr^{2+} and Ca^{2+} can be completely precipitated.

Q.19 Why do we sometimes get a white precipitate in group VI even if the salt does not contain Mg^{2+} radical?

Ans. The salt may contain Na^+ radical which may form white precipitate even if Mg^{2+} radical is absent.

Q.20 What is *aqua-regia*?

Ans. It is a mixture of conc. HCl and conc. HNO_3 in the ratio of 3 : 1 by volume.

Q.21 Name a cation, which is not obtained from a metal.

Ans. Ammonium ion (NH_4^+).

Q.22 How can you test the presence of ammonium ion?

Ans. Add NaOH to the salt and heat it. If NH_3 gas evolves, NH_4^+ ion is present. Pass this gas through Nessler's reagent, a brownish precipitate or colouration is observed.

Q.23 Why are the group V radicals tested in the order Ba^{2+}, Sr^{2+} and Ca^{2+}?

Ans. Tests of Sr^{2+} and Ca^{2+} are also given by Ba^{2+}. Similarly, Sr^{2+} also gives the test of Ca^{2+}. Thus, before confirming Sr^{2+}, we have to confirm the absence of Ba^{2+} and before confirming Ca^{2+} we have to show the absence of both the ions of Ba^{2+} and Sr^{2+}.

Q.24 Why does conc. HNO_3 kept in a bottle turn yellow in colour?

Ans. Due to the decomposition of HNO_3, NO is formed which is further oxidised to NO_2. The yellow colour is due to the dissolved NO_2.

$$4HNO_3 \xrightarrow{\text{Light}} 4NO_2 + 2H_2O + O_2$$

Q.25 Why should the solution be concentrated before proceeding to group V?

Ans. If solution is not concentrated, then the precipitation of the cations of group V will not occur completely with the group reagent $(NH_4)_2CO_3$.

Q.26 What do you understand by the term common ion effect?

Ans. Common ion effect is the suppression of dissociation of weak electrolyte in the presence of a strong electrolyte having a common ion. For example, in the presence of a strong electrolyte NH_4Cl, a weak electrolyte NH_4OH is less dissociated due to the presence of NH_4^+, a common ion between them. This fact is based on Le-Chatelier's principle.

$$NH_4Cl \longrightarrow NH_4^+ + Cl^- \quad \text{...(i)}$$

$$NH_4OH \rightleftharpoons NH_4^+ + OH^- \quad \text{...(ii)}$$

More NH_4^+ will shift the equilibrium backwards in reaction (ii) leading to the formation of more NH_4OH and hence, dissociation of NH_4OH is suppressed.

Q.27 Why is zinc sulphide not precipitated in group II?

Ans. Sulphides of group II cations are precipitated by passing H_2S gas through the acidified solution of HCl. Addition of HCl suppresses the ionisation of H_2S and lowers the concentration of S^{2-} ions, just enough to except the solubility product (K_{sp}) of group II sulphides but the precipitation of group IV sulphides like ZnS is prevented a s they have high (K_{sp}) values as compared to the sulphides of group II.

Q.28 Can we use glass rod instead of platinum wire for performing the flame test? Explain your answer.

Ans. No, we cannot use glass rod because glass contains sodium silicate which imparts its own golden yellow colour to the flame and hence, it will not give any accurate result.

Q.29 Why is dilute H_2SO_4 preferred over dilute HCl while testing anions?

Ans. On treating the salt with HCl, along with the gas evolved by the salt, HCl gas is also evolved. This can cause interference and the actual gas cannot be identified, whereas with H_2SO_4, no such problem arises.

Q.30 Carbon dioxide gas and sulphur dioxide gas both turn lime water milky. How will you distinguish between the two?

Ans. On passing through acidified $K_2Cr_2O_7$ solution, SO_2 turns $K_2Cr_2O_7$ green while CO_2 shows no effect.

Q.31 What is chromyl chloride test? How do you justify that CrO_2Cl_2 is acidic in nature?

Ans. This test is used to confirm the presence of chloride ions. During the test, the salt is mixed and heated with solid $K_2Cr_2O_7$ and conc. H_2SO_4. Red vapours of chromyl chloride (CrO_2Cl_2) are evolved. On passing them through NaOH solution, the solution acquires yellow colour due to the formation of Na_2CrO_4.

On acidifying this yellow solution with acetic acid and lead acetate, yellow ppt. of lead chromate is formed, confirming Cl^-.

$$4NaCl + K_2Cr_2O_7 + 6H_2SO_4 \longrightarrow 2CrO_2Cl_2 \uparrow + 2KHSO_4 + 4NaHSO_4 + 3H_2O$$

$$CrO_2Cl_2 + 4NaOH \longrightarrow Na_2CrO_4 + 2NaCl + 2H_2O$$

$$(CH_3COO)_2Pb + Na_2CrO_4 \longrightarrow \underset{\text{Yellow ppt.}}{PbCrO_4} \downarrow + 2CH_3COONa$$

CrO_2Cl_2 on reaction with water forms HCl and chromic acid which indicates its acidic nature.

$$CrO_2Cl_2 + 2H_2O \longrightarrow 2HCl + H_2CrO_4$$

Q.32 Why do bromides and iodides not give tests similar to chromyl chloride test?

Ans. Because instead of the formation of chromyl bromide and chromyl iodide, Br_2 and I_2 gases are evolved.

$$K_2Cr_2O_7 + 6KBr + 7H_2SO_4 \longrightarrow 3Br_2 \uparrow + Cr_2(SO_4)_3 + 4K_2SO_4 + 7H_2O$$

$$K_2Cr_2O_7 + 6KI + 7H_2SO_4 \longrightarrow 3I_2 \uparrow + Cr_2(SO_4)_3 + 4K_2SO_4 + 7H_2O$$

Q.33 Why is original solution for cations not prepared in conc. HNO_3 or H_2SO_4?

Ans. Conc. H_2SO_4 would lead to the precipitation of cations of group V as sulphate and conc. HNO_3 is an oxidising agent which on decomposition gives oxygen. When H_2S is passed, in the presence of HNO_3, a yellow precipitate of sulphur is obtained.

$$H_2S + 2HNO_3 \longrightarrow 2NO_2 + 2H_2O + \underset{\text{Yellow ppt.}}{S} \downarrow$$

Q.34 Why cannot conc. HCl be used as a group reagent in place of dil. HCl for the precipitation of 1st group cations?

Ans. The reason is that using conc. HCl would cause interference of $PbCl_2$ into the solution due to the formation of chloroplumbous complex by conc. HCl .

$$PbCl_2 + 2HCl \longrightarrow [PbCl_4]^{2-} + 2H^+$$

Q.35 Can we use ammonium sulphate instead of ammonium chloride in group III?

Ans. No, ammonium sulphate cannot be used in place of NH_4Cl in group III because it would cause precipitation of group V radicals as their sulphates in group III.

Q 36 Why is the reagent bottle containing sodium hydroxide solution never stoppered?

Ans. NaOH reacts with CO_2 from air to form $NaHCO_3$ and Na_2CO_3. Hence, NaOH bottles containing solution should not be stoppered as opening of them may become very hard and eventually becomes impossible with carbonate crust.

Suggested Experiments For Specimen Record of Salt Analysis

To analyse the provided salt for one anion and one cation present in it.

Materials Required

Boiling tubes, test tubes, test tube holder, test tube stand, delivery tube, corks, filter papers and reagents as per requirement.

Procedure

S.No.	Experiment	Observation	Inference
1.	**Physical examination** (i) Noted the colour of the given salt. (ii) Observed the smell of the salt.	(i) White (ii) No specific odour	Cu^{2+}, Fe^{2+}, Fe^{3+}, Ni^{2+}, Mn^{2+} and Co^{2+} may be absent. NH_4^+, S^{2-}, SO_3^{2-} and CH_3COO^- may be absent.
2.	**Effect of heating** Heated a pinch of the salt in a dry test tube and noted the colour of the gas evolved and change in the colour of the residue on heating and cooling.	(i) A reddish-brown gas evolved which turns $FeSO_4$ solution black. (ii) Colourless and odourless gas (CO_2) which turns lime water milky (iii) The sublimate is formed on the upper cooler parts of the test tube and colour of the sublimate is white.	NO_3^- may be present. CO_3^{2-} may be present NH_4^+ may be present.
3.	**Charcoal cavity test** Mixed a pinch of the salt with double the quantity of Na_2CO_3 and heated the mixture on a charcoal cavity in the reducing flame.	White residue	Zn^{2+}, Pb^{2+}, Mg^{2+}, etc., may be absent.
4.	**Cobalt nitrate test** To the above white residue, added a drop of cobalt nitrate solution. Heated it again in oxidising flame.	No characteristic colour.	Zn^{2+}, Mg^{2+} and PO_4^{3-} may be absent.
5.	**Borax bead test** Did not perform this test since, the given salt was white.		Cu^{2+}, Mn^{2+}, Co^{2+}, Ni^{2+} and Fe^{3+} may be absent.
6.	**Flame test** Prepared a paste of the salt with conc. HCl and performed flame test.	Persistent grassy green flame on prolonged heating.	Ba^{2+} may be present.
7.	**Dil. sulphuric acid test** Treated a pinch of the salt with dil. H_2SO_4 and warmed.	No gas is evolved.	S^{2-}, CO_3^{2-}, NO_2^- and SO_3^{2-} are absent.
8.	**Conc. sulphuric acid test** Heated a pinch of the salt with conc. sulphuric acid and then added it to a paper pellet.	A reddish-brown gas is evolved and it turns $FeSO_4$ solution black.	NO_3^- may be present.

S.No.	Experiment	Observation	Inference
9.	**Confirmatory test for NO_3^-** (Nitrate) (i) **Ring test** To 2-3 mL of the salt solution, add freshly prepared $FeSO_4$ solution. Now, add conc. sulphuric acid along the sides of the test tube carefully. (ii) **Copper chips test** Heated a pinch of the salt with conc. sulphuric acid and a few copper turnings.	A dark brown ring formed at the junction of the two liquids. Reddish-brown gas evolved.	NO_3^- is confirmed. NO_3^- is confirmed.
10.	Heated a pinch of salt with conc. NaOH solution.	No evolution of ammonia gas.	NH_4^+ absent.
11.	**Preparation of original solution** (OS) Shake a pinch of the salt with water. To a part of the original solution, added 1-2 mL of dilute hydrochloric acid.	Clear solution obtained. No ppt. formed.	Labelled it as original solution (OS) Group I absent (Pb^{2+} absent).
12.	Through a part of the above solution, passed H_2S gas.	No ppt. formed.	Group II absent Cu^{2+}, Cd^{2+}, As^{3+} ($Pb^{2+}$and Hg^{2+} are absent)
13.	To the remaining solution, added a pinch of solid ammonium chloride. Boiled the solution, cooled it and added excess of ammonium hydroxide solution.	No precipitation seen.	Group III absent (Fe^{3+} and Al^{3+} are absent).
14.	Through a part of this solution, passed H_2S gas.	No precipitation was seen.	Group IV absent (Zn^{2+}, Mn^{2+}, Ni^{2+} and Co^{2+} are absent)
15.	To the remaining ammoniacal solution, add ammonium carbonate solution.	White ppt. formed.	Group V present. (Ca^{2+}, Ba^{2+} and Sr^{2+} are present)
16.	**Confirmatory test for barium (Ba^{2+}) ions** Filtered the above white ppt. and dissolved the ppt. in hot dilute acetic acid. (i) **Potassium chromate test** To one part of the above solution, add few drops of potassium chromate solution. (ii) **Flame test** Performed flame test with the salt.	Yellow ppt. Persistent grassy green flame on prolonged heating.	Ba^{2+} is confirmed. Ba^{2+} is confirmed.

Result

The given salt contains

Acidic radical (anion) - NO_3^- (nitrate ion)

Basic radical (cation) - Ba^{2+} (barium ion)

Experiment 6.2

AIM

Detection of nitrogen, sulphur and chlorine in an organic compound.

Theory/Principle

Lassaigne's test for nitrogen, sulphur and halogens

This is the most important test for the detection of nitrogen, sulphur and halogens like chlorine, bromine and iodine. This test is also called **sodium fusion test**. It is done by using **sodium extract** or **Lassaigne's extract.**

Preparation of Lassaigne's extract

Sodium extract is prepared by heating dry sodium metal in a fusion tube until sodium metal melts to a shining globule. Then, a pinch of organic compound is added to it and the mixture is heated strongly so that the compound reacts with sodium metal. The fused mass is plunge into a China dish containing water and then the mixture is boiled and filtered. The filtrate so obtained is called **sodium** or **Lassaigne's extract**. This extract contains sodium salts of nitrogen, sulphur and halogens of the organic compounds, hence, these elements can be easily detected by Lassaigne's extract.

Chemistry of Lassaigne's test

Nitrogen present in the organic compound is converted into sodium cyanide during fusion.

$$Na + C + N \longrightarrow \underset{\text{Sodium cyanide}}{NaCN}$$

Similarly, sulphur is converted into sodium sulphide during fusion

$$2Na + S \longrightarrow \underset{\text{Sodium sulphide}}{Na_2S}$$

While halogens are converted into sodium halides.

$$Na + X \longrightarrow \underset{\text{Sodium halide}}{NaX} \qquad \text{(where, } X = \text{Cl, Br and I)}$$

Now, further tests are implemented to confirm the presence of the elements, N, S, Cl, Br and I in the compound. When organic compound contains both N and S,sodium thiocyanate (NaSCN) or sodium sulphocyanide is formed during the formation of Na extract which reacts with $FeCl_3$ to give blood red colour due to the formation of ferric thiocyanate.

$$Na + S + C + N \longrightarrow \underset{\text{Sodium thiocyanate}}{NaSCN}$$

$$3NaSCN + FeCl_3 \longrightarrow \underset{\substack{\text{Ferric thiocyanate} \\ \text{(Blood red)}}}{Fe(SCN)_3} + 3NaCl$$

Note *Chloroform and carbon tetrachloride should never be subjected to Lassaigne's solution test as it may result violent explosion.*

Materials Required

Item		Quantity	Item		Quantity
▪ Fusion (Ignition) tube	:	As per need	▪ Tripod stand	:	1
▪ China dish	:	1	▪ Bunsen burner	:	1
▪ Wire gauze	:	1	▪ Filter paper	:	As per need
▪ Test tubes	:	As per need	▪ Sodium metal (stored under kerosene oil)	:	As per need
▪ Test tube holder	:	1	▪ Distilled water	:	30 mL
▪ Glass rod	:	1	▪ Organic compound	:	100 mg

Soda lime (NaOH+ CaO), $FeSO_4$, HCl, $FeCl_3$, sodium nitroprusside solution $Na_2[Fe(CN)_5NO]$, lead acetate $(CH_3COO)_2Pb$, conc. HNO_3, $AgNO_3$ solution, $CHCl_3$ (chloroform) and chlorine water: As per need

Procedure

Preparation of Sodium Extract or Lassaigne's Extract

1. Take a small piece of dry sodium metal in a fusion tube.
2. Hold the fusion tube with a test tube holder and heat it gently till it melts and appears as shiny globule. [Fig. 6.7 (i)]
3. Add small amount of the given organic substance into it.
4. Heat it again till it becomes red hot.
5. Crush the red hot tube into a clean China dish, filled with distilled water and cover it with a wire gauze so that the unreacted sodium metal does not fly off. [Fig. 6.7 (ii)]

⚠ ALERT

- *Sodium metal is highly explosive, so, never keep the metal in open air.*
- *Chlorine is toxic by inhalation.*
- *Chloroform is harmful and toxic by inhalation.*

6. Repeat all the above mentioned steps with 2 to 3 fusion tubes to make concentrated sodium extract.
7. Use glass rod to break fusion tubes, if the tubes does not break itself.
8. Boil the contents of the China dish and filter it [Fig. 6.7 (iii)]. Label the filtrate as sodium extract or Lassaigne's extract [Fig. 6.7 (iv)].

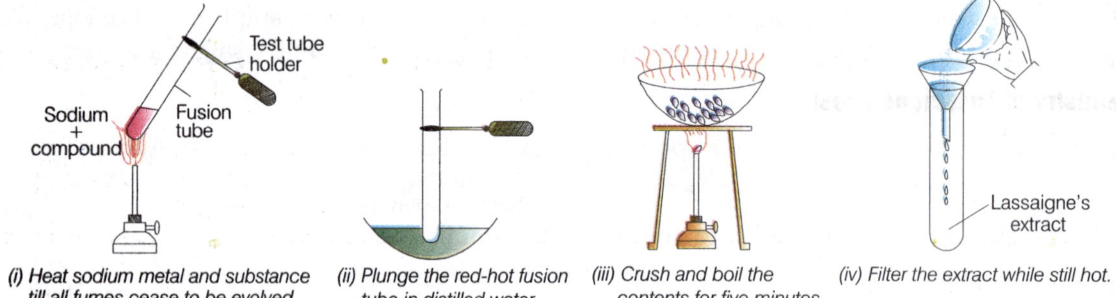

Fig. 6.7 *Preparation of Lassaigne's extract*

Detection of Nitrogen

The presence of nitrogen in an organic compound is detected by the following tests:

Experiment	Procedure	Observation	Inference	Chemistry involved
Soda lime test	Organic compound + soda lime (NaOH+ CaO) + heat.	Nitrogen present in an organic compound is converted into NH_3.	Pungent smell of NH_3 indicates the presence of nitrogen.	Organic compounds like urea (NH_2CONH_2) containing N on heating reacts with soda lime to evolve ammonia gas with pungent smell.
Lassaigne's test	Mix 1 mL of Na extract with 3-4 drops of freshly prepared $FeSO_4$ solution or add few crystals of ferrous sulphate in a test tube and warm it. Add few drops of $FeCl_3$ solution and acidify with dilute H_2SO_4 and warm.	A green precipitate is observed.	Appearance of greenish blue or Prussian blue colour confirms the presence of N in an organic compound.	$\underset{\text{From an organic compound}}{Na + C + N} \longrightarrow NaCN$ $FeSO_4 + 6NaCN \longrightarrow \underset{\text{Sodium (I) hexacyanidoferrate (II)}}{Na_4[Fe(CN)_6]} + Na_2SO_4$ $3Na_4[Fe(CN)_6] + 4FeCl_3 \longrightarrow \underset{\text{Iron (III) hexacyanidoferrate (II) (Prussian blue)}}{Fe_4[Fe(CN)_6]_3} + 12NaCl$

Detection of Sulphur

The presence of sulphur in an organic compound is detected by the following tests:

Experiment	Procedure	Observation	Inference	Chemistry involved
Sodium nitroprusside test	Add few drops of sodium nitroprusside solution in 1 mL of Lassaigne's extract.	A violet colour of sodium sulphonitropru sside appears.	A violet colouration indicates the presence of sulphur in the organic compound.	$2Na + S \xrightarrow{Fuse} Na_2S$ (From an organic compound) $Na_2S + Na_2[Fe(CN)_5NO] \longrightarrow$ (Sodium nitroprusside) $Na_4[Fe(CN)_5NOS]$ Sodium thionitroprusside (violet colouration)
Lead acetate test	To 1 mL of Lassaigne's extract, add dil. acetic acid and few drops of lead acetate solution.	A black coloured precipitate of PbS appears.	The formation of black precipitate indicates the presence of sulphur in the organic compound.	$Na_2S + (CH_3COO)_2Pb \longrightarrow$ (Lead acetate) $PbS\downarrow + 2CH_3COONa$ Lead sulphide (Black ppt.)

Detection of Nitrogen and Sulphur

The presence of nitrogen and sulphur when presents together in an organic compound is detected by the following tests.

Experiment	Procedure	Observation	Inference	Chemistry involved
Ferric chloride test	Acidify 1 mL of sodium extract with dil. HCl. Add Few drops of $FeCl_3$ solution and shake well.	Appearance of blood red colour of $Fe(SCN)_3$	A blood red colouration confirms the presence of both N and S in the organic compound.	$FeCl_3 + 3NaSCN \longrightarrow Fe(SCN)_3 + 3NaCl$ Blood red colour

Detection of Halogens

The presence of halogens like chlorine, bromine and iodine in an organic compound is detected by the following tests:

Experiment	Procedure	Observation	Inference	Chemistry involved
(i) **Silver nitrate test**	Add 2 mL of Lassaigne's extract in a test tube. Add 1 mL of conc. HNO_3 to the solution boil to expel all gases (HCN or H_2S) and cool the solution.	A pungent smelling gas is observed.	Halogens may be present.	If sodium cyanide is formed during the formation of sodium extract, it is decomposed by HNO_3 to form sodium nitrate ($NaNO_3$) with the evolution of HCN. $NaCN + HNO_3 \longrightarrow NaNO_3 + HCN\uparrow$ If sodium sulphide is formed, it is decomposed by HNO_3 to form $NaNO_3$ with the evolution of H_2S. $Na_2S + 2HNO_3 \longrightarrow 2NaNO_3 + H_2S\uparrow$

Note *If conc.* HNO_3 *is not added, then* NaCN *or* Na_2S *is not decomposed and they may interfere with the tests of halides since,* NaCN *gives a white precipitate with* $AgNO_3$ *while* Na_2S *gives a black precipitate.*

Experiment	Procedure	Observation	Inference	Chemistry involved
	Add $AgNO_3$ solution to the above cooled solution.	A white curdy precipitate is formed which is soluble in NH_4OH.	The white precipitate indicates the presence of chlorine in the organic compound.	NaCl formed during sodium extract formation, reacts with $AgNO_3$ to give white curdy precipitate of AgCl. $Na + \underset{\text{(From the compound)}}{Cl} \xrightarrow{\text{Heat}} NaCl$ $NaCl + AgNO_3 \longrightarrow \underset{\text{(White ppt.)}}{AgCl\downarrow} + NaNO_3$ $AgCl + 2NH_4OH \longrightarrow \underset{\text{Soluble complex}}{[Ag(NH_3)_2]Cl} + 2H_2O$
***Note** The solution obtained after dissolving precipitates of AgCl/AgBr/AgI in ammonium hydroxide should be acidify with 2M nitric acid and should be discarded quickly to avoid serious explosion.*				
		A dull/pale yellow coloured precipitate is formed which is sparingly soluble in NH_4OH.	Pale yellow precipitate sparingly soluble in NH_4OH indicates the presence of bromine in the compound.	NaBr formed during the formation of sodium extract, reacts with $AgNO_3$ to give dull/pale yellow precipitate of AgBr. $Na + \underset{\text{(From the compound)}}{Br} \xrightarrow{\text{Heat}} NaBr$ $NaBr + AgNO_3 \longrightarrow \underset{\text{(Pale yellow ppt.)}}{AgBr\downarrow} + NaNO_3$
		A dark yellow precipitate is formed which is insoluble in NH_4OH.	Dark yellow precipitate insoluble in NH_4OH indicates the presence of iodine in the compound.	NaI formed during the formation of sodium extract, reacts with $AgNO_3$ to give yellow precipitate of AgI. $Na + \underset{\text{From the compound}}{I} \xrightarrow{\Delta} NaI$ $NaI + AgNO_3 \longrightarrow \underset{\text{(Yellow ppt.)}}{AgI\downarrow} + NaNO_3$
(ii) **Layer test**	Acidify 1 mL sodium extract to concentrated HNO_3 and boil it for 1-2 minutes. Add a little of CCl_4/CS_2 followed by excess of chlorine water. Shake the solution vigorously.	Orange colour or purple/violet colour appears.	Appearance of orange colour in CCl_4 layer indicates the presence of bromine and the appearance of purple/violet colour indicate the presence of iodine.	$2Br + Cl_2 \longrightarrow 2Cl^- + Br_2$ $2I^- + Cl_2 \longrightarrow 2Cl^- + I_2$

PRECAUTIONS

- *Sodium metal being highly reactive should not be touched with fingers.*
- *Take only small amount of Na metal and dry it between the folds of paper before use.*
- *Only distilled water is used to prepare Lassaigne's extract.*
- *While performing test for halogens, test tube should be rinsed with distilled water before use.*
- *Always use freshly prepared aqueous solution of sodium nitroprusside as it is not stable.*
- *Make sure that the Lassaigne's filtrate should be clear and alkaline.*
- *Always use freshly prepared aqueous solution of sodium nitroprrside as it is not stable.*

Viva-Voce

Q.1 Why must the ignition tube be completely dry before fusion?

Ans. Any moisture in the ignition tube can react violently with sodium, posing a risk of splashing or explosion.

Q.2 What observation indicates a successful fusion during sodium extract preparation?

Ans. A vigorous reaction followed by formation of a red-hot mass that dissolves in water and gives a clear extract suggests successful fusion.

Q.3 What is the chemical form of nitrogen in Lassaigne's extract after fusion?

Ans. Nitrogen forms sodium cyanide (NaCN) upon fusion with sodium and carbon.

Q.4 What is indicated by the formation of a Prussian blue precipitate in the nitrogen test?

Ans. It confirms the presence of nitrogen in the organic compound.

Q.5 Why is ferrous sulphate boiled with Lassaigne's extract during nitrogen detection?

Ans. Boiling facilitates the reaction between NaCN and Fe^{2+} to form sodium hexacyanidoferrate(II), which further reacts with Fe^{3+} to give Prussian blue.

Q.6 Which colour change confirms sulphur using sodium nitroprusside solution?

Ans. The appearance of a violet colour confirms the presence of sulphur.

Q.7 Why is acetic acid used before adding lead acetate during sulphur detection?

Ans. Acetic acid acidifies the medium, allowing lead acetate to react properly and form black precipitate of lead sulphide (PbS).

Q.8 What does a blood red colour with ferric chloride indicate in Lassaigne's extract?

Ans. It indicates the simultaneous presence of nitrogen and sulphur in the organic compound as sodium thiocyanate reacts with Fe^{3+}.

Q.9 Why is it necessary to remove HCN and H_2S before performing halogen detection with $AgNO_3$?

Ans. HCN and H_2S interfere with $AgNO_3$ by forming white or black precipitates and giving false positives for halogens.

Q.10 How is chlorine distinguished from bromine and iodine using $AgNO_3$?

Ans. Chlorine gives a white precipitate of AgCl that dissolves in NH_4OH, unlike AgBr (partially soluble) and AgI (insoluble).

Q.11 What is the principle behind the layer test for halogens using CCl_4 or CS_2?

Ans. Halogens are oxidised by chlorine water and dissolve in organic solvents like CCl_4 or CS_2, showing characteristic colours—orange for Br_2 and violet for I_2.

Q.12 What role does air oxidation play in the Prussian blue test for nitrogen?

Ans. Oxygen from air oxidises Fe^{2+} to Fe^{3+}, which then reacts with sodium hexacyanidoferrate(II) to form the Prussian blue precipitate.

Q.13 Why should freshly prepared sodium nitroprusside be used in the sulphur test?

Ans. The reagent decomposes over time and its effectiveness in forming the purple complex reduces if it is not freshly prepared.

Questions From NCERT Lab Manual

Q.1 Why is sodium extract alkaline in nature. Explain.

Ans. Sodium extract is alkaline due to sodium hydroxide formed by the reaction of unreacted sodium metal during fusion with water.

Q.2 Why should sodium extract be boiled with concentrated nitric acid before using for the test of halogens.

Ans. To remove HCN or H_2S formed due to the presence of N and S, respectively.

Q.3 Can chlorine be liberated from sodium chloride solution by adding bromine water?

Ans. No, as bromine is less reactive than chlorine and cannot displace chlorine from sodium chloride solution.

Q.4 Can a sodium salt be used in place of sodium metal in the fusion reaction? If so, name the compound.

Ans. No, a sodium salt cannot be used in place of sodium metal in the fusion reaction. This is because of the following reasons

(i) Sodium metal has the ability to break the covalent bonds in the organic compound and form ionic compounds with elements like nitrogen, sulphur and halogens.

(ii) On the other hand, sodium salts such as, NaCl or Na_2SO_4 are already present in teh ionic form and do not have the reducing power to break the covalent bonds in the organic compound. Therefore, they cannot facilitate the necessary chemical transformations that sodium metal does during the fusion.

Q.5 Why is sodium extract prepared for the detection of elements in an organic compound?

Ans. Organic compounds don't furnish ions in solutions. Thus, in order to test the presence of elements in an organic compound it is fused with sodium to form sodium extract.

Q.6 Why chlorine water is added in the layer test for bromine and iodine? Can any other reagent be used in its place?

Ans. Chlorine has a higher reduction potential than bromine and iodine. Since, it acts as an oxidising agent and therefore it is used to oxidise bromide and iodide ions into bromine and iodine, which then dissolve in carbon disulphide to produce different colours. Yes, other reagents can also be used to oxidise bromide and iodide ion, though chlorine water is commonly used due to its effectiveness.

Q.7 Apply the concept of electrode potential to justify the occurence of the following reactions.

$$2Br^- + Cl_2 \longrightarrow 2Cl^- + Br_2$$
$$2I^- + Cl_2 \longrightarrow 2Cl^- + I_2$$

Ans. In both the reactions given above, Cl_2 is able to oxidise bromide (Br^-) ions and iodide (I^-) ions due to its higher standard electrode potential indicating its stronger oxidising power.

Further, these reactions are thermodynamically favourable as they involve the reduction of a stronger oxidising agent (i.e chlorine) and the oxidation of weaker reducing agents (i.e. bromide and iodide).

Project 1

AIM

Checking the bacterial contamination in drinking water by testing sulphide ions.

Theory/Principle

Water contamination occurs due to the presence of organic (urea, sugar, grease, soaps) and inorganic (ionic salts) impurities as well as microorganisms. Presence of microorganisms, specifically bacteria can be detected by the presence of sulphide ions. Sulphide ions present in water are produced when anaerobic bacteria decompose organic matter or reduce sulphates. Usually, effluents from paper mills, tanneries, domestic sewage and other chemical industries are responsible for the growth of bacteria and other microorganisms. These microorganisms are usually found in stagnant water.

Although, the water supply at our homes is already treated but due to the high degree of contamination in water, the permissible levels of the impurities in water are not achieved by water treatment processes. This results in health hazards and water-borne diseases.

Materials Required

- Titrating flask : 1
- Starch solution : 50 g
- Cadmium acetate : 0.025 M
- Iodine solution : As per need
- Distilled water : 500 mL
- Sodium thiosulphate ($Na_2S_2O_3$) : 0.05 M
- Zinc acetate : 50 g

Procedure

Collection and Fixing of Samples

Sulphides are readily oxidised, therefore care should be taken at the time of sampling to exclude air by flushing it with nitrogen or carbon dioxide. The best way is to 'fix' the sample immediately after collection. The fixing can be done by adding small volume of cadmium-zinc acetate solution.

⚠ ALERT

Handle conc. HCl very carefully as it is highly corrosive. Rest of the chemicals are of low hazard.

1. Dissolve 50 g of cadmium acetate and 50 g of zinc acetate in 1.0 L of water to form cadmium-zinc acetate solution.
2. Take 20 mL of cadmium-zinc acetate solution and add 80 mL of water to obtain a total volume of about 100 mL.
3. If the collected sample is acidic in nature, then neutralise it with little excess of alkali.

Titration of Fixed Solution

1. Take 100 mL of fixed solution in a titration flask, add 20 mL of 0.025 M iodine solution and immediately add 15 mL of HCl (1 : 1) solution and mix them together by **swirling** the flask.

2. Titrate the excess iodine against 0.05 M $Na_2S_2O_3$ by adding starch solution as indicator towards the end point.
3. Calculate the amount of sulphide ions in the original samples from the amount of iodine used in the reaction with H_2S.
4. Subtract the values of blank titration if available from the calculated values.

Chemical Reactions

$$I_2 + H_2S \longrightarrow 2HI + S$$

$$I_2 + \underset{\text{Sodium thiosulphate}}{2Na_2S_2O_3} \longrightarrow 2I^- + \underset{\text{Sodium tetrathionate}}{Na_2S_4O_6} + 2Na^+$$

Result

The water samples show the presence of S^{2-} ions and hence, the bacterial contamination.

PRECAUTIONS

- *There should not be any insoluble impurity present in the water sample.*
- *Clean all the apparatus thoroughly.*
- *Handle all the reagents carefully.*

Viva-Voce

Q.1 Which ion is present in sewage water due to the decomposition of organic matter by anaerobic bacteria?

Ans. Sulphide (S^{2-}) ion.

Q.2 How will you determine the total amount of dissolved organic impurities in sewage water?

Ans. By calculating Biological Oxygen Demand (BOD) or Chemical Oxygen Demand (COD).

Q.3 Why do sewages stink?

Ans. Due to the presence of sulphide ions in the form of hydrogen sulphide (H_2S) gas.

Q.4 Why cadmium zinc acetate solution is added before testing a water for bacterial contamination?

Ans. To fix the water sample for easy detection of sulphide ion so as to avoid the oxidation of sulphide ions.

Q.5 Where do sulphide (S^{2-}) ions come from in water contaminated by bacteria?

Ans. From the sulphur containing organic wastes and inorganic sulphates.

Q.6 Why sodium thiosulphate is doubly concentrated with respect to the iodine solution?

Ans. Sodium thiosulphate is doubly concentrated as each iodine molecule (I_2) reacts with two molecules of sodium thiosulphate ($Na_2S_2O_3$).

Q.7 Name any two water borne diseases caused due to bacterial contamination.

Ans. Typhoid and cholera.

Project 2

AIM

To study the methods of purification of water.

Theory/Principle

Purity of water obtained from different natural sources is different. The type of contamination and impurity present depends upon the source from which water is obtained. Potable water should be free from turbidity, colour, odour and bacteria. It should also be free from hardness.

The purest form of water is considered to be rain water but when it comes in contact with acidic contaminants like gases and dust particles of air, minerals and soil contamination, it becomes impure.

The human consumption of contaminated water may lead to many diseases and infections. Besides drinking purposes, we require pure water for various other purposes like, in chemical analysis.

Thus, it is essential to treat water for the removal of these contaminants. The process of removal of impurities from water so that the water becomes fit for human consumption is called **water purification**. There are various methods for the purification of water. These remove impurities and contamination to different extent. There are some advantages and disadvantages in using these methods.

Comparsion of various methods of purification will provide an idea about obtaining water of specific purity for a specific purpose. The water treatment is done on a large scale and the various steps for treatment of water for purification, are described below:

Steps for Treatment of Water

1. Boiling

Boiling water for 15-20 minutes kills many harmful microorganisms and also decomposes calcium or magnesium bicarbonates into insoluble carbonates which precipitates easily thereby, decreasing the hardness of water. Drinking boiled water save us from stomach infections.

2. Distillation

This technique involves boiling of water to produce water vapours which are then condensed to get pure water. The impurities are left behind in the boiling water. Distillation gives 99.9% pure water.

3. Coagulation and Sedimentation of Impurities

Artificially controlled sedimentation basins are used for the removal of suspended impurities which are not completely removed on storage. In these basins, artificial stimulation for the coagulation of impurities is provided through introduction of active chemicals known as **coagulants**.

The primary aim of coagulants is to provide a nucleus for agglomeration of suspended particles and increase their specific gravity to cause more rapid coagulation to form large particles which can be easily settled down. The phenomenon of joining of small particles to form larger settleable particles is known as **flocculation** and the larger formed particles are called **floc**.

The commonly used coagulant used is ordinary alum or aluminium sulphate. It is one of the best and almost universally applied chemical for coagulation. Some other common coagulants are iron (III) sulphate or chloride, lime, etc. When impure water is treated with calculated amount of coagulant, the suspended impurities settle down at the bottom of the tank. A layer of sludge is formed at the bottom of the basin (or tank) and removed from time to time.

4. Filtration

When all the visible suspended particles have settled down, then, water is filtered most commonly through a sand column. A layer of activated carbon is kept above the sand which removes colouring matter and odour imparting bad taste to water. The suspended impurities are trapped in pores of sand particles or adhere to sand. Thus, the sand filter renders water free of particulate matter. The sand filter may be reused by cleaning the trapped matter. The filter is cleaned by **back flushing**. In this process, the water is passed through the filter in the direction opposite to the normal flow of water. The adhered particles come out with opposite flow of water making the filter ready for reuse.

5. Disinfection

Filtered water still may have pathogens such as bacteria, virus and protozoans. The process of rendering water free from harmful living bacteria is known as **disinfection**. Hence, filtered water is disinfected from the pathogens by chlorine gas, ozone or UV treatment.

Chlorine gas and sodium hypobromite are the most widely used disinfectants as they are cheap and their action is rapid. These are effective in killing bacteria but have limited effectiveness against protozoans. Both of these leave strong disinfectant residuals in the water even when water enters the distribution system.

The major disadvantage of using chlorine gas or sodium hypochlorite is that they react with organic compounds in the water and form harmful chemical by products like trihalomethanes and haloacetic acid, both of these are potential carcinogenic. Chlorine also imparts some offensive odour and taste to the water.

Ozone is used in many developed countries as it is a very strong and wide spectrum disinfectant. It is most effective against all protozoans and work well against all the other pathogens. It does not form any harmful by-products. There is no bad odour or taste imparted to water. This method does not leave any residual matter in water.

Ultraviolet (UV) **radiation** can also be used as disinfectant. It is very effective and can destroy even viruses. The major advantage of UV radiation is that like ozone it also leaves no disinfectant residual in water. It is used in aqua-guards (water purifiers) these days.

6. Water Conditioning

This method is used for reducing the effects of hard water. In this technique, water with high concentrations of hardening salts is treated with sodium carbonate (soda-ash) which precipitates out the excess salts through common-ion effect.

7. Reverse Osmosis (RO)

You have seen 'RO' systems installed in your homes or in schools to get pure water. This RO treatment removes salts and coloured compounds from water. It involves passing of impure water through semipermeable membrane by applying high pressure to obtain water free from impurities. In this process, the minerals and coloured compounds are removed from water. It is also used for purifying sea water.

8. Ion Exchange

Ion exchange system uses zeolite resins to replace Ca^{2+} and Mg^{2+} ions with Na^{+} ions. Some synthetic ion exchange resins can remove all the ions from water and the water obtained is completely free from ions, i.e. deionised water. It is used for research purposes.

Materials Required

As per your need.

Procedure

1. Make different groups of students with 3-5 students in each group.
2. Each group must study the water treatment methods used in their houses and nearby locality. Students may also find out level of purity achieved by various techniques in use, for purification of drinking water.
3. Record your observations and discuss them with other group members and your teacher.

Observation

The various water treatment methods used in locality *A* are ...... and in locality *B* are ....

PRECAUTIONS

- *Before starting the project, study all the techniques well.*
- *Allot a specified work to each student of the group.*

Viva-Voce

Q.1 Which method is employed for the removal of large debris from surface water?

Ans. Screening method.

Q.2 How will you clean a rapid sand filter?

Ans. The rapid sand filter is cleaned by back flushing, i.e. by passing water through the filter in the direction opposite to the normal direction.

Q.3 Name some water purification methods used in the houses.

Ans. Filtration, RO systems, etc.

Q.4 Name a commonly used resin in ion-exchange method.

Ans. Zeolite resin.

Q.5 What is plumbo-solvency?

Ans. It refers to the dissolution of lead from lead pipes through which water is being carried.

Q.6 Name a commonly used coagulant for water filtration.

Ans. Potash alum.

Q.7 Why activated charcoal is used in carbon filtering process?

Ans. Because activated charcoal have large surface area and helps to adsorb the impurities from water.

Q.8 Differentiate between osmosis and reverse osmosis.

Ans. Osmosis is passing of a solvent (like impurities) through semipermeable membrane, in a direction where the solute (like impurities) concentration is low. While in reverse osmosis, the solvent (water) is passed into opposite direction through semipermeable membrane by applying high pressure.

Project 3

AIM

Testing the hardness, presence of iron, fluoride, chloride, etc., depending upon the regional variation in drinking water and study of the causes of presence of these ions above permissible limit.

Theory/Principle

Quality of drinking water is very important for human health and life. The presence of iron, fluoride, chloride etc., in water may cause several health problems if they are present above permissible limits. e.g. If fluoride is present above permissible limit, people of the region may suffer from fluorosis.

Hard water contains the dissolved salts of calcium and magnesium ions. In low concentrations, these ions are not harmful but in higher concentrations, these ions interfere with the cleansing action of soaps and increase the corrosion of steel pipes.

The strength of hardness in water depends on the extent of concentration of hardening ions present in water. Usually, hardness is due to $CaCO_3$ hence, the unit of hardness is expressed as mg $CaCO_3/L$ which is equivalent to ppm $CaCO_3$. A basic classification of hard water is given below

Classification of hard water

Hardness (ppm $CaCO_3$)	Type
<15 ppm	Very soft water
15-50 ppm	Soft water
50-100 ppm	Medium hard water
100-200 ppm	Hard water
> 200 ppm	Very hard water

Estimation of Hardness

The hardness of water can be estimated by **volumetric analysis technique**, i.e. **complexometric titration** by using disodium salt of **EDTA** (ethylene diamminetetraacetic acid) as **titrant** and eriochrome black-T, i.e. **EBT** as an **indicator**.

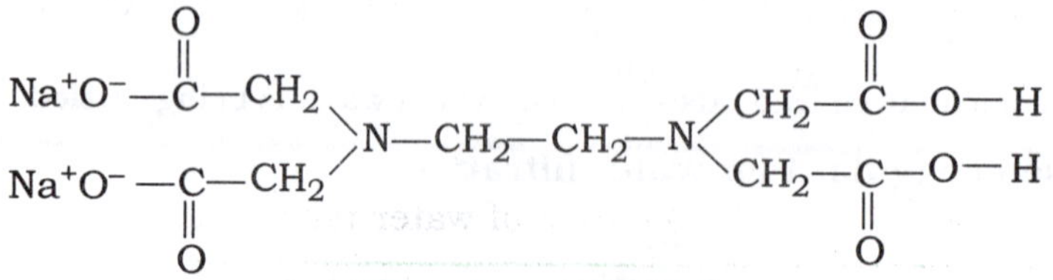

$$(Na^+\,{}^-O-C(=O)-CH_2)_2N-CH_2-CH_2-N(CH_2-C(=O)-O-H)_2$$

Disodium salt of EDTA

EDTA is a weak acid and dissociates into Na^+ and H_2Y^{2-} ions [Y = ethylene diamine tetraacetate ions]. In aqueous solution, Ca^{2+} and Mg^{2+} ions react with this H_2Y^{2-} ions to form stable 1 : 1 complexes in the solution. The pH of this solution should be ≈ 10. A buffer solution of ammonia and ammonium ions is used to maintain pH around 10. End point is detected by using EBT as an indicator, it forms complex ions with Mg^{2+} and Ca^{2+}. EBT indicator is sky-blue in colour but it forms a wine-red coloured complex, $[Mg\text{-}EBT]^{2+}$, with Mg^{2+} ions present in the water sample.

$$Mg^{2+}(aq) + EBT(aq) \longrightarrow [Mg\text{-}EBT]^{2+}(aq)$$

Sky- blue Wine- red

Therefore, in the starting of titration, when EBT is added to hard water, it combines with Mg^{2+} of hard water and get turned into wine-red colour. When the titrant H_2Y^{2-} is added, it forms complex with Mg^{2+} and removed Mg^{2+} from $[Mg\text{-}EBT]^{2+}$ complex, resulting in sky-blue colour from wine-red colour at the end point.

$$[Mg\text{-}EBT]^{2+}(aq) + H_2Y^{2-}(aq) \longrightarrow MgY^{2-}(aq) + 2H^{+}(aq) + EBT(aq)$$

Wine- red Sky- blue

Thus, H_2Y^{2-} solution consumes whole of the Mg^{2+} ions and liberates eriochrome black-T which has blue colour.

At the end point, Mg^{2+} must be available in the solution. Thus, a small amount of Mg^{2+} (in the form of salt) is added to the buffer solution and an equivalent amount of Na_2H_2Y is also added so that the added Mg^{2+} ions do not affect the amount of H_2Y^{2-} used during titration.

Note *Testing for the presence of iron, fluoride and chloride ions, etc., requires complex procedure and high end equipments which is difficult at this level.*

Materials Required

- Funnel : 1
- Beaker (100 mL) : 1
- Conical flask (100 mL): 1
- Burette : 1
- Pipette (25 mL) : 1
- EDTA standard solution (0.01 M) : As per need
- EBT indicator : As per need
- Buffer solution of pH 10 : As per need
- Samples of hard water : As per need

Procedure

1. Take 100 mL of the hard water sample in a 200 mL beaker. Remove all the suspended impurities of the hard water sample by simple filtration.
2. If the water sample is acidic to litmus, then add 1 M NH_3 dropwise until it becomes basic.
3. Wash and clean the burette, rinse it with standard solution of EDTA and then fill the burette with the same. Note down the initial reading.
4. Pipette out 10 mL of hard water sample in the conical flask. Add 1 mL of the buffer solution [having pH = 10] and 2 drops of EBT indicator. The colour of the solution would become wine-red.
5. Titrate it with standard solution of EDTA taken in the burette. Stop adding the solution from burette when wine-red colour disappears and the solution in the conical flask turns blue in colour. This indicates the end-point of the titration. Note down the final reading and repeat the titration to get concordant readings.
6. Similarly, proceed with other hard water samples.

Observation

Molarity of Na_2H_2Y standard solution = 0.01 M Volume of water taken = 10 mL

S. No.	Initial burette reading	Final burette reading	Volume of Na_2H_2Y used (mL)
1.			
2.			
3.			
4.			

Concordant reading = ... mL

Similarly, record for other samples in the same manner.

Calculation

Let the volume of EDTA used be x mL

Molarity of EDTA used = 0.01 M

Moles of EDTA used $= \frac{M \times V}{1000} = \frac{0.01 \times x}{1000}$

Moles of EDTA = Moles of $Ca^{2+} = \frac{0.01\,x}{1000}$

Total hardness is expressed in terms of Ca^{2+} ions as $CaCO_3$.

$\therefore$ Moles of EDTA used = Moles of Ca^{2+} ions $= \frac{0.01x}{1000}$

Mass of equivalent $CaCO_3 = \frac{0.01\,x}{1000} \times 100 \times 1000\text{mg} = x$ mg (Molar mass of $CaCO_3 = 100$)

$\therefore$ 10 mL of sample of water contains $CaCO_3 = x\,\text{mg}$

Mass of $CaCO_3$ per litre of water sample $= \frac{x}{10} \times 1000 = 100\,x$ mg/L

Total hardness = Strength of $CaCO_3$ present per ppm of water sample = $100x$ mg/L

Similarly, calculate the hardness of other water samples.

Result

The hardness of different water samples are estimated as :

Sample A : .... Sample B : .... Sample C : ...., etc.

PRECAUTIONS

- *Remove all insoluble impurities from the samples of water by filtration.*
- *Make the water sample basic to litmus by adding ammonia before starting the titration.*

Viva-Voce

Q.1 What is the unit of hardness of water?

Ans. As, the hardness of water is expressed in terms of Ca^{2+} ions of $CaCO_3$. Thus, the unit of hardness of water is mg of $CaCO_3$/L

Q.2 How the hardness of water can be estimated?

Ans. It can be estimated by using volumetric analysis technique.

Q.3 Which indicator is used for titrating water sample against Na_2H_2Y standard solution?

Ans. Eriochrome black-T (EBT)

Q.4 Which complex is formed when water sample is treated with indicator?

Ans. $[\text{Mg-EBT}]^{2+}$, a wine-red colour complex is obtained.

$$\underset{}{Mg^{2+}(aq)} + \underset{\textit{Sky-blue}}{\text{EBT}(aq)} \longrightarrow \underset{\textit{Wine-red}}{[\text{Mg-EBT}]^{2+}(aq)}$$

Q.5 Why buffer solution is used in this titration?

Ans. A buffer solution of ammonia and ammonium ions is used to maintain pH of water about 10.

Project 4

AIM

Investigation of the foaming capacity of different washing soaps and the effect of addition of sodium carbonate on their foaming capacity.

Theory/Principle

Soaps and detergents are those substances which are used for cleaning purposes. Soaps are sodium or potassium salts of higher fatty acids containing long chains of 15-18 carbon atoms. Some common examples are sodium stearate, sodium palmitate, sodium oleate, etc. When soap gets dissolved in water, it forms foam or lather which carries away dirt and grease by forming emulsion when excess of water is added.

The **cleansing action** of soap basically depends upon the foaming capacity of soap, i.e. the extent to which it forms lather. The foaming capacity of different soaps can be easily compared by considering the time taken for the disappearance of foam produced in different soap solutions of same concentration.

Lesser is the time taken for the foam to disappear, the lower will be the foaming capacity of a soap sample. Limitation of usage of soap is that it cannot be used in hard water because hard water contains certain metal ions as Mg^{2+} and Ca^{2+}. These ions react with soap and form a curdy white precipitate known as **scum**.

e.g.

$$2C_{17}H_{35}COONa + Ca^{2+} \longrightarrow \underset{\text{Calcium sterate (white precipitate)}}{(C_{17}H_{35}COO)_2Ca} \downarrow + 2Na^+$$

$$\underset{\text{Soap}}{2C_{17}H_{35}COONa} + Mg^{2+} \longrightarrow \underset{\text{Magnesium stearate (white precipitate, scum)}}{(C_{17}H_{35}COO)_2Mg} \downarrow + 2Na^+$$

This scum does not form emulsions and hence, are not able to remove oil, fat or grease from clothings thus, reducing the cleansing capacity of the soap.

Na_2CO_3 can be used to remove hardness of water as it causes the precipitation of Ca^{2+} and Mg^{2+} ions in the form of their carbonates.

$$Ca^{2+} + Na_2CO_3 \longrightarrow CaCO_3 \downarrow + 2Na^+$$

$$Mg^{2+} + Na_2CO_3 \longrightarrow MgCO_3 \downarrow + 2Na^+$$

Therefore, addition of sodium carbonate to the soap solution removes Ca^{2+} and Mg^{2+} ions and finally, increases the foaming capacity of soap.

Materials Required

- Test tubes : As per need
- Glass rod : 1
- Beakers (250 mL) : As per need
- Graduated cylinder (25 mL) : 1
- Stopwatch : 1
- Burner : 1
- Tripod stand : 1
- Different brands of soap : As per need
- Distilled water : As per need
- A sample of hard water : As per need
- Na_2CO_3 : As per need

Procedure

Investigation of foaming capacity of different washing soaps

1. Weigh 1 g each of the different samples of soap.
2. Dissolve all these samples separately in 100 mL of distilled water taken in different beakers labelled as *A, B, C, D* and *E*.
3. Warm the solutions to dissolve the soap completely.
4. Now, take 2 mL of the soap solution from beakers *A, B, C, D* ... etc., in separate 20 mL test tubes labelled as *A′*, *B′*, *C′*, *D′* and *E*. respectively. Arrange all these five test tubes on a test tube stand.
5. Add 10 mL of distilled water to the test tube *A′* close the mouth of the tube with the help of a cork and shake it upside down for 2 min for making 20 regular strokes, so that foam increases uniformly. Keep it back in the test tube stand.
6. Foams will be produced in the test tube *A′*. Note down the height (or length) upto which foam produced rises in different soap solutions and record the observation in the table. Also, note down the time taken for the foam to settle down or disappear.
8. Repeat the steps 5 and 6 with other samples of soaps as well and record your observations in tabular form.

Effect of addition of sodium carbonate on the foaming capacity of a given sample of soap

1. Weigh 1 g of a given sample of soap and keep it in a beaker.
2. Add 20 mL of distilled water to this beaker and dissolve the soap completely. Warm, if required.
3. Make a solution of sodium carbonate in another beaker by dissolving 0.5 g of it in 50 mL of distilled water.
4. Take 1 mL of soap solution in three separate test tubes labelled as 1,2,3.
5. Add 10 mL of hard water in test tube 1, 10 mL of distilled water in test tube 2 and 5 mL each of hard water and Na_2CO_3 solution in test tube 3.
6. Shake each of the test tube for equal time-period and compare the height upto which foam produced rises in different soap solutions with and without the presence of Na_2CO_3.
7. Also, note the time taken for the disappearance of foam in each test tube.

Observation

Investigation of foaming capacity of different washing soaps

Amount of soap taken = 1.0 g

Volume of distilled water added = 100 mL

Volume of soap solution taken in each test tube = 2 mL

Volume of distilled water added to the soap solution = 10 mL

Time for which each test tube shaken = 2 min

S.No.	Soap sample	Time taken for disappearance of foam (in seconds)	Length of the foam produced (in cm)
1.	Lux		
2.	Liril		
3.	Pears		
4.	Lifebuoy		
5.	Hamam		

Effect of addition of sodium carbonate on the foaming capacity of a given sample of soap

Amount of soap taken = 1.0 g

Volume of distilled water added = 20 mL

Volume of soap solution taken in each test tube = 1 mL

S.No.	Sample taken	Time taken for disappearance of foam (in seconds)	Length of the foam produced (in cm)
1.	Hard water (10 mL)		
2.	Distilled water (10 mL)		
3.	5 mL hard water + 5 mL Na_2CO_3 solution		

Conclusions

1. The soap for which the time taken for the disappearance of foam is maximum, has maximum foaming capacity.
2. Foaming capacity of hard water increases on adding sodium carbonate to it.

Result

1. The foaming capacity of different soap samples is in the order ......>......>...... etc.
2. The length of the foam produced in different samples is in the order ......>......>...... etc.
3. The height upto which foam rises in different soap solutions with and without the presence of Na_2CO_3 increases in the order ......>......>...... etc.

PRECAUTIONS

- *Shake all soap solutions for equal time with equal force.*
- *Soap must be completely dissolved in water before performing the experiment. It may be warmed a little for complete dissolution of soap.*
- *If warmed, then cool the soap solution to the room temperature before starting the experiment.*
- *Equal volume of soap solution must be added in each test tube.*
- *Use same distilled water for every sample because foaming capacity of a soap also depends upon the nature of water used.*

Viva-Voce

Q.1 Soaps are sodium or potassium salts of higher fatty acids. How many carbon atoms do these fatty acid molecules consist?

Ans. Usually 15-18 carbon atoms.

Q.2 Why hard water does not form foam with soap?

Ans. Hard water does not form foam with soap because Ca^{2+} and Mg^{2+} ions present in hard water prevents the release of stearate or palmitate ions by forming curdy white precipitate with these ions.

$$2C_{17}H_{35}COONa(aq) + Ca^{2+}(aq) \longrightarrow (C_{17}H_{35}COO)_2Ca(s) + 2Na^+$$

$$2C_{17}H_{35}COONa(aq) + Mg^{2+}(aq) \longrightarrow (C_{17}H_{35}COO)_2Mg(s) + 2Na^+$$

Q.3 In which kind of natural source of water, soap is likely to form more lather?

Ans. Rain water, as they are least likely to consist hardening agents (like Ca^{2+}, Mg^{2+}, etc.)

Q.4 What is meant by foaming capacity of soap?

Ans. The tendency of a soap to form lather or foam for a long period of time is referred as foaming capacity of a soap.

Q.5 What is the effect of addition of Na_2CO_3 on foaming capacity of soap?

Ans. Foaming capacity of a soap increases on the addition of Na_2CO_3 solution in water.

Project 5

AIM

To study the acidity of different samples of tea leaves.

Theory/Principle

Tea is one of the favourite beverages in India. Tea acts as respiratory, cardiac and muscle stimulant on its drinker. These all properties are mainly because of the presence of caffeine and theophylline (an alkaloid) in tea leaves.

The amount of caffeine in tea leaves varies from 2-5% depending upon the climate and the soil in which the plant is grown. Earlier, these compounds were supposed to be responsible for the taste, colour and flavour of tea.

But now, it has been proved wrong. Pure caffeine is a white tasteless substance. It clearly indicates that, some other compounds are responsible for the taste, colour and flavour of tea. These are due to the flavouring agents and tannins (polyphenolic compounds).

The relative amounts of these substances are different in different varieties of tea leaves, and this is the reason, why their flavour and taste are different. The variation of taste of different samples of tea can be correlated to its acidity because acidity reflects on the tannins content of tea.

In this project, we will estimate the concentration of acids (like tannic acid) present in different tea samples and the effect of addition of acids or bases on the colour of tea extract. Tannic acid is a weak acid which can be estimated by titrating it with strong base (NaOH) by using phenolphthalein as an indicator.

Materials Required

- Different samples of tea leaves : As per need
- Distilled water : As per need
- *M*/50 NaOH : As per need
- Phenolphthalein : As per need
- Conical flask (100 mL) : 1
- Burette : 1
- Burette stand : 1
- Beakers (500 mL) : As per need
- Filter papers : 5
- HCl, NaOH and NH_4OH solution : As per need
- CH_3COOH : As per need

Procedure

Estimation of Concentration of Acids Present in Tea

1. Weigh 10 g of the sample of tea leaves.
2. Prepare the extract of each sample separately in 200 mL of distilled water. For this, boil different samples of tea leaves with distilled water for a fixed time period.
3. Take 5 mL of tea extract in a conical flask and dilute it with 20 mL of distilled water.
4. Shake the solution well for homogeneous mixing and titrate it against *M*/50 NaOH solution using phenolphthalein as an indicator.
5. Similarly, titrate other tea extracts with *M*/50 NaOH solution.
6. Calculate the concentration of acids present in different samples of tea leaves in terms of molarity.

7. Take the tea extract in the burette if the colour of the extract causes problem and sodium hydroxide solution in the conical flask. Add phenolphthalein as an indicator if sodium hydroxide solution is taken in conical flask. The colour change will be from pink to colourless.
8. Note down the initial and final reading of the burette.

Effect of Acids and Bases on the Colour of Tea Extract

1. Take five filter paper strips and mark them as *A, B, C, D* and *E*.
2. Dip all the strips in any one sample of tea extract and then take them out.
3. Now, put two drops of dil. HCl, acetic acid solution, NaOH solution and NH_4OH solution on strips *A, B, C* and *D* respectively.
4. Compare the change in colour of these strips with reference to the colour of the strip *E*.
5. Repeat the experiment with other samples of the tea extract.

Observation

Estimation of Concentration of Acids Present in Tea Volume of NaOH used = 20 mL

S.No.	Initial burette reading	Final burette reading	Volume of tea extract used
1.			
2.			
3.			
4.			

Effect of Acids and Bases on the Colour of Tea Extract

S.No.	Name of acid and base	Colour in Sample 1	Colour in Sample 2	Colour in Sample 3	Colour in Sample 4	Colour in Sample 5
1.	HCl					
2.	CH_3COOH					
3.	NaOH					
4.	NH_4OH					
5.	Tea extract only					

Calculations

Using molarity equation, molarity of tannic acid in tea can be calculated.

Result

Estimation of Concentration of Acids Present in Tea

The increasing order of acid present in tea samples is ....

Effect of Acids and Bases on the Colour of Tea Extract

The sample .... is least affected by acid sample and the sample .... is least affected by base. The sample .... is most affected by acid and the sample .... is most affected by base.

PRECAUTIONS

- *Brew the tea for the same duration of time for every sample.*
- *Add equal volume of same boiling water in each cup.*
- *Clean the glass rod well before using it for each liquor.*
- *Note down pH of the liquor carefully.*
- *Put the brewed tea leaves in a dustbin.*

Viva-Voce

Q.1 Name the major constituents of tea leaves.

Ans. The major constituents of tea leaves are caffeine, tannins and theophylline.

Q.2 Why are different tea differs in taste?

Ans. Due to the presence of different amounts of tannins in different samples of tea leaves.

Q.3 How does tea affect the human body?

Ans. It acts as cardiac, respiratory and muscle stimulant on the drinker.

Q.4 Which compounds are responsible for the flavour and colour of tea?

Ans. Flavouring agents and tannins (polyphenolic compounds).

Q.5 Why phenolphthalein is used as an indicator in this experiment?

Ans. Because phenolphthalein changes colour in basic medium and thus help to detect the end point in acid-base titration.

Q.6 Why does the colour of tea change with acids and bases?

Ans. It is because the tea contains natural pigments like tannins, which are pH-sensitive.

Project 6

AIM

Determination of the rate of evaporation of different liquids.

Theory/Principle

A process in which liquid molecules get converted into gaseous molecules at any temperature below its boiling point is called **evaporation**. Rate of evaporation of a liquid is defined as the amount of the liquid evaporating per unit time.

Materials Required

- Weighing tubes : 4
- Weight box : 1
- Balance : 1
- Water : As per need
- Acetone : As per need
- Ethyl alcohol : As per need
- Benzene : As per need

Procedure

1. Take five clean and dry weighing tubes and mark them as *A*, *B*, *C*, *D* and *E*.
2. Weigh each weighing tube with its stopper.
3. Pour 10 mL of given liquids like, ethanol, ether, tetrachloromethane, acetone in different weighing tubes. Weigh each weighing tube again and find the mass of the liquid taken in each weighing tube.
4. Remove the stoppers of the weighing tubes and keep them at room temperature for one hour. Exactly after one hour, close the mouth of all the weighing tubes with their stoppers and weigh them one by one.
5. Relate the difference in rates of evaporation of liquids with their chemical constitution and variation in intermolecular or intramolecular interactions.

Observation

Room temperature = ...°C.

Time allowed for evaporation = 3600 s.

S. No.	Liquid taken	Weight of weighing bottle + liquid		Loss in weight of liquid after evaporation, $(w_1 - w_2)$ g	Rate of evaporation $\left(\frac{w_1 - w_2}{3600}\right)$ gs^{-1}
		Before evaporation, w_1 (g)	After evaporation, w_2(g)		
1.	Ethanol			—	
2.	Ether			—	
3.	Tetrachlorome: lane			—	
4.	Acetone			—	

Result

Ether has the highest rate of evaporation. The rates of evaporation are in the order : Ether > acetone> tetrachloromethane > ethanol.

Thus, ether has weaker intermolecular forces of attraction while ethanol has stronger intermolecular forces of attraction.

PRECAUTIONS

- *The temperature and the surface area should be same for the evaporation of each liquid.*
- *Weighing tubes of almost same size and shape should be used.*
- *Use same measuring cylinder for measuring all the volumes.*
- *Liquid should not be split while pouring.*

Viva-Voce

Q.1 Name few factors that affect the rate of evaporation of a liquid.

Ans. Nature of the liquid, surface area, temperature, composition of the environment, etc.

Q.2 What is the relation between the rate of evaporation of a liquid and the variation in its surface area?

Ans. More is the surface area of a liquid, higher is its rate of evaporation.

Q.3 What is the rate of evaporation?

Ans. The rate of evaporation of a liquid is defined as the amount of liquid evaporating per unit time.

Q.4 Give two uses of the process of evaporation in daily life.

Ans. (i) Clothes dry faster in summers than in winters.

(ii) It is easier to drink hot tea from the saucer than from the cup.

Q.5 What will be the correct order of rate of evaporation of water, benzene, ethanol, diethyl ether and acetone?

Ans. The liquid having weaker intermolecular forces has greater rate of evaporation. In terms of temperature, rate of evaporation of a liquid increases with the decrease in its boiling points.

∴ Diethyl ether > acetone > ethanol > benzene > water.

Q.6 Why do different liquids evaporate at different rates?

Ans. It is due to the differences in their intermolecular forces and molecular structure.

Q.7 Why is the surface area kept constant in this experiment?

Ans. To ensure fair comparison by eliminating surface area as a variable.

Q.8 How is the rate of evaporation calculated?

Ans. By dividing the loss in mass (grams) by the time (in seconds).

Project 7

AIM

To study the effect of acids and bases on the tensile strength of fibres.

Theory/Principle

Fibres are long, thin, thread like polymers which can be woven into fabrics. These fibres possess strong **intermolecular forces** between the chains. These forces can be dipole-dipole interactions and hydrogen bonds, e.g., in case of polyesters, the intermolecular forces are dipole-dipole interactions while in case of polyamides (like nylon), the intermolecular forces are hydrogen bonding.

Tensile Strength

The strength of the fibre is often expressed in terms 'tensile strength'. It may be defined as the extent to which a fibre can be stretched without breaking. It is a measure of the minimum weight required just to break the thread. It may be measured by taking threads of different materials and stretching them by adding weights gradually till it breaks. The weight required to break the thread gives the tensile strength of the fibre. In the given project, we will first compare the tensile strength of different fibres and then, study the effect of acids and bases on the tensile strength of different fibres.

Materials Required

- Slotted weights : As per need
- Tweezer : 1
- Weight hanger : 1
- Clamp : 1
- Clamp stand : 1
- Hook : 1
- Acid [1M and 5M of HCl] : As per need
- Base [1M and 5M of NaOH] : As per need
- Different types of fibres : As per need

Procedure

1. Cut out five samples of equal length (nearly 20 cm) of fibre of each type.
2. Tie one end of any one fibre (like cotton thread) with a ring fixed on an iron stand and the other end with a hanger which carries the weights to keep the fibre gets straighten.
3. Now, start adding weights onto the weight hanger and observe the stretching of the thread. Increase the weights gradually on the weight hanger till the breaking point is reached. Note the minimum weight required to break the cotton thread.
4. Repeat the steps 2 and 3 with other threads made up of different materials (e.g., Wool, silk, terylene, etc.) and compare their tensile strength.
5. Now, to study the effect of acids and alkalies on the tensile strength of fibres, dip each type of fibre in dilute HCl or dilute NaOH solution of equal strengths for equal intervals of time.
6. After a small but fixed interval of time, the fibres are removed from the solution, washed with water and dried in the sun.
7. Determine again the tensile strength of the dried fibres by repeating steps 2, 3 and 4.

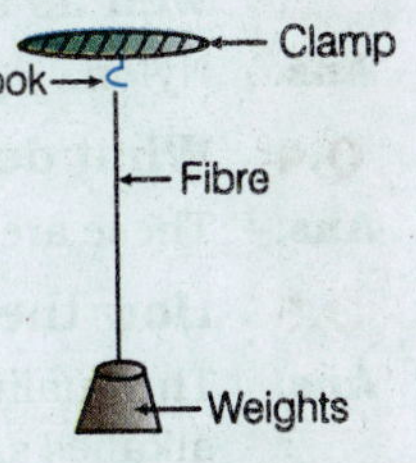

Observation

Length of fibre = 20 cm; Strength of the acid = 1 M HCl and 5 M HCl

Strength of the base = 1 M NaOH and 5 M NaOH

S.No.	Type of fibre	Original tensile strength [Before soaking]	Tensile strength of soaked fibre (g)			
			1 M HCl	5 M HCl	1 M NaOH	5 M NaOH
1.	Silk					
2.	Cotton					
3.	Wool					
4.	Nylon					

Conclusion

The order of increasing weights required at the breaking points of threads will be the order of increasing tensile strengths.

Result

1. The tensile strength of the given fibres is in the order ....
2. The tensile strength of a fibre is affected by the acid and alkali. The order of the tensile strength of soak fibre is ....

PRECAUTIONS

- *All fibres should be of same length and thickness.*
- *The volume and molarity of acids and bases should be same.*
- *Threads should be completely dipped and dried before tying their ends to hook and hanger carrying weights.*
- *Take same set of weights in every experiment.*
- *Add small weights (1-2g) near the breaking point.*

Viva-Voce

Q.1 What are the two types of fibres?

Ans. Natural and synthetic fibres.

Q.2 What do you mean by tensile strength of fibres?

Ans. It is the extent upto which a fibre can be stretched.

Q.3 Name a fibre whose strength almost remains same even after soaking in acid as well as alkali.

Ans. Nylon.

Q.4 What do you understand by the term regenerated fibres?

Ans. These are altered natural fibres, e.g. rayon is obtained from cellulose.

Q.5 How the quality of fibres can be judged?

Ans. The quality of fibres can be judged on the basis of its specific gravity, action in water, acids, alkalies and other chemicals, tendency to undergo oxidation, etc.

Project 8

AIM

To study the acidity of fruit and vegetable juices.

Theory/Principle

Fruits and vegetables juices contain free acids and minerals which are very essential for the growth and maintenance of our body.

The amount and kind of mineral and free acids present in juices varies from fruit to fruit and vegetable to vegetable. In the given project, firstly we have to determine the amount of acids present in various fruits and vegetables, and then to detect the presence of iron, carbohydrate, protein and sugar in vegetables and fruits.

The acid present in fruits and vegetables can be tested with the help of **pH paper** or **universal indicator**. The acid content can be calculated by titrating a known quantity of juice with $M/100$ KOH.

Materials Required

- Test tubes : As per need
- Test tube stand : 1
- Glass rod : 1
- Dropper : 1
- Universal indicator or pH paper : As per need
- $M/100$ NaOH or KOH solution : As per need
- Burette : 1
- Burette stand : 1
- Pipette : 1
- Conical flask : 1
- Phenolphthalein as indicator : As per need
- Fehling's solution *A* and *B* : As per need
- Tollen's reagent : As per need
- Molisch reagent : As per need
- Ninhydrin reagent : As per need
- Biuret reagent (i.e. NaOH and $CuSO_4$) : As per need
- Fruits and vegetables juice : As per need
- Other laboratory reagents : As per need

Procedure

Estimation of Acid Content

1. Take out the juice of few fruits and vegetables (apple, orange, amla, lemon, radish, cane sugar) by crushing them.
2. Keep the juice samples in different test tubes.
3. Dip pH paper in the juices and determine the pH of different samples of juices.
4. Determine their acid content by titrating a known quantity of juice with $M/100$ potassium hydroxide solution using phenolphthalein as an indicator.
5. In case of dark coloured juices, dilute them with enough distilled water to get sharp end point during titration.
6. Compare the acid contents of juices by comparing their acid values.
   (Acid value of vegetables and fruits is the number of milligrams of potassium hydroxide required for neutralising the acids present in one gram of vegetable/fruit)

Tests of Proteins, Fats, Carbohydrates (Starch and Sugar) Mineral Content (Ca, Fe, Mg, P)

Test of Proteins

Following tests can be performed :

1. **Xanthoproteic test** Add concentrated HNO_3 to the sample of juice taken in a test tube and boil it for few minutes. Formation of yellow precipitate takes place. Cool the test tube under running tap and then add few drops of 10 M NaOH solution, appearance of an orange colour confirms the presence of proteins.
2. **Ninhydrin test** Add 2-3 drops of ninhydrin solution to the 2 mL of juice taken in a test tube and heat it. Appearance of blue colour confirms the presence of proteins.
3. **Biuret test** Add 3 mL of 5% NaOH and 2 drops of 1% $CuSO_4$ solution to the juice sample. Warm the mixture for about 5 min. Appearance of violet colour confirms the presence of proteins.
4. **Millon's reagent test** Add 2 drops of mercuric nitrate solution and 1 drop of dilute H_2SO_4 to a sample of juice and then boil it. Cool and add 1 drop of sodium nitrite solution and warm again. A red colouration confirms the presence of proteins.

Test of Fats

Fats are tested by acrolein test. The procedure for this test is depicted below :

1. Take 2 mL of juice sample in a test tube.
2. Add few crystals of $KHSO_4$ to it, then heat the mixture.
3. A pungent irritating odour indicates the presence of fats.

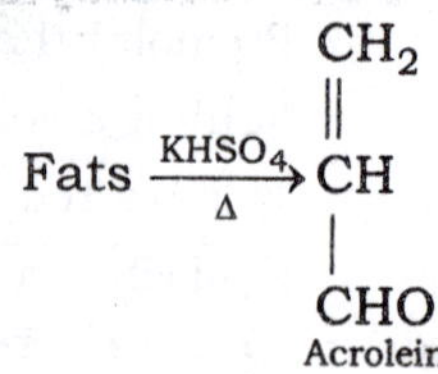

Test of Carbohydrates

Following tests can be performed to test the presence of carbohydrates:

1. **Molisch's test** Shake 1 mL of the juice with Molisch reagent, i.e. 1% solution of α-naphthol in ethanol and add conc. H_2SO_4 along the sides of the test tube. A purple coloured ring is formed at the junction of two layers which confirms the presence of carbohydrates.
2. **Tollen's reagent test** Add Tollen's reagent (i.e. ammoniacal silver nitrate solution) to the juice sample and keep the test tube in the water bath. Formation of brown or grey precipitate or silver mirror confirms the presence of a reducing sugar.

$$\text{Carbohydrates} + 2\,[Ag(NH_3)_2]^+ + 3OH^- \longrightarrow \underset{\text{Silver mirror}}{Ag\downarrow} + H_2O$$

3. **Fehling's solution test** Mix equal volumes of Fehling *A* and Fehling *B* reagents, then, add 2 mL of the juice sample to it. Shake well and keep the test tube in a water bath. Red precipitate of Cu_2O appears which confirms the presence of reducing sugar in the juice sample.

$$\text{Carbohydrates} + Cu^{2+} + OH^- \longrightarrow \underset{\text{Red ppt.}}{Cu_2O} + H_2O$$

4. **Benedict's test** Add 1 mL of Benedict's reagent (i.e. copper (II) ions complexed with citrate ions) to a sample of juice and heat the mixture to boiling in a water bath for 2 min. The formation of an orange-red precipitate due to the formation of copper (I) indicates the presence of carbohydrate.
5. **Iodine test for starch** Add 2-3 drops of freshly prepared 0.02 M iodine solution to a sample containing starch. Appearance of violet colour indicates the presence of starch.

Determination of Mineral Content

Different tests can be performed for determining different minerals.

1. **Test of calcium** Add NH_4OH and ammonium oxalate to the juice sample, white precipitate confirms the presence of calcium.
2. **Test of iron** Add 2 drops of conc. HNO_3 to the juice sample, boil it and then cool it. Add potassium ferrocyanide solution to it. Blood red colouration confirms the presence of iron.
3. **Test of magnesium** Add NH_4OH and ammonium phosphate to the juice sample taken in a test tube. Scratch the sides of the test tube with a glass rod. Formation of white precipitate confirms the presence of magnesium.
4. **Test of phosphorus** Add conc. HNO_3 and 1 mL ammonium molybdate to the juice sample. A yellow precipitate confirms the presence of phosphorus.

Observation

S.No.	Name of juice sample	pH	Proteins	Fats	Carbohydrates	Minerals			
						Ca	Fe	Mg	P
1.	Lemon								
2.	Apple								
3.	Orange								
4.	Amla								
5.	Radish								
6.	Cane sugar								

Result

Juice of .... is highly acidic, fats are present in ...., carbohydrates in .... and proteins in .... juice. .... juice contains minerals.

PRECAUTIONS

- *Juice should not contain any suspended matter or insoluble impurities.*
- *Only use fresh juice samples for the test.*
- *Use distilled water for making all solutions.*

Viva-Voce

Q.1 How will you test the presence of carbohydrate in a juice sample?

Ans. The presence of carbohydrate can be confirmed by using Molisch's reagent, Tollen's reagent and Fehling's reagent solution.

Q.2 How will you test the presence of starch in a juice sample?

Ans. Add 2 mL of juice in a test tube and add few drops of iodine solution to it. Blue colour confirms the presence of starch in the juice sample.

Q.3 Which coloured precipitate is obtained in Biuret test to confirm the presence of proteins?

Ans. Violet coloured precipitate.

Q.4 What is Molisch's reagent?

Ans. It is the 1% solution of α-naphthol in ethanol.

Q.5 Which vitamin is present in citrus fruits like orange, lemon, etc?

Ans. Vitamin-C

Q.6 What happens when fats present in juice sample react with the crystals of $KHSO_4$?

Ans. Acrolein is formed which has pungent and irritating odour. The equation is as follows.

$$\text{Fats} \xrightarrow[\Delta]{KHSO_4} \begin{array}{c} CH_2 \\ \| \\ CH \\ | \\ CHO \end{array}$$

Acrolein

Q.7 How is the presence of iron tested in the sample?

Ans. By heating the juice with conc. HNO_3 and then performing the iron test by using suitable reagents.

Q.8 Why is the juice sometimes diluted before titration?

Ans. To make the end point of the titration clear, especially in dark-coloured juices.

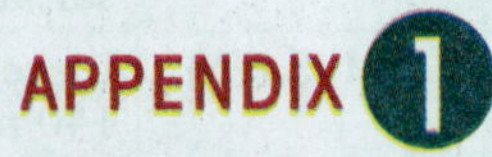

APPENDIX 1

Important Laboratory Reagents

A. Strengths of Concentrated Acid Solutions

S.No.	Acid	Specific gravity	Percentage by mass	Approximate strength
1.	Glacial acetic acid, (CH_3COOH)	1.05	99.5	17 M
2.	Hydrochloric acid, (HCl)	1.18	37	12 M
3.	Nitric acid, (HNO_3)	1.41	70	16 M
4.	Sulphuric acid, (H_2SO_4)	1.84	96	18 M
5.	Phosphoric acid, (H_3PO_4)	1.69	85	14.8 M

B. Preparation of Commonly used Dilute Solutions of Acids

S.No.	Name of acid	Concentration	Method of preparation
1.	Dil. sulphuric acid, (H_2SO_4)	1.25 M [2.5 N]	Add 70 mL of conc. H_2SO_4 slowly and with constant stirring in 250 mL of distilled water. Cool and make up the volume to 500 mL.
2.	Dil. hydrochloric acid, (HCl)	2.5 M [2.5 N]	Add dropwise 215 mL of conc. HCl in the distilled water and make up the volume to 550 mL.
3.	Dil. acetic acid, (CH_3COOH)	2.5 M [2.5 N]	Add 140 mL of glacial acetic acid slowly and with constant stirring in distilled water. Cool and make up the volume to 500 mL.
4.	Dil. nitric acid, (HNO_3)	2.5 M [2.5 N]	Add 160 mL of conc. (HNO_3) to distilled water and make up the volume to 500 mL.

Note *Concentrated acids are directly used as supplied.*

C. Preparation of Commonly used Dilute Solutions of Bases

S.No.	Name of base	Concentration	Method of preparation
1.	Dil. sodium hydroxide, (NaOH)	2.5 M [2.5 N]	Dissolve 100 g of NaOH pellets in 500 mL of distilled water.
2.	Dil. potassium hydroxide, (KOH)	2 M [2N]	Dissolve 125 g KOH pellets in 500 mL of distilled water.
3.	Dil. lime water, ($Ca(OH)_2$)	0.02M [0.04 N]	Shake 2-3 g of calcium hydroxide [$Ca(OH)_2$] with 1 L distilled water filter the solution after sometime and keep in a reagent bottle.
4.	Dil. ammonium hydroxide solution, (NH_4OH)	2 M [2N]	Pour 26.6 mL of conc. ammonia solution in distilled water and make up the volume to 1 L.
5.	Dil. ammonia solution	15 M [15 N]	Used as directly supplied.

D. Preparation of Salt Solutions

S.No.	Name of the salt	Concentration	Method of preparation
1.	Ammonium acetate, (CH_3COONH_4)	2M (2N)	Dissolve 154 g of the ammonium acetate salt in distilled water and dilute to 1 L.
2.	Ammonium carbonate, $(NH_4)_2CO_3$	1.7 M (3.5 N)	Dissolve 160 g of ammonium carbonate in 140 mL liquor ammonia and make up the solution to 1 L with distilled water.
3.	Ammonium chloride, (NH_4Cl)	5 M (5N)	Dissolve 267.5 g of the salt in distilled water and dilute to 1 L.
4.	Ammonium molybdate, $[(NH_4)_6Mo_7O_{24}\cdot 4H_2O]$	0.5 M	Dissolve 100 g of molybdate salt in a mixture of liquor ammonia solution and add 250 g of ammonium nitrate and dilute to 1 L with distilled water.
5.	Ammonium oxalate, $[(COONH_4)_2]$	0.5 M	Dissolve 71 g of ammonium oxalate salt in distilled water and dilute to 1 L.
6.	Ammonium sulphate, $[(NH_4)_2SO_4]$	1 M(2 N)	Dissolve 132 g of the salt in distilled water and dilute to 1 L.
7.	Ammonium thiocyanate, (NH_4CNS)	0.25 M (0.5 N)	Dissolve 38 g of the salt in 1 L water.
8.	Calcium chloride, ($CaCl_2$)	0.5 M (0.5 N)	Dissolve 55 g of the salt in distilled water and dilute to 1 L.
9.	Copper sulphate, ($CuSO_4\cdot 5H_2O$)	0.5 M (0.5 N)	Dissolve 125 g of crystalline salt in 500 mL water, add 3 mL concentrated sulphuric acid and dilute to 1 L.
10.	Cobalt nitrate, ($Co(NO_3)\cdot 6H_2O$)	0.15 M (0.075 N)	Dissolve 44 g of the salt in distilled water and make up the volume to 1 L.
11.	Disodium hydrogen phosphate, ($Na_2HPO_4\cdot 12H_2O$)	0.3 M	Dissolve 120 g of the salt in distilled water and make up the volume to 1 L.
12.	Ferric chloride, ($FeCl_3\cdot 6H_2O$)	0.33 M	Dissolve 90 g of the salt in distilled water containing 10 mL of conc. HCl and make up the volume to 1 L.
13.	Ferrous sulphate, ($FeSO_4\cdot 7H_2O$)	0.5 M	Dissolve 140 g of the salt in about 500 mL water, add 7 mL of conc. H_2SO_4 and dilute to 1 L.
14.	Lead acetate, $[(CH_3COO)_2Pb]$	0.5 M	Dissolve 200 g of lead acetate salt in 500 mL of distilled water containing 15 mL acetic acid and make up the volume to 1 L with distilled water.
15.	Magnesium sulphate, ($MgSO_4\cdot 7H_2O$)	0.25 M	Dissolve 60 g of the salt in 1 L water.
16.	Mercuric chloride, ($HgCl_2$)	0.25 M (0.5 N)	Dissolve 70 g of the salt in small amount of distilled water and make up the volume to 1 L.
17.	Potassium chromate, (K_2CrO_4)	0.25 M (0.5 N)	Dissolve 49 g of the salt in distilled water and dilute to 1 L.
18.	Potassium dichromate, ($K_2Cr_2O_7$)	0.15 M (1 N)	Dissolve 49 g of the salt in distilled water and make up the volume to 1 L.
19.	Potassium ferrocyanide, $[K_3[Fe(CN)_6]$	0.15 M (0.5 N)	Dissolve 46 g of the salt in distilled water and dilute to 1 L.
20.	Potassium ferricyanide, $(K_4[Fe(CN)_6]$	0.2 M (0.5 N)	Dissolve 55 g of the salt in distilled water and dilute to 1 L.
21.	Potassium iodide, (KI)	0.5 M (0.5 N)	Dissolve 83 g of the salt in distilled water and dilute to 1 L.

S.No.	Name of the salt	Concentration	Method of preparation
22.	Potassium permanganate, ($KMnO_4$)	0.06 M (0.3 N)	Dissolve 10 g of the salt in 1 L distilled water. Heat the solution and filter it through glass wool.
23.	Potassium thiocyanate, (KSC)	0.5 M (0.5 N)	Dissolve 49 g of the salt in distilled water and make up the volume to 1 L.
24.	Silver nitrate, ($AgNO_3$)	0.1 M	Dissolve 17 g of the salt in 250 mL of distilled water and store it in a brown coloured bottle.
25.	Sodium acetate, ($CH_3COONa{\cdot}3H_2O$)	3 M (3 N)	Dissolve 408 g salt in distilled water and make the volume of solution 1 L by diluting with water.
26.	Stannous chloride, ($SnCl_2{\cdot} 2H_2O$)	0.25 M	Dissolve 55 g of the salt in 200 mL fo conc. HCl by heating. Dilute with distilled water to make up the volume to 1 L. Add several pieces of metallic tin into the solution
27.	Calcium chloride, ($CaCl_2 \cdot 6H_2O$)	0.25 M	Dissolves 55 g of the hydrated salt in distilled water and make the volume of solution 1 L by diluting with water.

E. Preparation of Common Lab Reagents

S.No.	Name of the Reagents	Concentration	Method of Preparation
1.	Bromine water, (Br_2)	0.5 N	Prepare saturated solution by shaking 11 mL of liquid bromine with water keep it in a dark bottle.
2.	Chlorine water, (Cl_2)	3 N	Prepare chlorine gas by treating solid $KMnO_4$ with conc. HCl. Saturate one litre of distilled water with chlorine gas and keep the solution in a dark coloured bottle.
3.	Dimethyl glyoxime, ($C_4H_8O_2N_2$)	1 %	Dissolve 1 g of the white needle shaped solid dimethyl glyoxime in 100 mL ethyl alcohol.
4.	Diphenyl amine, $(C_6H_5)_2NH$	0.5 N	Dissolve 0.5 g of the solid diphenyl amine in 85 mL of conc. H_2SO_4 and dilute it with distilled water to 100 mL.
5.	Hydrogen peroxide, (H_2O_2)	—	Used as 3 % commercial solution
6.	Iodine solution, (I_2)	0.1 N	Dissolve 12.7 g of iodine in a solution of 20 g of pure KI in 30 mL of water and dilute to 1 L with water.
7.	Magnesia mixture	—	Dissolve 55 g hydrated magnesium chloride and 70 g ammonium chloride in 650 mL water and add 350 mL conc. ammonia.
8.	Nessler's reagent ($K_2[HgI_4]$)	—	Dissolves 3.5 g potassium iodide in 10 mL water. Add 1.7 g mercuric chloride solution slowly to the prepared KI solution until a permanent precipitate occurs. Dilute the precipitate to 100 mL with 10% diluted NaOH solution.

S.No.	Name of the Reagents	Concentration	Method of Preparation
9.	Alkaline solution of Nessler's reagent, (K_2HgI_4)	—	Dissolve 10 g of KI solution in 10 mL of ammonia free water. Add saturated $HgCl_2$ solution 160 g per litre in small quantities at a time and shake the solution until a slight permanent precipitate forms. Then add 80 mL of 9 N NaOH solution and dilute to 200 mL. Allow to stand overnight and decant off the clear liquid.
10.	Sodium nitroprusside, $[Na_2(Fe(CN)_5NO)]$		Dissolve 4 g of the solid in 100 mL of distilled water.
11.	Yellow ammonium sulphide, $[(NH_4)_2S_x]$	6 N	Take about 200 mL of conc. ammonia solution in a bottle and saturate it with H_2S gas. Add 10g of sulphur and 200 mL of conc. NH_4OH. Warm gently and shake well until sulphur is completely dissolved. Dilute the solution to 1 L with distilled water.
12.	Buffer solution in non-aqueous media [for EDTA titration]	—	Dissolve 67.5 g of ammonium chloride in 570 mL of conc. NH_3 solution and dilute of 1 L.
13.	Eriochrome black-T in non-aqueous media (indicator for EDTA titration)	—	Dissolve 0.5 g of solid eriochrome black-T in methanol and make up the volume to 100 mL.

APPENDIX 2

Solubility of Some Important Organic Cations

Name of anion	Symbol	These ions form soluble compounds (solubility greater than 0.1 M) with these cations	Soluble compounds (solubility less than 0.1 M)
Nitrate	NO_3^-	Most cations	None
Acetate	CH_3COO^-	Most cations	Ag^+
Chloride	Cl^-	Most cations	Ag^+, Pb^{2+}, Hg_2^{2+}
Bromide	Br^-	Most cations	Ag^+, Pb^{2+}, Hg_2^{2+}
Iodide	I^-	Most cations	Ag^+, Pb^{2+}, Hg_2^{2+}
Sulphate	SO_4^{2-}	Most cations	Br^{2+}, Sr^{2+}, Pb^{2+}, Ag^+
Chromate	CrO_4^{2-}	Most cations	Br^{2+}, Sr^{2+}, Pb^{2+}, Ag^+
Sulphide	S^{2-}	NH_4^+, alkali metal cations and alkaline earth metal cations	Most other cations
Hydroxide	OH^-	NH_4^+, alkali metal and alkaline earth metal and Ba^{2+} and Sr^{2+}	Most other cations
Carbonate	CO_3^{2-}	NH_4^+ and alkali metal cations	Most other cations
Phosphate	PO_4^{3-}	Except Li^+	

APPENDIX 3

Solubility Product Constant of Some Common Compounds

S.No.	Name of compound	Formula	Solubility product constant, K_{sp}
1.	Barium sulphate	$BaSO_4$	1.0×10^{-10}
2.	Barium oxalate	BaC_2O_4	2.3×10^{-8}
3.	Aluminium hydroxide	$Al(OH)_3$	1.8×10^{-5}
4.	Calcium hydroxide	$Ca(OH)_2$	5.5×10^{-6}
5.	Calcium oxalate	CaC_2O_4	2.7×10^{-9}
6.	Calcium carbonate	$CaCO_3$	2.8×10^{-9}
7.	Copper (II) sulphide	CuS	6×10^{-37}
8.	Lead chloride	$PbCl_2$	1.6×10^{-5}
9.	Lead chromate	$PbCrO_4$	2.8×10^{-13}
10.	Magnesium hydroxide	$Mg(OH)_2$	1.2×10^{-11}
11.	Magnesium oxalate	MgC_2O_4	8.5×10^{-5}
12.	Lead sulphate	$PbSO_4$	1.6×10^{-4}
13.	Lead sulphide	PbS	8.0×10^{-21}
14.	Magnesium carbonate	$MgCO_3$	3.5×10^{-8}
15.	Silver chloride	AgCl	1.0×10^{-10}
16.	Silver chromate	$AgCrO_4$	1.1×10^{-12}
17.	Silver iodide	AgI	5.5×10^{-17}
18.	Zinc sulphide	ZnS	2×10^{-25}
19.	Zinc oxalate	ZnC_2O_4	2.8×10^{-8}
20.	Silver phosphate	Ag_3PO_4	1.3×10^{-20}

APPENDIX 4

Preparation of Some Indicators and Test Papers

A. Preparation of Some Important Indicators

S.No.	Name of indicator	Preparation	Strength
1.	Phenolphthalein	In 100 mL ethyl alcohol dissolve 1g of phenolphthalein.	1 %
2.	Methyl orange	In 1 L of distilled water, dissolve 1g of the solid.	0.1 %
3.	Methyl red	Dissolve 1g of the solid in 600 mL of ethyl alcohol and dilute with 400 mL of water.	0.1 %
4.	Starch solution	Make a paste of 1 g of starch with cold water. Pour this drop by drop into 100 mL of boiling water and continue to boil for few minutes. Allow to stand until cool. Decant off clear solution.	1 %
5.	Litmus solution (blue)	Add 100 g of salicylic acid to 100 mL of the strach solution.	1 %
6.	Litmus solution (red)	Add two or three drops of dil. HCl to the prepared blue litmus solution until it changes to red.	1 %

B. Preparation of Test Papers

S.No.	Name of the test papers	Method of preparation
1.	Dichromate paper	Dissolve a crystal of solid potassium dichromate, ($K_2Cr_2O_7$) in a test tube containing water soak the filter paper sheet in it and dry in air and cut into small strips.
2.	Lead acetate paper	Dissolve 10g of lead acetate in 100 mL water in a beaker or China dish, soak the filter paper sheet in it, dry it away from H_2S and cut into small strips.
3.	Litmus paper	Soak a filter paper sheet in litmus solution dry in shade and cut into small strips.
4.	Starch paper	Soak filter paper sheet in starch solution, dry and cut into small strips.
5.	Starch iodide paper	Mix equal quantities of starch solution and potassium iodide in a beaker or China dish, soak a filter paper sheet in it and dry in air and cut into small pieces.
6.	Turmeric paper	Boil 0.5 g of powdered turmeric and 25 mL water in a beaker, cool and filter. Soak a filter paper in filtrate, dry in air and cut into small strips.

C. Some Common Indicators and their pH Ranges and Colours

S.No.	Indicators	pH range	Colour in acid medium	Colour in alkaline medium
1.	Phenolphthalein	8.2 - 9.8	Colourless	Pink
2.	Methyl orange	3.1 -4.4	Red	Orange
3.	Methyl red	4.4 - 6.2	Pink	Yellow
4.	Cresol red (acidic)	0.2 - 1.8	Orange	Yellow
5.	Cresol red (basic)	7.0 - 8.8	Orange	Purple
6.	Litmus	5.0 - 8.0	Red	Blue
7.	4 - nitrophenol	5.4 - 7.5	Colourless	Yellow
8.	Eriochrome black T	7 - 11		Wine red
9.	Bromothymol blue	6.0 - 7.6	Yellow	Blue

APPENDIX 5

Equivalent Weights of Common Chemicals

A. Equivalent Weights of Common Acids

Acids	Chemical formula	Molecular weight (MW)	Equivalent weight (MW/Basicity)
Monobasic			
1. Hydrochloric acid	HCl	36.5	$\frac{36.5}{1} = 36.5$
2. Acetic acid	CH_3COOH	60	60 / 1 = 60
Dibasic			
3. Anhydrous oxalic acid	COOH | COOH	90	90 / 2 = 45

Acids	Chemical formula	Molecular weight (MW)	Equivalent weight (MW/Basicity)
4. Hydrated oxalic acid	$COOH\cdot 2H_2O$ | $COOH$	126	126 / 2 = 63
5. Sulphuric acid	H_2SO_4	98	98 / 2 = 49
Tribasic			
6. Phosphoric acid	H_3PO_4	98	98 / 3 = 32.67

B. Equivalent Weights of Common Bases

Bases	Chemical formulae	Molecular weight (*MW*)	Equivalent weight (*MW*/Acidity)
Monoacidic			
1. Sodium bicarbonate	$NaHCO_3$	84	84 / 1 = 84
2. Potassium bicarbonate	$KHCO_3$	100	100 / 1 = 100
3. Sodium hydroxide	$NaOH$	40	40 / 1 = 40
4. Potassium hydroxide	KOH	56	56 / 1 = 56
Diacidic			
5. Calcium carbonate	$CaCO_3$	100	100 / 2 = 50
6. Barium hydroxide	$Ba(OH)_2$	171	171 / 2 = 85.5
7. Sodium carbonate	Na_2CO_3	106	106 / 2 = 53
8. Potassium carbonate	K_2CO_3	138	138 / 2 = 69
Triacidic			
9. Ferric hydroxide	$Fe(OH)_3$	107	107 / 3 = 35.7

C. Equivalent Weights of Some Common Oxidising and Reducing Agent

Compound	Chemical formulae	Molecular weight (*MW*)	Ionic equations	Number of electrons lost or gained (*n*)	Equivalent weight (*MW/n*)
Anhydrous oxalic acid	$COOH$ | $COOH$	90	COO^- | $\longrightarrow 2CO_2 + 2e^-$ COO^-	2	90 / 2 = 45
Hydrated oxalic acid	$COOH$ | $\cdot 2H_2O$ $COOH$	126	COO^- | $\longrightarrow 2CO_2 + 2e^-$ COO^-	2	126 / 2 = 63
Mohr's salt	$FeSO_4\cdot(NH_4)_2SO_4\cdot 6H_2O$	392	$Fe^{2+} \longrightarrow Fe^{3+} + e^-$	1	392 / 1 = 392
Potassium permanganate	$KMnO_4$	158	$MnO_4^- + 8H^+ + 5e^- \longrightarrow Mn^{2+} + 4H_2O$	5	158 / 5 = 31.6
Sodium thiosulphate	$Na_2S_2O_3$	158	$2S_2O_3^{2-} \longrightarrow S_4O_6^{2-} + 2e^-$	1	158 / 1 = 158

Experiment No.________ Date ________ Page No. ________

Teacher Signature________________

Experiment No.________ Date ________ Page No. ________

Teacher Signature________________

Experiment No.________ Date ________ Page No. ________

Teacher Signature ________

Experiment No.________ Date ________ Page No. ________

Teacher Signature ________________

Experiment No.________ Date ________ Page No. ________

Teacher Signature ________

Experiment No.________ Date ________ Page No. ________

Teacher Signature ________________

Experiment No.________ Date ________ Page No. ________

Teacher Signature________________

Experiment No.________ Date ________ Page No. ________

Teacher Signature ________

Experiment No.________ Date ________ Page No. ________

Teacher Signature ________________

Experiment No.________ Date ________ Page No. ________

Teacher Signature ________________

Experiment No.________ Date ________ Page No. ________

Teacher Signature ________

Experiment No.________ Date ________ Page No. ________

Teacher Signature ________________

Experiment No.________ Date ________ Page No. ________

Teacher Signature ________________

Experiment No.________ Date ________ Page No. ________

Teacher Signature ________________

Experiment No.________ Date ________ Page No. ________

Teacher Signature ________________

Experiment No.________ Date ________ Page No. ________

Teacher Signature ________________

Experiment No.________ Date ________ Page No. ________

Teacher Signature________________

Experiment No.________ Date ________ Page No. ________

Teacher Signature ________________

Experiment No.________ Date ________ Page No. ________

Teacher Signature ________

Experiment No.________ Date ________ Page No. ________

Teacher Signature ________________

Experiment No.________ Date ________ Page No. ________

Teacher Signature ________________

Experiment No.________ Date ________ Page No. ________

Teacher Signature ________________

Experiment No.________ Date ________ Page No. ________

Teacher Signature ________

Experiment No.________ Date ________ Page No. ________

Teacher Signature ________

Experiment No.________ Date ________ Page No. ________

Teacher Signature ________________

Experiment No.________ Date ________ Page No. ________

Teacher Signature ________________

Experiment No.________ Date ________ Page No. ________

Teacher Signature ________

Experiment No.______ Date ______ Page No. ______

Teacher Signature ______

Experiment No.________ Date ________ Page No. ________

Teacher Signature ____________

Experiment No.________ Date ________ Page No. ________

Teacher Signature ________________

Experiment No.________ Date ________ Page No. ________

Teacher Signature ________________

Experiment No.________ Date ________ Page No. ________

Teacher Signature ________________

Experiment No.________ Date ________ Page No. ________

Teacher Signature ________________

Experiment No.________ Date ________ Page No. ________

Teacher Signature ________________

Experiment No.________ Date ________ Page No. ________

Teacher Signature ________________

Experiment No.________ Date ________ Page No. ________

Teacher Signature ________________

Experiment No.________ Date ________ Page No. ________

Teacher Signature ________

Experiment No.________ Date ________ Page No. ________

Teacher Signature________________

Experiment No.________ Date ________ Page No. ________

Teacher Signature ____________________

Experiment No.________ Date ________ Page No. ________

Teacher Signature ________

Experiment No.________ Date ________ Page No. ________

Teacher Signature ________________

Experiment No.________ Date ________ Page No. ________

Teacher Signature ________

Experiment No.________ Date ________ Page No. ________

Teacher Signature ________

Experiment No.________ Date ________ Page No. ________

Teacher Signature ________________

Experiment No.________ Date ________ Page No. ________

Teacher Signature ________________

Experiment No.________ Date ________ Page No. ________

Teacher Signature ________

Experiment No.________ Date ________ Page No. ________

Teacher Signature ________

Experiment No.________ Date ________ Page No. ________

Teacher Signature ________________

Experiment No.________ Date ________ Page No. ________

Teacher Signature ________________

Experiment No.________ Date ________ Page No. ________

Teacher Signature ________________

Experiment No.________ Date ________ Page No. ________

Teacher Signature ________________

Experiment No.________ Date ________ Page No. ________

Teacher Signature ________________

Experiment No.________ Date ________ Page No. ________

Teacher Signature ________________

Experiment No.________ Date ________ Page No. ________

Teacher Signature ________________

Experiment No.________ Date ________ Page No. ________

Teacher Signature ________________

Experiment No.________ Date ________ Page No. ________

Teacher Signature ________________

Experiment No. ________ Date ________ Page No. ________

Teacher Signature ________

Experiment No.________ Date ________ Page No. ________

Teacher Signature ________________

Experiment No.________ Date ________ Page No. ________

Teacher Signature ________

Experiment No.________ Date ________ Page No. ________

Teacher Signature ________

Experiment No.________ Date ________ Page No. ________

Teacher Signature ________________

Experiment No.________ Date ________ Page No. ________

Teacher Signature ________

Experiment No.________ Date ________ Page No. ________

Teacher Signature ________

Experiment No.________ Date ________ Page No. ________

Teacher Signature ________________

Experiment No.________ Date ________ Page No. ________

Teacher Signature ________________

Experiment No.________ Date ________ Page No. ________

Teacher Signature ________________

Experiment No.________ Date ________ Page No. ________

Teacher Signature

Experiment No.________ Date ________ Page No. ________

Teacher Signature________________

Experiment No.________ Date ________ Page No. ________

Teacher Signature________________

Experiment No.________ Date ________ Page No. ________

Teacher Signature ________________

Experiment No. ________ Date ________ Page No. ________

Teacher Signature ________________

Experiment No.________ Date ________ Page No. ________

Teacher Signature ________________

Experiment No.________ Date ________ Page No. ________

Teacher Signature ________________

Experiment No.________ Date ________ Page No. ________

Teacher Signature ________________

Experiment No.________ Date ________ Page No. ________

Teacher Signature ________

Experiment No.________ Date ________ Page No. ________

Teacher Signature ________________

Experiment No.________ Date ________ Page No. ________

Teacher Signature ________________

Experiment No.________ Date ________ Page No. ________

Teacher Signature ________________

Experiment No.________ Date ________ Page No. ________

Teacher Signature ________

Experiment No.________ Date ________ Page No. ________

Teacher Signature ________________